T0195767

FOCUS ON BETTER

A REAL DEAL GUIDE TO BECOMING A MATCH FOR
SUSTAINED HAPPINESS, SUCCESS, AND FULFILLMENT.

SELF EMPOWERMENT.

BETTER THINKING.

A BETTER LIFE

ANDRE A. VAN LUN

authorHOUSE

AuthorHouse™
1663 Liberty Drive
Bloomington, IN 47403
www.authorhouse.com
Phone: 833-262-8899

Published by AuthorHouse 08/11/2020

ISBN: 978-1-7283-6666-1 (sc)
ISBN: 978-1-7283-6668-5 (hc)
ISBN: 978-1-7283-6667-8 (e)

Library of Congress Control Number: 2020912061

This book is dedicated to Nicole Khristen Van Lun. You are the love of my life. Who you be has awakened greatness within me. You have stretched me, challenged me, and loved me to realizing my version of "better". There is no way that I would be the man that I am without your love. I am grateful to you for who I will become in your presence. You have been and still are my favorite human! I am blessed beyond measure to know you and be your husband. Our twins are lucky to have your DNA.

To Drece Delainey Van Lun and Nico Anthoy Van Lun, before you were born the very possibility of your existence caused me to grow. Your presence in my life has awakened me to a level of love that I never knew existed. Thank you! Drece you are already the sweetest and most loving baby I have ever met. Nico you have a strength coursing through you that reminds me of mine and assures me that the world is blessed to have you here. I am honored to love and guide you two gorgeous souls until my last day.

Last but not least, this book is dedicated to Travis Farnell. You have been my angel and my rock for over three decades. Thank you for taking a chance on Adam and I. God has put us together for a reason. The thousands of people who I have impacted with the work that I do have you to thank as well. Without the many lessons that you have imparted on me I would have undoubtedly become another hood statistic of failure. One person believing in a child can change not only their trajectory in life, but the entire trajectory of their family line for generations. That is exactly who you have been for me. I love you more than words can even express. This planet needs more loving humans like you. My beautiful little family is better because you allowed God to move through you. Thank you!

CONTENTS

CONTENTS

PREFACE

Traditional education hasn't successfully addressed the balancing of personal fitness, personal finances, critical thinking, and cultivating extraordinary relationships. No one teaches turning those ingredients into the soup, of being a well-adjusted adult human being. During your hunt for balance you will inevitably encounter failure. Hopefully, you will lick your wounds quickly. You take the lessons that you have painstakingly discovered, and begin the entire process again. After a few thousand times of tumbling through this process you may gain some powerful insights. You'll have tons of experience, raised scars, and hopefully some grand wins on your mantle to peruse and admire fondly. This book just may cut down on the attempts you'll have to endure.

It seems that I have lived many lifetimes all neatly rolled up into my forty one years on the planet. My first life was spent being a traumatized, super-sensitive, empathic young boy. I was the one and only child produced of a handsome and religious Caribbean man, who stepped out on his marriage, to have fun with a vibrant around-the-way-Caribbean-girl in New York City. They both decided to place my asthmatic, younger half-brother, and I, into foster care. I basically raised and fended for us as we navigated the system. Survival consumed every sleeping and waking moment that I can remember back then. I'd also like to humbly share that, since then, nearly everything that I have ever focused on achieving, with great desire, has come to be my reality. Today, I live a life surrounded with beautiful circumstances, people, and experiences that eclipse what I could ever have dreamt of experiencing while going through my darkest of times.

It wasn't all luck. I actually know how I did it. I have the receipts from the many mentors that I've hired in the past. I have scars in my mind and on my body from hard fought lessons. For twenty four years I have helped people achieve, what they felt was impossible, with their minds and their bodies. I have done so as a fitness expert and an executive life-strategist. Over this time of working with some of the busiest and most successful people on the planet I have been able to extract some very powerful information. My life's work is to share the powerful principles that I have accumulated with the people in the world who need it. My content, seminars, workshops, and books help people tap into dormant potentials and possibilities. My hopes is that they then go on to live powerful, intentional, and fun lives. This book is for leaders willing to do the internal work.

I believe that exercise and healthy eating is something that is paramount to humanity flourishing. I will use the prism of fitness and nutrition to outline triumphs and struggles that myself and my clients have lived. My hope is that these stories and methodologies equip you with tools that can be used universally in many areas of life and living. Most of the population finds healthy eating and consistently exercising challenging. I have found that it is the difficult and rewarding things that we do in life that call us to evolve. When it comes to doing difficult things on a consistent basis and until a desired outcome is achieved I am an expert. Adversity was the first toy that I can remember ever receiving. I swam in the seas of ugly circumstances for more than half of my life. Now I get to suck down mouthfuls of sweet nectar by living a life that I love and enjoy to the max! I have worked so much on me and traversed so much ground emotionally, psychologically, and physically that I feel a duty to share what I have learned. I have used the distinctions and lessons that I've learned along the way, not only to help myself, but to help thousands of others to reconnect with the best parts of who they are and live intentional and authentic lives.

Fitness is only a single important ingredient in the gumbo of us human beings living our best lives. Fitness is leverage. It is a conduit for us to achieve higher vibrations and higher levels of being. The wisdom that is accessed through moving our bodies with the intent to improve and grow is endless. Fitness can make visible to each of us the strength that is within us. Owning that strength really reminds us all of who we really are. The movement of our bodies and usage of the body's wisdom is so important. Our bodies affect all areas of life and living. Our bodies are our chariots. They carry us through this expression of God and man that we call life. Fitness literally saved my life. Fitness helped me to find meaning and value in life. Exercise fostered, in me, a sense of self-worth that society doesn't usually afford orphans.

As a child who was very self-aware and living under the stress of being abandoned and abused, I felt a deep coldness growing in me. I hated it. I had a hard time mentally reconciling the cold world around me with the fact that deep within me I felt that human suffering was an unnecessary reality. The structure and discipline needed to make the human body thrive through training helped me to build character, confidence, and purpose. Pain helped me make sense of it all. I have used structure and discipline to fuel my work and how I live. Fitness has allowed me to be a part of improving the lives of others. Unfortunately, in society fitness has been framed and packaged in a way that relegates it as a luxury that occupies certain people's free time. Free time is something that absolutely none of us have. Life is too short not to be who you are meant to be. Being physically fit and healthy sets the stage for an elevated quality of life. It also creates an avenue for true self-expression. My body was that first and only thing that I discovered I had control of as a child. I built a strong body that I felt could carry my mental and spiritual burdens.

In recent years our physicality has been tossed aside in favor of technological pursuits. I can facetime clients their workouts and mental distinctions around the world now! Yet, those same workouts do not usually get wholly done without me being present. Technology is essential to the advancement of humanity but at the same time technological advances have cost many of us our physical wellbeing. Daily life doesn't demand that we physically work as hard as we used to in centuries past. There is an app for making everything easier. On top of that, restaurant delivery services like Door Dash, Uber Eats, and Grub Hub make food that is slowly killing us in tasty fashion, far too easy to access. Without obsessive effort to infuse balance between advances in technology and health and wellness a gap continues to widen. That gap I am referring to is the gap between how fit and healthy our minds and bodies are and the speed that life is happening at. Life is happening faster, we all feel it speeding up as technological connectivity increases. The question is, will we possess the levels of health and wellness necessary to navigate a world that is increasingly becoming faster and increasingly more stimulating? Having we practiced being present, focused and discipline where need be? For so many of us that answer is no. Our only hope is to defiantly live an existence that is conscious, intentional, and healthy.

In a world filled to the brim with distractions. Carving out time to improve the function of our bodies and minds puts an end to the separation from our souls that this era of living can cause. Becoming familiar with pain through exercise puts you in touch with the most primal and real parts of who you are. The burning, the involuntary thoughts and the clarity that self-inflicted physical challenge provides is priceless. The controlled chaos of taking muscles to failure or panting from exertion physically connects the mind and soul. As a kid witnessing the growth that can happen in my body due to training I got to know me. I tested my limits both mentally and physically. I learned at age twelve that it will be my mind that is most often that first to break when taking on challenging tasks. I also learned that when my mind and body sync up that I was an unstoppable force. Those lessons made an orphaned child who was in multiple foster homes and group homes before age seven, know deep within his heart, that he was getting out of the ghetto and making a positive mark on the planet in some way, shape or form. I sensed that I had what it took within me to transform my circumstances.

Getting to know what kind of physical adversity I could withstand at an early age is what has saved me from the perils of growing up in the foster care system. It informed how I became able to overcome the PTSD associated with the sexual, physical, and mental abuse that I endured in foster care as a child. It shaped how I responded to racism that I endured both systemically and on a personal level. Knowing my own inner strength prepared me to handle rejection on two separate occasions from the man who fathered me. The strength that I witnessed in myself while drenched in sweat and trembling under more weight than I had ever lifted before, fueled my self-esteem and confidence at a time where no one else on the planet acknowledged anything great within me. Wanting a better life fueled my ability to sacrifice my childhood to protect myself and my younger brother from the unfortunate situation we had to navigate. The confidence that I created in the gym and on the track has informed me to help thousands of others overcome psychological hurdles that have historically stopped them from being fully expressed in other areas of life and living. I always had a sense of urgency built into the way that I lived. My response to the fear of losing stability was incessantly hunting for ways to pull myself out of the situation that I found myself born into.

The seeds of inner-confidence and self-reliance were planted within me while exercising hard in a low ceilinged, dusty, concrete basement in Bedford Stuyvesant, Brooklyn, New York City during the cocaine era in the mid 1980's. What I learned there has helped me start businesses, win awards/accolades, graduate college, speak on stages, serve in the US Army, own a US patent, marry the woman of my dreams, navigate the hoods of New York City, cope with racism in the workplace and in the suburbs, graduate college, write four books, pen hundreds of published articles, train thousands of bodies and minds all over the globe, and become the man that I am today. I now help leaders and successful visionaries develop themselves and continue to bridge the gap between where they are and their visions for themselves. I also learned to understand the hypocrisy of being human. I watched people struggle with years old issues and not make any progress. I also witnessed the havoc that a negative environment can wreak on good human beings.

In order for me to "get myself" I had to put myself into a very raw and vulnerable state. Getting pinned under the weight of an old school vinyl and cement weight set helped me get a good glimpse of what kind of kids I was. Much like my life, I had to find a way out from underneath the weight of the world because "no one was there to save me". My fitness journey has been a metaphor for living ever since. Challenging my body in a consistent fashion has brought me many opportunities. Pushing my body towards and past my own perceived limitations has given me a new world of possibility to live into. It has made me defiant to the status-quo. My trained and healthy body gave me a beautiful yet invisible bullet-proof suit of armor to navigate a world that constantly told me on every level that: "I don't belong", "I don't matter", "I will never amount to anything", "People that look like you and come from where you come from do not normally turn out well", "just give up." "Black men are (you name it)_____", "You'll just be another statistic.", "You can't win", "You are not good enough." "You don't deserve a great life filled with abundance." "Surviving life is all that you can aspire to." These are all phrases that I heard about me growing up. Sometimes I heard these things from people directly. I also, over the years, had bolstered many of these limiting thoughts and cues into ironclad beliefs in my own mind. They became my truth. I said them to myself. This was a result of how

I was treated and what I noticed and soaked up as a child. We all have navigated some trauma that leads to us carrying limiting "truths" that mentally and spiritually stunt our growth.

The doubt and angst that I encountered may be the same or different than your experience, but I can assure you that as a human, you have heard someone else negatively define who you are. I can also guarantee that if you haven't, then you have done it to yourself at some point in life. Limiting beliefs and depression due to life's negative circumstances has touched all of our lives. Fitness has been one of the many, many, tools that I have personally and professionally used to overcome this. I had one of the most chaotic minds. It now has evolved into living a very intentional, peaceful, and fulfilled life. I can tell you that life may never be perfect, but it can definitely be loaded with many elements that you desire to experience. You must make the time to intimately get to know you. When looking to develop yourself, fitness can kill limiting beliefs and help you reconnect with the real you.

I hope to awaken you to what can accomplish in your life by challenging "who you be". A tough workout is challenging "who you be". By making your muscles tremble, allowing effort to contort your face, and squinting through perspiration, you get to redefine who you are on every level of what it means to be human. I want dreams to be awakened in you and bubble out of your mouth, eyes, and ears. Acknowledge who you are becoming in the moments that you challenge yourself and fail. You should be aware of exactly how it feels to you, internally, when you do win. Do you experience euphoria or anxiety? Does it make you feel uneasy to win? Why? Nothing is more fulfilling than aligning your real life with the ideal vision of you that is held within your mind's eye. I would love for you to possibly discover a new way to become the intentional sculptor of your wellbeing, and your life, by reading this book.

Imagine the impact that you'll make in your life and the lives of those that encounter you. Imagine your contribution to the planet. I can't place enough emphasis on how important it is for you to know and nurture the real you. Learn to employ compassion and self-care when it comes to dealing with your reawakening process. In terms of personal growth, I am totally unrecognizable, not only to myself, but also to those who've known me for a long time. I have witnessed so many others that have done the work within this book and flourished as well. Trade in the idea that doing difficult but beneficial things aren't worth the effort. Adopt the idea that only you can powerfully sculpt yourself inside and out. I hope this book aids in that endeavor and provides insights on ways to make the popular phrase "living our best life!" a reality that you can embody for life.

CHAPTER 1

NEARLY DROWNING HAS LESSONS

"Tangible outcomes are always the product of
intangible forces at work."

I love the depth and gravity explored in the heading above. Your perception of something has a direct effect on the actions that you take towards said person, place, or thing. I prefer pools to the beach. To me pools seem more controllable and less wild than the ocean does. As a kid, and even now as an adult, I don't particularly like sand getting into every orifice of my body. Who's with me? Sand filled crevices on my body have always posed a problem for me. I find peace in the illusion of control that a pool provides. Sand creeping into ones ass-crack erases that illusion immediately.

In the late nineteen eighties Reese beach in New York almost killed me as a kid. The sandy ocean bottom that I was walking on, in the murky gray-blue water, suddenly vanished and the next thing you know I was inefficiently treading water all by myself. When the ocean floor vanished underfoot, shit hit the fan! Panic ensued, and my useless treading instantaneously transformed into helpless splashing. I felt something brush my leg in that dark water too! Waves washed over my head unmercifully as I uncontrollably gulped salt water and sunk to the bottom of the ocean. One of the older foster kids that I grew up with pulled me to safety by one of my arms. Sean saved my life! I gasped for air, I spit up water, felt sick to my stomach, and had one hell of a headache the rest of the day. That evening was one of the first times in my life that I contemplated how it must feel to die.

That happened when I was about eight years old or younger. Even now, at age forty one, there is a certain amount of fear that I undoubtedly face when approaching beaches. It changed my whole perception of beaches. I was forced to respect and fear the beach at an early age and it stuck with me for life. An intangible memory of a near death experience altered my actions for a lifetime. One of the main reasons that I love Miami Florida so much is that every hotel has a pool as well as full access to the beach. If I am with someone else that loves the beach I can always spend a little time with them at the beach and then sneak off to the pool and hang out in close proximity. Oddly enough, a bucket list item of mine today is to swim in every ocean on the planet. I have already done two of five so far.

When faced with a drowning death I set an audacious goal to swim in every ocean on the planet. This is counterintuitive thinking at its finest. That goal grew on me as a result of looking failure and fear in the eye. One lesson that I learned deep within my bones, from training and exercising, is that failure should always spark you to make another attempt. Your new attempt will be armed with new information and the power of experience. Being relentless, and smart, always pays off. Failure should trigger a sense of defiance. Defiance of the limitation that you encountered the last time that you made an attempt. It is the only way to make progress. Every workout is defiance against past weaknesses and limitations. As a child in foster care there were many times that I felt weak and limited growing up. I found that defying my physical limitations always produced results. I even asked my adoptive mom if I could learn how to swim. Becoming stronger and more capable became addictive to me. I asked my adoptive mother (Travis Farnell, the angel who took a chance on adopting my brother and I) "What would it take to improve my life and move out of the ghetto?" She said "First and foremost you need an education." I then took the "never quit" mindset that I learned from exercising and nearly drowning and I applied it to school and learning in the classroom. I got to the root of creating change and success. Let's get to the root of why fitness is such a major struggle are of life for so many of us.

Shoveling new remixes of diets, waist shapers, pills, social media's radical diet and workout plans, will not solve the many health related problems that Americans face. Before we can start using the plethora of tools we have to build a healthier and better life, it is important to first look at the real underlying and intangible issues that fuel the disconnection that we have had with fitness. What are the current ideologies that make us sicker and fatter? The fitness industry is allegedly here to help eradicate unhealthiness in America. *Who have we all been that "fitness" is?* Why does fitness in its current state help so few? Why are we fatter and sicker? Why does fitness grow as an industry while we become sicker? I think it has a lot to do with how we collectively view fitness. If we don't change the social narrative and context around the word "fitness" this phenomena will continue to happen.

It's funny, that as a 24 year veteran fitness professional I believe that the current idea of "fitness" and how it is traditionally marketed is somewhat off-putting to the people who need it most. If I am being one hundred percent real, shorter more intense workouts, useless gadgets, pills, and creating Spartan like lifestyles is failing us. As an educator and life strategist who helps people make behavioral changes from the inside out, I see the real reasons why people struggle with certain things. I think that how we see life and fitness has to be altered both psychologically and spiritually. As a recovering perfectionist who has looked for success to validate my entire existence I hated repeatedly failing as a fitness professional. When it comes to fitness I think the failure cycle that people experience has a lot to do with fitness being taken at face value. The fit have been getting fitter. Two thirds of Americans fall into the classification of over fat now. Almost half of those people are obese. We need a more thought filled approach to being fit, healthy, and being our "best selves". We need to make fitness into a loveable habit worthy of adoption.

Mainstream American society's idea of fitness started out with strongmen, gymnasts, and circus freaks. The buff body builders and bikini girls used to lead the way. Jane Fonda aerobics, Richard Simmons, Jack Lalanne's feats of strength, and people who were outside of the norm soon became the face of fitness. Fitness trickled into sports performance. Major Leagues sports teams soon adopted fitness to become bigger, stronger and faster. Fitness as we know it then snaked its way into the look of the modern Hollywood's leading man. Leading action stars started beefing up like Arnold Schwarzenegger, John Claud Van Dam, and Sylvester Stallone. Stars like Dwayne "the Rock" Johnson, Chris Helmsworth and Hugh Jackman are all action stars currently developing physiques of action heroes. Daniel Craig the latest James Bond was also athletic and buff. Instagram models and trainers now carry the fitness torch for the masses. Everyday people still see fitness as something for *those people.* Subconsciously, for most people, it is still a pipe dream to get into really good shape and sustain it.

These days Instagram, YouTube influencers, celebrities, & fitness enthusiasts lead the way doing impossible workouts and exercises mostly for show. It is all gobbled up by the masses as entertainment. How do we change that? Fitness needs a PR team to revamp its' image and collectively shift the consciousness of America. Maybe the teams that worked for Bill Clinton and spun his version of the "deep throat" fiasco, could re-inspire our approach to fitness. Fitness is not viewed by most as a powerful and malleable way to add to the experience of being a human. On a personal level, we each have to create our own new narrative around living healthier.

Moving our bodies is an integral slice of our "wellbeing" pie. It is beneficial to find a way to make it climb up the hierarchy of our personal values list. Even though fitness has many faces on it today, it doesn't yet own the visage of our hopes, dreams, and potentials. It isn't yet connected to the sense of purpose that is at the very core of our beings. Even with all of its transformation and inclusion, fitness has not yet perceived as something to be cherished. The average person in America and on the planet doesn't readily connect how exercise adds to life other than looking sexier and feeling better. We have somehow separated moving our bodies and achieving better health, from adding more life and energy to all that is truly important to us. Fitness is adding life and energy to living. I believe that more and more of us are waking up to the psychological benefits of fitness. There are no words that I can type that would paint the bond that exercise has created between myself and sanity. It is because I discovered fitness and clung to it that I am alive and somewhat sane today. I have excised so much pain, self-doubt, trauma, heartaches, tragedy, and disappointments out of my life by using physical challenge and discipline to my advantage. I have witnessed thousands use a new grasp on fitness to do the same.

"Fitness" should be positioned in our society as an access point to creating our very best experience of life. Everyone is entitled to experiencing a life that they love. Living a life that is "fine" or simply "bearable" is not what any of us are here to do. Fitness should be seen as an opportunity to increase our capabilities and positively impact how we show up in life. Our current prevalent perception will not solve the problems that we currently face in America with regards to obesity and other preventable disease. We must focus on better, because perception often becomes reality. Focusing on better thinking, doing and being will equate to better living. As long as fitness is a section of life that happens "over there", or "only one day when you have time", it will never be seen as a "go to" tool that we select when life is undoubtedly life. A healthy body adds to us being our best. Health adds to all that is important in our lives. Being fit is not necessary for those content with a lifetime of settling. When it comes to fitness aiming for "better" is the main fuel source. We should all work to begin to shift the perception of how exercising, eating healthier, mentally releasing stress, and positively handling anxiety occurs to us.

SELF-CARE BEGINS WITH SELF-LOVE

Fitness is an individual practice within self-care. Taking care of ourselves first, is an area of weakness for most of us. Especially the really good among us. Self-care is essential. There is an unsaid mental programming among humanity that states: "When life gets busy and overwhelming, automatically drop yourself to the last spot on your list of priorities. Better yet, erase yourself from your own to-do lists." We often settle for being "fine" and just "okay". We try to justify, and get used to, not being as fit or healthy as we could be. Furthermore for centuries, self-neglect has been rewarded in our society. The harder we work without taking time to refuel or recover, the better. Driving ourselves into the dirt has been mislabeled as discipline and work-ethic. Exercising is still seen by many of us as wasting time. So many people feel guilty when they take time from something else, in order to make exercise and their own health a priority. Mother's and father's feel guilty for investing in themselves.

At the same time, daily movement is paramount to the thriving of all human beings. It is a paradox. Thriving is a truly different concept than just "getting by" or "surviving". Subconsciously, many don't believe that flourishing in life is a viable option. I am here to tell you that it is! A pervasive feeling of unworthiness plagues humanity. It is good to remember some powerful "old school" tenants to live by. One should lean on self-discipline, practicing consistency, living in integrity, and developing character in order to overcome crippling beliefs.

In this book the word "fitness" can be interchanged for any hard-to-do, for you, activity or behavior that will grant you immense greatness as a reward for doing it consistently and faithfully. I'm here to tell you that there truly are, ways of thinking, doing, and being that translate into unfathomable success. You can have thorough enjoyment of your life on every level. I have transformed my life into such an existence. I have traveled that road from adversity to advocacy for the wellbeing of others. Bliss and balance can be achieved without being strung out on illegal drugs or using other unhealthy mechanisms to get there.

Addressing limiting mindsets while moving the human body is powerful. The majority of the people who need to work with great fitness experts or life coaches do not. "Fitness" subconsciously shows up as a subsection of life that really doesn't fit in with what they deem important. It's low on the value scale. It's marketed in a manner that turns off the people who would benefit most. The numbers show that shredded bodies and inspiring words aren't enough to make people get up, get active, and more importantly, reevaluate their priorities. I am convinced that for the majority of people who are not as fit as they'd like to be, beliefs implanted in their subconscious mind are at war with what they know they should be doing. Psychologists would refer to this as cognitive dissonance.

In my opinion this internal mental war is the real reason that so many struggle with achieving great success in life. We know exactly what to do and the proper actions to take to win. We also struggle with having subconscious beliefs that make taking consistent action hard for us to do. Each of us have areas of life affected by cognitive dissonance. Smokers who know that cigarettes are poison, suffer from cognitive dissonance. When our behaviors and our knowing do not match, there is stress and outcomes in life that do not suit us. This slowly drains our batteries as humans. It leads to inaction around important things and sustained action becomes impossible. The birth of procrastination occurs because of unchecked bickering beliefs and misaligned actions.

Have you ever begun a project with boundless vim and vigor? After a while you find yourself losing energy. Self-sabotage sets in. You avoid the harder tasks. Obstacles grow in size. Ultimately you embrace procrastination. Then finally you quit all efforts altogether. Take a couple of seconds to reflect on an area of life where you are stuck in this sequence. Right now, you may be shaking your head in agreement feeling like "Damn, I need to do better." I promise you that it is fixable. The problem is that a belief or set of beliefs in your subconscious paradigm is at total odds with the activity that you must perform to win. That belief has been hard wired in place over years and years of living and seeing it true. The fact that it is a hidden belief is what has hampered you for years. Hidden limiting beliefs fuel cyclical failure and self-sabotage. When you act in accordance with the hidden belief or beliefs, there is a strange comfort there. Even when you continuously lose. All kinds of alarms are set off internally when you try to do things that challenge this hidden deep rooted negative belief. Make the time to hunt within and discover it. Aim to alter the subconscious limiting belief that you may have. Then and only then, can you freely adopt new and beneficial habits. Sometimes it takes a certain level of courage and vulnerability to uncover what is really holding you back. The more we look for the offending subconscious belief the more it runs away to hide. Many times it takes the insights of another human with a whole new perspective to help you see things differently and move on. We have been trained to work alone. Now is not the time for that mindset consult those who know you and love you.

In my life I have had to identify and eradicate many subconscious paradigms. After I discovered them I had to drag them onto the stage that is my conscious mind and shine a spotlight on them. Once the identified demons are laying exposed on the stage of your conscious mind, it's important to trace the affects that they have had on life, both positive and negative. Sometimes the positives are very hard to locate but they are there. Two paradigms that I was unaware existed in my life for years but were killing my efforts at success were the paradigms that *"I don't deserve to have it all"*, and that *"It is impossible to happy for any sustained period of time."*

For years, when I got to the brink of breaking through in any area of life I would find a way to subtly kill the process. I would go all the way through the steps and do ninety seven point nine percent of the work. Then I'd subconsciously stop and kill the seed of success. I noticed this trend while in my twenties. I took a powerful look at my money in my twenties. I found that earning money was not a hard thing for me to do. I inherited my work ethic from my adopted mother Travis Farnell. She came to America from Guyana South America with two dollars in her pocket and built a successful and significant life from the ground up. I worked hard as a trainer from before the sun came up until after it went down for years. I single handedly built a business that I was proud of. I soon became aware of the fact that when I made more money than I was used to, I felt a huge surge of panic in my being. I'd feel a rush in my cells to spend it. It was like a driving force to become poor again took over me. Instead of receiving the money and then looking forward to investing it into something and put my dollars to work for me and my family's future, like I do now. I'd feel urged to spend it. Spend it I did. I bought tons of expensive things from TV's, to clothes, rims, to jewelry and watches. I bought a bunch of things that I did not need. Living in the New York City Metro area allows you to blow a ton of money super quickly.

I was buying bottles in the club. I was serial dating, and spending anywhere from fifteen hundred to three thousand dollars a weekend in clubs and restaurants. Eventually, I got into trouble with credit cards and owed almost thirty thousand dollars! I had to start over again, and again, each month growing my wealth. Deep down inside all I wanted in my life was financial security. My true desires and my actions didn't match. Furthermore, I had never in my life witnessed the behaviors and habits of someone with real wealth. I was in my early to mid-twenties having the time of my life! All this time I held and desired the major goal of being financially free by age thirty five. That didn't happen. Talk about cognitive dissonance! The spending that I was doing didn't match that goal. I spent rather than invested. I bought a brand new car off the lot all cash. I saw it in the New York City Car Show at Jacob Javits Convention Center and bought it a few months later. I also bought a three thousand dollar TV without even blinking. I had a blaring problem. Young Dre' was self-sabotaging in a huge way. I found that two major subconscious beliefs drove this behavior.

Number one, I subconsciously believed that being black and wealthy without being an entertainer or playing a ball sport was impossible. I also believed that being able to work only because "I choose to" and not "because I have to" was something that was out of my reach as a black man. It was a pipe dream to me. Financial freedom was something that I felt *I wasn't worthy of and didn't deserve.* Secondly I also subconsciously believed that *life was all about pain and struggle.* I was totally unaware that those two beliefs were running my show. Eventually I got totally fed up with my reality. I gathered up the energy to hunt down, internally, what was at the core of me sabotaging my finances.

Not feeling worthy of living a life where there is no lack of money, was something that I acquired over years and years of observing society and slowly padding that belief as a kid. Growing up in poverty in the ghettos of NYC and Connecticut showed me that I was a part of a group of people in America who weren't worth anything. It was the poor people. More times than not those poor people were black and brown. They looked just like me. Poor black people always stayed poor. I never had anyone who looked like me and developed wealth speaking to me growing up. I had no models. My perception as a kid, and unfortunately well into my adulthood was that being black without a sports scholarship or being discovered for entertainment talent meant that you couldn't develop wealth. Coming from where I came from you can't beat the system, so why try? I believed that for my entire life I would struggle to make ends meet. My mom worked really hard and moved us to live in a "Blue Ribbon" school district. This was in a white community when I was thirteen. They ate French fries, fresh sandwiches with produce, and studied from recent edition books every day. All of our food came from out of cans in the schools that I attended. Golf was a thing they did in gym class. For a very long time I felt that society had set it up for me to lose and there was no way that I could win.

Everything about the environment where I grew up, the history I was taught in schools, how I witness the poor and specifically black people treated while growing up in America maimed my idea self-worth. As an adult, I consciously knew that I could become a success but my idea of success was also negatively affected by my childhood. As I served in the military and went on to graduate college subconsciously, I still believed that as a black man in America I was not worth much. Unknowingly, I still believed that I was born the wrong color. I also believed that I didn't deserve to hit my goals of financial freedom. That reality was set aside for people who didn't look like me. That was so deeply entrenched in my psyche without me knowing it. I had witnessed life being a struggle for so long, and for so many people around me, that I never took any time to enjoy it. I never acknowledged the wins in my life. I didn't acknowledge any of the beauty of being alive either. I was in mode survival mode my entire life. Struggle and pain became too normal for me. Those two fueled my weaknesses and my strengths. I wrongly believed that without pain and struggle, I would lose my strength and determination. I felt I would lose my edge. I believed that I would lose my strength and resilience. The only sense I had of myself, came from overcoming odds. I subconsciously feared I wouldn't know myself without pain and struggle. Every fiber in my being wanted to enjoy a life where my passive income paid all of my living expenses, but I subconsciously prevented it on every front. Financial freedom meant no more financial pain. Would I even know me without it? It plagued me to the point where I couldn't even embrace prosperity when it flooded into my life. I ran from opportunities to win. Can you relate?

I wore my self-worth when I wore my expensive watches. I ate my self-worth in the best restaurants around the globe. I didn't *know* my own self-worth. Discovering me took time, research, expansion as a human, and a great will to understand why fulfillment was so elusive. I had to learn to love myself enough to give myself permission to heal. I had created a life that, on the outside, looked like the American dream. After all the hard work that it took to build a business, graduate college, buy a house and car, travel and train people all over the world. I was left feeling drained and unfulfilled.

I had to stop degrading all of my achievements down to dumb luck. I had to learn to acknowledge and accept praise. I didn't believe the testimonials from my clients. I had to learn that empowering people and adding inspiration into other people's lives was a unique and valuable skillset that I owned. Would you believe that I even felt guilty accepting payment from clients? I thought that my gifts and knowledge around training bodies and minds to succeed weren't valuable. I doubted my own value, even though evidence of who I really was, and how I helped others was everywhere

One of my biggest lessons was learning to embrace winning. A lot of us have this issue. I had to become okay with having a different story than so many that I grew up with. I had learn to transplant the two paradigm stories **1.** *I don't deserve prosperity and a life of purpose.* **2.** *Life is unhappy and all about pain and struggle.* In order to adopt the right money habits and, in turn, begin building wealth for myself. When I drug these beliefs out into the open I was able to see the damage they caused in all areas of my life. I could see where and why hesitation and self-doubt had clipped my wings. I was able to decide that their reign of terror in my life was over. I decided to move differently. I decided to love me in the true sense of the word. I loved me enough to create new habits.

You can't do anything about, what you don't know, that you don't know. I now live into a brand new paradigm. I live into **1.** *"I do deserve a life of prosperity and purpose."* and that **2.** **"Life is to be enjoyed."** My entire life reflects these two truths now. I affirm them mentally hundreds if not thousands of times a day. My bank account and investment portfolio do too. My beautiful wife, the programs and workshops that I've created, the quiet confidence and peace that I now enjoy reflect the intangible work that I have put in. By discovering, reflecting and then executing things a little differently, you can transform your entire life experience.

CHAPTER 2

TRUE TRANSFORMATION HAPPENS
FROM THE INSIDE OUT

In my own money story, I outlined my difficulty with money and finances in my twenties. It wasn't until I began regarding being broke at the end of the month as a horrible problem, did I adopt different actions. I had an "A Ha" moment! I'd never realize my goal of financial freedom if I kept my self-worth attached to buying whatever I wanted, whenever I wanted it. Before this point If you asked me why I blew every dollar I got I couldn't tell you. I decided to get to the root cause of why I kept throwing away money on frivolous things. I worked daily on detaching my self-identity from how many things I could afford. I also I decided to change my perception around being broke. I made up my mind that it was an unacceptable reality for me. I stopped expecting a future filled with lack. I imagined daily an abundant future with more money than I could ever spend. One where I checked the progress of my investments every morning. I drew a line in the sand around my finances. My new story of my reality prompted me to do the difficult but necessary internal work. A new story fueled my actions. I made financial freedom the only acceptable reality for me to live into. My new perception fueled me to unpack and deal with my own psychological baggage around self-worth. I had been depressed most of my life and didn't know it. I could not find the discipline to continually do all that needed doing in that area of my life until I learned to denounce my own story around being broke and in debt. Self-sabotage around money were fueled by a story of scarcity and hardship around money. I had mentally grown to accept a version of normal that involved starting over from scratch financially every week. It was modeled for me all my life, in every foster home that I ever lived in. Over time, I adopted a new normal where wealth building became the center piece of living.

You have limiting mental processes going on right now that you are unaware of. Matter of fact, we all do. They quietly prevent us from enjoying so many great life experiences. As long as these hindering thought processes remain hidden they have power in our lives. The purpose of me writing this book is to shine the spotlight of awareness onto our blocks and inactions. Then you can make new choices that will virtually alter your life with fitness, and so much more. You can then implement just about any exercise routine or eating regimen with a new motivation and commitment that lasts! Your world really opens up when you look and feel the way that your "inner Self" desires you to look and feel.

I'm asking you to be open to trying on this book's simple methods and distinctions. If something does not apply to you, feel free to leave it behind. Make sure you look inside of yourself thoroughly as you read and apply the techniques within this book. Steal lessons from the stories and analogies in this book. Apply them to your own life experience. You will understand how and why you and others have failed in the past at shifting certain things in life. My hope is that you enjoy a new found power and strength around making and sustaining change. This power should be accompanied by a sense of empathy and compassion for yourself and others. Most of us do not need more information. We simply need a shift in thinking. Take notes as you read and do all of the **ACTION** points.

MIND MANAGEMENT

"Actions, behaviors and habits display what a
person's true underlying thoughts are"

Every day, people think to themselves or make the statement that they are "sick and tired of feeling and looking the way they do." Yet they take no sustainable action. They may even get a gym membership, go to the gym for three weeks, then lose momentum and stop exercising all together. At some point, one has to be sick and tired of this merry-go-round. The key to changing this insanity is to be ready to build a better connection with yourself on a mental and spiritual level. *This book outlines how people all over the world think and then act to bring the bodies of their dreams into existence.* This book will provide fully tried and tested tools to implement on a mental level that will translate into fit and healthy bodies now and for the long run. It is about time that someone approached health and fitness from the source addressing "the mind" and our inner beings as the main source of power in the efforts of achieving the fit bodies that so many desire.

Are you willing to accept and embrace change? Not the kind of change that happens when the body is placed under stress of weights or rigors of running, but the change that occurs when you put in the effort to truly hear yourself and live a life of purpose and intentional creation. Everyone reading this book can redefine what they want in life, and then go out there and get it. With practice, we can all gain the ability to think things into existence and continually take actions to make them happen in reality. No matter what the world throws at us we can all flourish. You can experience and have the things that you love and quit settling for the things that you only "like" because it is there. Living like this takes practice, willpower, self-love, compassion, and the ability to be real with yourself. The reason you now have this book in your hand is that something inside of you needs to express itself. Something that is not satisfied with "Where you are" right now. A part of you sees the potential for more.

Something inside of you wants to achieve all of the things that matter to you. Full expression and access to your higher self are pushing you to turn these pages. Getting into great shape, building wealth, or have better relationships may be the desire. Behind doing these things is a thirst to better share who you are with your world. Being able to positively alter and assume control over the physical expression of who you are, will exponentially enhance every other aspect of your life. You may already see that connection. Society has programmed us to seek out practical/ quick sound bite solutions for deeper issues. We have lost the ability to see the place that our mindsets play in our state of physical well-being. I created this book because I wanted to bring the connection between the mindset, soul and physical health to the center of our consciousness. It is sometimes important to drag things from the dark to the light so we can deal with them powerfully. Then one can move on and achieve what they want. It is important in the human experience that we are able to manifest things in our lives we have historically believed impossible. I believe it is essential to cultivate favorable mindsets to carry from day to day and from situation to situation. You have total control over the mindset that you carry through life. You are the Chief Executive Officer of your mind and therefor your life. This book will hopefully raise a state of self-awareness and provide some tried-and-true tools that people who are very successful utilize. A person whose mental processes are blocked by the noise of the world is a person who literally has no control over one's own mind. Without the mind there aligned properly with the goal, hoping and wishing is the best you can do to create the life of your dreams.

POWERFUL LIVING

"You are the architect of your life experience...
You get to choose who you will be in every facet
of life"

My name is Andre Anthony Van Lun and I am a human being. I am a simple human being who has lived through a myriad of circumstances both positive and negative. I have navigated them just like every other human being on this planet. I believe that what you take from circumstances you go through and carry with you is what matters most. A unique and honest perspective is what I have to offer you here in this book. Don't take anything written in this book as the "truth" just because it is in print. As human beings, we have a whole lot of things in common, we are not as different as you may think. I have gone through many different circumstances which most people would deem negative. At the same time, I am not simply a sum of my circumstances. We are all today, what we chose to become yesterday. Whether you chose knowingly or not, you have chosen your present state of being. In this very moment, we are all pure possibility. I accepted full responsibility for what I experience in life. Most people do not do this. The most popular way to live is to unwittingly drag limiting mindsets and clumsily cultivated beliefs through life, receiving whatever random outcomes these potent mindsets yield. I choose to live a life of intentional creation.

I no longer live a life that runs completely on chance and circumstance.

I used to live like this and I know one thing for sure. That existence sucked! It's like living inside of a washing machine. Circumstances and environmental forces left unguided, sets us up to receive the worst. I decided it was time to seize creative control over most aspects of my life. Although circumstances I cannot control still swirl around me, I still surf life happily. Because of this, what I do and who I am touches the lives of many. I am fortunate enough to know that I am armed with a message of internal empowerment that I must share with others. We each have something unique inside of us to give to the world.

If life is an ocean, we should learn how to surf. It is far better than being focused on trying to shift the waves of the ocean. Surfing is selecting and amplifying the thoughts that you want to entertain while tuning out continual deluges of negative ideas and beliefs from others. Protect your peace! Do not allow the noise around you to become the noise within you. Blocking out certain energies gives you the ability to surf wisely through life. You will become awakened to your own mental strength. That strength will lead you to taking daily purposeful action. In order to get the most of the distinctions laid out in this book, you must be willing and open to learning how to surf instead of being helplessly tossed about in the ocean. Be open to enjoying inner peace. Remember to apply the action points, stories, and anecdotes directly to your life. Refer to them after the book is done.

"Amazing" is how I refer to myself and my disposition when people ask me "How are you doing today?" I live into it, no matter what the day throws my way. Sure, like every human on the planet I have days that totally suck. The only difference is that when I do, I knowingly choose to think better thoughts. I place focus on taking better actions that turn everything around.

Embracing gratitude every morning helps to set a tone for each day of my life. Every human that can read these words has something to be grateful for. Gratitude is the energy that makes increase and abundance possible. Gratitude is light to a dark room. I no longer wallow or settle for feeling bad for long periods of time. Negative feelings are to be acknowledged, understood and let go. I have practiced being grateful and focused on 'better" for years. I now live a life where my words, thoughts, and actions are aligned with what I want to experience in life. Much of my life was not this way. I worked against me experiencing my own best life for years. My mind was loaded with thoughts and energies of lack and inadequacy. The best life that you can live is one where your words, actions, and thoughts are aligned. I am whatever I say I am. I one hundred percent live my word. The entire world should be able to experience a version of life that thrills them. I am not special. I, at some point, felt so bad and depressed that I genuinely made feeling good and creating a great life a non-negotiable obsession.

WE ARE ALL WORKS IN PROGRESS

By stating that I enjoy great balance in my life and love the life I live. I'm not bragging. I'm sharing my reality and what's possible. Living a life of deliberate creation is not reserved for a select few people. It is reserved for those who want to happen to life instead of having life happen to them. When life happens to you it is usually not kind. When going through the darkest periods of life I never thought I'd be writing words on paper about living a beautiful life of balance, purpose and fulfillment.

I started this race called life as an orphaned black male who grew up in multiple New York City Tri-State area ghettos. I spent my formative years in the foster care system bouncing, from home to home with a plastic takeout bag filled with all of my belongings. At the same time I belonged nowhere, exactly. I also had to care for a sick younger brother along the way. We went through some of the most abusive situations and lived in some of the roughest, most destitute areas of New York City. My brother and I did this during the eighties crack era. This is when cocaine was sprinkled into various ghettos across America. Now it is common knowledge that government agencies aided the proliferation of cocaine in poor black communities like mine. The black family structure and the neighborhoods were decimated. I saw my first dead body before age ten. I managed to evolve from that kind of place, to being known around the world as one of the elite leadership and fitness coaches on the planet. I am sure that the success that I have experienced occurred as a result of what I actively entertained in my mind. The mindsets that I have assumed over time are the reasons that I am not another sad statistic. One thing that

I can tell you for sure is that I spent way too much time being unhappy. Don't waste your time being unhappy!

There is a prevalent social agreement among the have-nots that says that, "You can't possibly have it all". I believed wholeheartedly in this fallacy most of my life. I believed that pain and suffering was the price to pay for being alive. I had to shatter that phony "truth". That one belief, stops so many who come from humble beginnings from taking the first step toward pursuing their dreams. We become too used to failure and hardship. It cripples even those who are dripping with potential. Society as a whole suffers due to that lack of contribution.

I have twenty three years of experience mentoring leaders and those called to do, be, and make greatness happen on this planet. I love working with high achievers. I love people who are already working from purpose and are looking to achieve more balance and impact. The prism that I have primarily used to do this is health/wellness, fitness, and strategic life coaching. You can call me a life-strategist. I specialize in helping workaholics and people who historically believed that they are "too busy" to integrate exercise and healthy eating into their daily routines. Most of my work is psychological. It feeds me on a personal level to teach it. I am, myself what most would call a workaholic. I make a living as a life strategist, leadership coach, and fitness expert. I have worked with thousands of clients: celebrities, athletes, rock star corporate executives of Fortune 100 companies, entrepreneurs, business owners, as well as everyday people wanting to get a handle on balance and fulfillment. I have also owned and run three businesses myself.

I am a professional member of the NSCA (National Strength and Conditioning Association) and I have been certified by the American College of Sports Medicine as a health fitness specialist. I was also awarded by the American Heart Association for saving a life. I have been a writer for bodybuilding.com, Men's Health Magazine's Fitness Council. I was featured on MTV, INC magazine, MSNBC magazine, SHAPE magazine, Bloomberg, Business Week and TV networks. I have hundreds of articles and videos spread all over the internet helping people psychologically, and physically tap into their best selves. One of my greatest accomplishments is saving a life with an AED. A guy thought that he would get a workout in on a Monday morning but his heart had other plans. I ended up having to hook electrode pads up to his twitching wet body and shock him twice. We saved his life with the use of an automated external defibrillator. He never looked me in the eye or spoke to me again as we casually passed each other. I guess he was embarrassed. His ego wouldn't allow him to face his mortality by shaking my hand when he saw me. My ego made me lifelong over achiever. My own ego caused me to hunt for a feeling of validity and self-worth through working with great and established brands. I hunted and stacked the accolades to say "Hell Yeah! I am worthy." I am valid. I am worth something. Inadequacy fueled my success for so long. Ego was behind a lot of my drive.

Also at the heart of it all, I love being a part of helping to transform the mindsets, bodies, and souls of leaders. I had to develop a strong sense of ego to survive where I started in life. Ego makes for a good servant but a terrible master. If you allow ego to take control of your life you will be miserable. Through all of the accolades I still felt emptiness. I had to chastise my ego many times over the years. It took me a long time to understand that our ego is the source of all feelings of inadequacy. Making this connection changed the game. Being self-centered is where most humans start. Knowing this is when my trajectory changed. My fuel for doing my work was switched out. I identified my purpose at an early stage, leaned into my strengths, and never put them down. All humans have a function and purpose to lean into. I believe that if we all live our functions to the best of our abilities, that we elevate the overall health of the planet. Many times putting down the ego is necessary for growth.

I was around twelve years old when I decided to take charge of my body. I was a newly adopted foster kid, I hated not being in charge of anything happening in my life. I grew up feeling that life was unfair, tumultuous, and not fun. I was thick into the process of survival and all I ever witnessed was the hardest parts of life. Most of my life people helped us out on the back of good will and financial gain. Many of them sucked! Just when I'd get used to one environment I would inexplicably be yanked from it and told to start anew. From one home and one set of rules, to another over and over again. I felt like a burden. I felt this even after being adopted by Travis Farnell. She never made me feel like this, but I did anyway. It was engrained. My past circumstances shaped me. Independence and autonomy was something that I craved. My body was the only thing that I found that I could control. I have never been super out of shape for any extended period of time. I have been an athlete, avid exerciser, amateur bodybuilder, and a fitness model for most of my life. I have been involved in exercise, fitness and its teaching in many shapes and forms for over twenty seven years now. Exercise has been my therapy. I was exposed to exercise and training rather early. It awakened different super powers within me, it stuck. I identified with the pain and reward of it all. My entire life was painful and ugly. Can you identify with that journey? In those early years. I made a huge discovery.

Fitness was a psychological tool that added balance to me. We should all find a practice or anchor that adds to our sanity. In this day and age I suggest that we find three. Exercise kept me sane. It granted a dopamine hit and sent a certain type of electricity coursing through my body. It was a self-imposed difficulty that, over time, made me more capable than other people. It made me more resilient. The structure of weight training and strength development became a way that I poured into myself when only one other person did. Every workout subconsciously stated to myself that I was important. This was contrary to what society said of me being a young, unwanted, poor, black, kid in America. It was opposite of what was portrayed in the filthiness of the hoods that I lived in. It flew in the face of what my biological parents said to me by abandoning me. Every run, forced repetition, and all of the sweat I could conjure up translated into me telling myself that "I am a person of worth." It turned into me saying to myself at an early age that "I am too important to go to jail". It made me dare to apply to college. It lead to me serving in the military and starting businesses of my own. The respect that I got from others by building my body, psychologically, meant to me at a very young age, that I could alter other people's perspectives of me by taking care of myself and making myself strong. I found a thing that made me outwardly admirable. Doing what you're called to do in this lifetime opens doors. It's attractive to others Finding and committing to a calling can be the spark and validation needed to create a life you love.

These lessons I learned are a glimpse into the kinds of lessons that I have taught to my clients for years. Clients whose lives have been forever altered. Experiences, research, and extensive reading of scientific studies helped me to uncover psychologically how and why fitness and exercise would stick for some, and why it is such a struggle for others. Exposing these underlying causes helps turn fitness into a consistent priority in many people's lives. Adherence usually has nothing to do with a "certain type of workout" or eating only "certain types" of foods. Although all of that is important, our actions are result of internal processes of the mind and soul. I still face the hurdles of procrastination and hesitance in certain areas of life that others may thrive at. No human is perfect, or maybe we all are. Success stories are the result of discovering and conquering certain habitual mindsets. At some level we are all battling the age-old-struggle of consistently doing something that is universally beneficial, but at the same time, personally dreadful.

I struggle to this day, with delegation of tasks that I feel "Only I can do". I procrastinate to the point of paralysis when it comes to asking for help. Yet, we all need others in order to live fulfilling and happy lives. I spent many years sitting on muted potentials as a result of latching onto to the idea that "I must do all things on my own. I was convinced that trusting others to come through for me is an exercise in stupidity. Some people didn't have that life experience. They delegate without a problem. I have always struggled with trusting others to do what they've promised me they'll do. I have gone unsupported in so many critical areas of my life. People have failed or betrayed me on so many occasions. I became jaded and disconnected. I know now that nothing great was created by a single person on an island. Greatness takes the efforts of a group of gifted individuals moving in unison.

Since I became aware that great distrust existed deep within me I work to defy it. I have worked through daily thoughts of great cynicism and pessimism when it comes to others. It has been one of the hardest mindsets for me to alter. I think it was passed to me in-utero through my DNA. For me, the environment that I was born into nurtured the generational traumas within me. The mindsets that moved me forward in life were mostly geared for survival. One of them was "Don't trust anyone but yourself". This and other mindsets moved me away from being able to "focus on better" through collaboration. I had a hard time imagining what "better" would even look like. The dichotomous struggle of "expecting the worst" while simultaneously working towards "better" eventually became my lens for attaining success. This mindset served me and sabotaged me at the same time. I'd experience some success, but it came at the expense of enjoyment, self-expression, and inclusion of others. Fear of the other foot dropping is like having an emergency brake engaged while driving a car in a race. Never trusting enough to delegate, does not align with my goal of helping millions and making millions. I still work through trust and fear of loss issues. Not one of us is perfect. I am still a work in progress. I have made tremendous personal progress. Doing the inner work is hard, but so worth it. Trust me, over time it gets easier.

I love studying human similarities and differences. I almost became an anthropologist while studying at Montclair State University. I loved a class I took called "Human Variation." The head of the Anthropology department asked me to switch my major from Exercise Physiology to Anthropology. I declined. Studying people, history, and cultures was a love of min but, I couldn't see making a living at it. I couldn't believe that I could be financially successful doing something that intrigued and excited me. I didn't even do any research into discovering what applications anthropology had in the real world. I never even looked into what top grossing anthropologists earned. I naively created a story in my head of me crawling around in the sand, carefully brushing dust away from bone fragments and pottery. I created that unpalatable story in my mind. It served as a wall not to explore the unknown. Back then, I believed that I could never have my cake and eat it too. Pain was woven into my DNA. I believed that if it didn't hurt me in some way, shape or form, that it wasn't real. Looking back this was sad. I guess that was why I was pursuing a career as an actor and a model in New York City at that time. The struggle, constant rejection, poverty, and the pain of acting were more familiar and comfortable to me than exploring a whole new world that organically intrigued me. Now, I say give me all of the cake! I am eating it all!

In another life I was a very guarded city kid raised on Reggae and 80's Hip-Hip blaring in the streets. Our idols were the flashy drug dealers on every corner. I have also been the only black kid attending a blue ribbon white school in a small moderately racist town called Spotswood, New Jersey for three years. By the time I made it to college. I had lived a life of two extremes. Venturing off into the land of anthropology still felt impossible for me. Anthropology was intriguing because I had first-hand experience of a large gamut of cultures. I wanted to understand people better. I love humans in all of our shapes, sizes, colors, and stupidities. I still felt that I didn't belong in the world of anthropology. I didn't feel worthy to play in that game.

This is why models are so important. Before 1998 I never knew anyone who looked like me, who was in the field of anthropology. I wasn't aware of anyone black making a living that way. There was only one black male professor I had ever met. He was a lot older than me and he said that I had a knack for it. I scored straight A's in my anthropology classes without much effort. He said that I had the curiosity it took to be successful in the field. To this day I actually study ancient societies and anthropological history in my free. Back then, as a nineteen or twenty year old it felt like an overly white field of study that I didn't belong in. I created that story in my mind. My whole existence may have been different if I didn't. When have you created a story in your mind that has cut off all possibility of growth for you? I have since learned that the "truth" is what you choose for it to be. It isn't absolute. I implore you to use your mind. It is at the top of the list of extremely powerful tools worth mastering. Challenge your "truths" and always question how they got there.

ARE YOU READY TO RUN... MENTALLY?

"If you do not wield your mind as a carpenter wields his tools, you'll miss out on the opportunity to intentionally build a life."

We have all been mentally conditioned. Some of that conditioning serves us well, while some of it is poisonous to our continued growth as humans. In the beginning it takes a lot of thinking and focus to adopt new and beneficial habits. How we are conditioned plays a big role. Until the new habit becomes second nature, the mind painstakingly controls the continuous taking of the new action. There will be no long lasting results if you cannot make it through this transitional time period. Doing what it takes to be healthy and fit is one of those pursuits that does not stop.

Even when the goal of becoming fit has been achieved, there is no finish line. Maintenance is always necessary. That means that the motivations behind the actions must run deep. Many of us don't consider our own inner workings when tackling new and difficult tasks that are mandatory for success.

Taking a drop dead honest inventory of ourselves is step number one. Knowing how far you are from achieving a goal is important as well. It gives you a chance to make a fair assessment of the amount of energy that it will cost for you to achieve a thing. When I was twenty nine years old I decided that I would run a marathon before I turned thirty. I had never run more than three miles before setting this goal. I was also in bodybuilding shape at the time. That means I was five foot eleven two hundred and ten pounds with less than ten percent body fat. I'd never run more than three miles because I hated running. I hated running because it was difficult for me. With every step I took I struggled with breathing. I never got to the runners high that so many people speak of. I still run today and I can only count two times that I may have felt euphoric while doing it. I was as far from being able to run a marathon as a person could be. That's why I chose to sign up and run twenty six point two miles. A marathon was further than twenty six point two miles away from me. My habits and training up until that point, made it feel as though I was planets away from crossing the finish line.

I knew training to run it would be hard, but I never knew how much I'd learn about myself in the process. Unfortunately, I only gave myself nine weeks to train from it. The real reason I was running the marathon was because every decade of my life I like to issue myself a challenge. It reminds me of how far I've come internally and how far I still have to go. It commemorates the progress of living a decade. I always pick something personally hard to attempt. Deep inside of me I felt I couldn't do it. I had to physically incentivize myself as well. I bought a limited edition Invicta Russian Diving watch that I had seen while on vacation in the Bahamas with my then girlfriend. (She's since became my wife Nicole.) I vowed not to wear it until I conquered the marathon. I knew that I had negative mental programming to override in order to do it. I got a glimpse of who I could become in the painful process of training my body to run a marathon. I envisioned becoming a person capable of navigating any physical or mental pains. I even envisioned myself becoming a person able to overcome old patterns of thinking by conquering a marathon. The effort was worth it!

I lost seven toenails in training for the marathon. I lost over thirty pounds of fat and muscle. I was relentless! I also chose (very stupidly, I might add) not to alter the rigors of my work out schedule, or diminish the physical nature of my three jobs. At the time I was a mobile physical trainer running a business, a health and wellness coach for a fortune 100 company, and a corporate group exercise instructor.

I remember being insanely focused on thinking and making my training runs happen each day. I researched a marathon training program and stuck to it like my life depended on it. I melded my mind to become singular in regards to running. I ran in all weather. I hated doing that the most. I ran in rain, sleet, cold, whatever weather New Jersey could throw at me in January and February I ran through it. I flipped a switch on having a singular focus. This was my inner resilience made real. We all are faced with doing things that are difficult but beneficial. What will be your marathon? What self-imposed challenge can you select that will make you grow into a better person? I had to tap into the very fiber of my being to be able to make it through the training. I got to see and remind myself of who I really was, and what kind of material I was made of. If you place yourself under stress and undertake a difficult- for-you project, you will awaken a powerful awareness and knowing of yourself. You set the stage to create an unshakeable belief in you as well as the God in you.

The world tries to wear that down. Our society is hard on our sense of self-belief. We are programmed to look for all of the answers in life in places outside of ourselves. Someone is always selling us the remedy we need. Only you can reconnect with the soul knowing that our inner guidance and strength is already within us. It just takes intense focus. It takes us being inquisitive around who we are being as humans. From time to time do difficult things that force you to question that fabric of who you are. We gain so much as a result of the challenge. The self-belief that can be cultivated through struggle is insane. The awareness raised around who you really are and who you can become is invigorating. Life should be invigorating... Is yours?

I thought about how I'd feel after completing the marathon. I recommitted to achieving it again and again every single hour of every single day. I learned that when I become focused on doing a thing that it is like the jaws of a pit-bull locking on prey. I never let up! See, making the decision to run the marathon only once wasn't going to be enough. They don't tell you this but for the hard things you must commit many times. When up to doing something that is psychologically unattainable, due to who you fundamentally are, you must recommit to the task regularly, over and over and over again. You can't just say it aloud one time or write it down in a book and put the book in a closet and forget about it. If you do that you won't gather enough energetic momentum to see the task through. Repetition is what creates enough momentum to get you over the finish line. Repetition controls who you become. Consistently recommitting to the goal makes the goal achievable to our subconscious mind.

If running came easily to me, I could afford the option of not thinking about it until I had to. I could also afford feeling comfortable. In the beginning I was uneasy about it and I had to train my mind to focus. I talked myself into running each day. I had to coax myself past the blood blisters that formed on the pads of my feet and hurt like hell. I learned to buy good sneakers and even better socks. I had to navigate bloody nipples from the friction of t-shirts rubbing on them for my long runs. Electrical tape works wonders on that front! I had to find relief for chaffed thighs. The self-talk that I developed during this time period is what got me through plantar fasciitis and chronic pain in my knee. That same self-talk has fueled success in many areas of my life since then.

With regards to the goals that we set for ourselves to achieve we do not all start at the same place. Being real with where you are starting from matters a lot. When it came to running I was far, far from being a marathoner. I would have quit if I expected a marathon to be easy. Being compassionate with yourself when you fail or experience temporarily pain in pursuit of a worthy goal! Being realistic affords you that room. There were so many times that I felt drained by the effort it took to run the seven, fifteen, or eighteen mile training runs. There were many times I set out to accomplish the distance of the day and had to stop short from fatigue, injury, or feeling sick. I had to forgive me in that moment and look forward to finishing the next training run. I became more organized with my time. I employed the use of small naps each day. Tired was an understatement. I often didn't feel really healthy either. I ultimately depressed and challenged my immune system to the point where I broke out in hives and experienced flu like symptoms for a year. I touched the edges of what was physically possible for me. I still had lots of work to do on my ability to show myself compassion.

There came a point in training, even though it was hard, where I know that I was going to finish the marathon in one piece. I grew to know that it wasn't going to finish me. Towards that end of my training runs, running for two hours a day became something that I just did. It was the air that I breathed. I even hated it less. I didn't need to obsess over the prospect of running anymore. I had broken through. For the time being running had become a part of me. This wasn't luck, but it was through intention that a fifteen mile run became easy for me to do. To accomplish something that presents as difficult for us, we must nurture it into becoming a habit.

All of the things associated with long distance running became my new normal after nine weeks of training. The blisters, the clothing, the food, wrapping my feet, and the early wake ups, all became my new "regular". By the end of marathon training I not only liked the idea of a marathon, I couldn't wait to run it. I knew down to my very cells that I could do it. I was in a new body too. I was 30lbs lighter and faster than I had been in years! I ran the marathon nonstop in the time of four hours and fourteen minutes. My confidence around everything else in my life also skyrocketed! Most people exercise and eat in hopes of getting into great shape. They should be doing both in efforts of creating a grand experiment. They should be training to see how much better they can become as an entire human being. After doing a difficult physical thing, people should be asking themselves what tools can I take and use, from what I've just learned about myself? For humans, the power of creation lay in our dedication to see things through. Discipline is the answer. On the surface, our bodies seem to work as one unit, but in reality, we are a series of many complex systems and components. The mind and soul happen to be among the most important components. For the vast majority of fitness products, smart marketing and sales people are the real winners.

WHEN WILL WE UN-LEARN?

*"The most difficult thing is to Unlearn ways of
being that no longer serve us."*

Obesity is on the rise worldwide, and especially in America. One point five billion humans are estimated overweight in the world according to the World Health Organization. Another 43 million children under the age of 5 are categorized as obese. I would like to point out that at this point in history, there are more gyms, exercise studios, and obesity centers on the planet than there ever were. There are more fat loss guides, exercise gadgets, boot camp classes, more health foods, trainers, health conscious Mega super markets, weight loss shows, body contouring clothing, 90 Day challenges, creams, fit video games, exercise apps. And the list goes on. I regret to inform you that all of these answers to the epidemic of obesity are surface solutions to a much greater problem. These so-called practical remedies give the same result as rubbing very expensive lotion on a broken arm hoping to fix it. Without the proper mindset to continuously implement all of the various exercise solutions, in continuous fashion, there will be no lasting changes. Surface solutions translate into billions of dollars flooding into the companies that develop them. There are very few lasting solutions for the people who need them.

I would like to be the first to say that many of these fitness solutions could be great. The problem is that most will implement a certain tactic for a short period of time and then inevitably lose steam. If you are like most people who struggle with physical fitness you have likely tried many of exercise products and programs. Some of them do work. They work as long as you have the gusto, vim and vigor to implement them. So many of them flat-out suck! Even great information has no impact if you are not mentally ready to receive and implement it. Take a second to think about how many times you have personally been on this roller coaster ride. Almost everyone that I know has lost weight, added muscle, definition, and been in better shape at some point in time. Not many are able to sustain these changes over time. This is because their minds have not changed while they were taking actions. Their new body was the result of simply doing. Their normal has remnants of their old ways of being. They took actions but never graduated into "a new way of being". Doing and being are not the same thing... Being has the soul attached to it. When considering every viable solution available, some options will work for many, but no single solution will work for everyone. Remember I am using fitness as a prism here. People often use no discernment when choosing what course of action they should take in many areas of life.

At the end of the day what truly works are the following: 1. Regular consumption of a healthy natural diet. 2. Developing coping tools for creating a great mental state of being. 3. Consistent execution of a sound and challenging exercise program. These three things will bring out the best body and health in each of us. Let me point out that almost everyone knows this. Eat less processed garbage and more naturally occurring foods. Exercise more and add muscle by participating in strength training program one to two times a week. If you are not eating the most nutrient rich diet, supplement your foods with a good multivitamin. I believe that most people also know this by now. On a whole, we do not actively registered it and acted from it yet. There should at least be as much light shown on nutrition and health as there has been on COVID 19 virus. A good thing to look at is why do our actions defy logic on so many occasions? There is a huge correlation between sensory overload and unhealthy eating. Along with the sharp increase in obesity there is also a large increase in cases of depression.

BUSY IS MAKING US FATTER

"Busy" has long been a badge of honor in our society and utterly impossible to avoid. It is also making us fatter. A very popular study outlines how decision making ability plummets as mental fatigue increases. Our minds are now more connected to more happenings than ever before. Ten horrific happenings from across the globe can enter your mind-space before you even have your first cup of coffee. Our "to-do" lists are longer and they are filled with more things and situations to navigate than ever before. We know so much, about so many different things, that it leaves us less space to be mentally nimble. That causes us to make poor decisions in our everyday lives. These choices usually happen to be around what matters most to us. One study from a prestigious University follows two groups of participants.

One group was tasked with remembering a four digit number. The other group is asked to remember a seven digit number. They each attended a healthy eating seminar. After the course of the study the groups were asked to select a healthy desert choice. They were given either fresh fruit or chocolate cake to choose from. The group that had seven numbers to remember were 50% more likely to select chocolate cake than the group that was only required to remember four numbers. Imagine what happens in a busy life filled with daily food decisions. How many of us are tasked with remembering and taking action on hundreds of things daily. The volume of information that we take in these days is staggering. I always recommend to my high achieving clients who are already successful and want to take it to the next level, to do all of their higher thinking tasks in the beginning of the day.

The mind works very similarly to a muscle. It becomes fatigued as the day progresses. Decision making both large and small can become compromised by the end of the day. Can you identify with this? Hopping from real life, to the news, to social media, to family issues etc. it is no wonder why we can lose control of their own minds. Most people find themselves in a state of mental fatigue which translates into poor decision making around food and exercise. That is their perpetual version of normal.

If you never rest a muscle, or have no clue of how much load it can support, you throw away both safety and efficiency while using it. The same is true of our minds. There must be time set aside for practicing concentration and focus. Five or ten minutes where you practice being present and focused on only one thing. Eventually you will be able to do so for extended periods of time. It is also important to know our own bandwidth. Each of us have different mental thresholds for how much high level thinking we can effectively do. Some people can sustain hours of mental work straight. Some of us can maintain only a few minutes. Get to know the measure of your mind. Become reacquainted with it. Practicing mindfulness and meditation are like taking the mind in to be serviced and washed. DO them both.

Make time for your mind to recharge. This is especially true for those people who have type "A" personalities like I do. Our minds never rest, they run and run and run. That can result in us putting ourselves in positions that we have to apologize for later. Things tend fall through the cracks. That wreaks havoc on the mind of a recovering perfectionist. It caused anxiety. Too many of us have also allowed the noise and rigors of life to drown out the sound of our own inner voice. That wise, calm, consistent voice we all have. This is the guidance system that leads people to experiencing the best version of themselves and their best life. Never allow it to be drowned out. It is our true north!

HABITS VS GENES

"You are what you habitually do"

As research on the human body progresses, outcomes tend to show that the oversimplified concept of too many calories in and not enough calories out isn't the only major determinant of our body fat levels. The idea that weight and fitness levels have anything to do with each other, is also misinformation. It is easy to say that you will be fat if you eat more calories than you burn, and that you will be thin if you eat less calories than you burn. This explanation makes sense in only a rudimentary way. The problem is that the human body is not a container that you can simply empty out or fill up. Humans are complex organisms. There are hormones and systems at work that regulate what the body does with the calories you eat. These hormonal conditions can change like the weather. Stress affects everything. Due to this finding, the way that you exercise becomes an even smaller slice of the pie when it comes to enjoying extraordinary health and wellbeing.

I believe that scientists and exercise physiologists of the future will find that the mental disposition of a person has so much more impact on our physical health than we could ever imagine. There are times when you can eat a lot of food and not gain weight and there are times when you can eat less and gain weight. Recent studies have begun to show that repeated actions and habits have more of an effect on a person's life than their own genetic predispositions. DNA expression is more fluid than once thought. Habits and lifestyle are shown to have a profound effect on the expression of our genes.

It is almost common knowledge now, that our lifestyles can alter genetic expression in our bodies. Things such as environmental factors, exercise and nutrition have been shown to affect which switches get flipped on or flipped off in our genetic sequences. Epigenetics studies gene expressions that takes place without the actual sequence of our DNA being changed. There are so many factors that translate into which traits in our DNA either express or remain dormant. Some of the latest research in epigenetics is showing that some of the lifestyle changes that we make now will affect not only our genes, but also can become heritable changes. This means that predispositions can be handed down to the next generation due to habit and lifestyle changes of the previous generation. Your habits, good or bad may not only affect you, but your offspring before they are even born. This has been found to be true for both positive expressions like lowered risk of heart disease, certain cancers etc. It is also true for negative genetic expressions such as diabetes, cancers, obesity etc. Our habits are that powerful! The choices that we make now can genetically affect our grandchildren. Their habits will do the same. The power of making smart choices in our lives has been undervalued. I recently started watching TV again and the fact that prescription drugs now have commercials and focus group-tested names is disturbing. We are being programmed to expect to need them as we age. A war is going on.

No one is hopeless when it comes to getting into better shape or looking and feeling great! What happens in life may be out of your control, but how you process feelings, the actions that you take, and the direction of your thinking is up to you. The way that we feel and our stress levels also play a large part in how we look and feel as human beings. Even families of large stature, that may be obese, usually have one or two family members of smaller stature or normal weight. The smaller individuals in a family may have the same overall bone structure and genetically inherited fat deposits, but they just haven't taken the actions to fill up those fat deposits. Who they are as humans steps in to decide the meat suit they will wear. Ever wonder why there are fat dogs and cats that are pets? Wonder no more... Take a look at their owner's eating habits.

On the other hand, some people eat less and gain more. The question to ask is... What is the mental environment running in that person's body, at this particular moment? What is the skew of their predominant thoughts and emotions? What habits are in place that lead to the expressions in reality that they see? If we struggle with weight issues, if there is no money left at the end of the month, if your relationships always fall apart, you can trust and believe that there are consistent ways of being and thinking that are attracting those outcomes to you. All things that manifest in our reality have intangible origins. This would mean that one of the most valuable things that we can do is to take time to look inward. Ask yourself these questions: "What is my overall mindset towards life like?" "How am I coping with stress and anxiety now? "Do I speak in terms of expecting weight gain, sickness, being broke, or being alone?" Is there balance in my life?" If every human is mentally and metabolically driving a car. Are you driving Lamborghini Aventador or an old beat up 1997 Ford Festiva through life? What kind of car would your mindset and expectations match up with? How do your daily habits align? Do they coincide with what you want to achieve with their body? Everything you do and think should be in unison with what you want to achieve. Creating alignment is so important.

Everything is energy, the seen world is created by a lot of unseen factors. Your body's wellbeing is also included in this universal law. The way you see the world can elevate or degrade the condition of your health and fitness levels. It controls how well you literally and figuratively move through life. Your body's metabolic environment and mindset are different but they are usually aligned. A person's mindset (conscious or subconscious in nature) creates a person's actions and habits. Habitual ways of being can ultimately control one's fitness levels, our finances, and the kinds of relationships that we enjoy with others. If the mindset is changed, the environment of a person's body can be changed. That means that each one of our existences can be altered significantly.

CHAPTER 3

IGNORANCE ISN'T ALWAYS BLISS

> "What you don't know, that you don't know, can hurt you."

"When the frying pan is hot enough, and you are fed up, you will do whatever is necessary." I served in the US Army. At the time, I saw it as a way to get set up to go to college. My mother always insisted that she didn't have the money to send me to school. She told me that when I first met her at age eight. I really didn't expect her to anyway. In my mind, her work was done when I became a man. I was seventeen and I was certain that I could easily find my way in the world. I had already overcame so much in life by that age that I was certain I could carve out a life. I was accepted to multiple colleges and had partial or full scholarships as a student athlete. I had earned some pure academic scholarships as well. I chose to go to the military because I had a fascination with weapons. Guns, knives, swords, explosives name it, I love it all. If it is beautiful and dangerous I was drawn to it. The military seemed like a good way for me to get school paid for without getting my neck broken playing football. By the time I was shipping off for Basic Combat training I was having constant headaches and lower-back pain from playing football. I was good but not naturally gifted at playing the game. I evaluated the amount of work it would take me to get into the NFL and I said "hell no". I was already in pain all of the time. I'd have to grow my body, I'd have to train up my speed, and the head-aches were insane. Sometimes I would wonder if I had a tumor. I played with anxiety the whole time, and never really got into the flow while playing in high school. I ended up enlisting in the US Army.

Unbeknownst to me my recruiter wrote "not applicable" on most of my benefits. The no down payment on a home benefit was waived. The Montgomery G. I. Bill was marked N/A as well. I got no college benefits. I was seventeen and the recruiter turned out to be a slick salesman. I wanted to move onto the next chapter of my life and leave home. My mom wanted whatever I wanted, so, we signed away all of my benefits. I didn't find that out until after I had already completed Basic Combat training in Missouri. I was then sent to Virginia for Advanced individual Training as a Unit Armorer and weapons specialist. After active duty was over I was in the reserves. I unfroze some of my academic scholarships and made the attempt to get into college. I settled on going to Montclair State University even though there were some bigger schools that accepted me. I wanted to go to a school close to my mom. That way I could help her with keeping an eye on the other three kids in the house. She was working the night shift twelve to sixteen hours a day raising my siblings all alone. It was at that time that I was informed of my ineligibility for any college benefits. I reviewed my original contract and low and behold "N/A" was scribbled across all benefits. My mom's and I's signature was right there too. I paid for my first few semesters with cash from my savings account. Then, like the son of a true Caribbean immigrant, I got three other part time jobs to make up the rest. I also maxed out TAG grants and took out the maximum student loans. My struggle with debt started in college. To this day I still pay student loans monthly. Fine print and ignorance is a motherfucker. The story goes much deeper, but I will end that story there in order to jump into some of the benefits that entering the military had. It changed my fabric as a human being. Looking back, I see a lot of naivety, but I also see so many lessons. Here are some lifelong lessons that ignorance afforded me

I went into the army as an enlisted private E-1. That is the lowest rank that you can come in as, in the Army. It was also my first time out of the New York City Tri state area. Everything was new to me. I was in Ft' Leonard Wood Missouri. I was just outside of the Ozark Mountains. A New York City and New Jersey kid (My only exposure to the woods was the fresh air fund for at-risk youth) was whisked away and dropped into the woods with people of all races and cultures. We were all wrapped up ogether under the blanket color of camo and the American Flag.

It was a whole new chapter of living. You are secluded on a base with only men and woman in training. You become a cog in a machine. Your persona is erased in the first few weeks. Your ego is challenged and broken. Those who can't conform are singled out and tossed to the side.

They are paid special attention with physical training to exhaustion, shame, and a never ending stream of yelling and berating. When I was younger when faced with opposition and hardship I naturally balled up in anger. I grit my teeth and fought through it no matter what. From the first kid I punched in the face, until that point in life, I had been ridiculously strong and very defiant under pressure. At the same time, I'd become a pro at internalizing both rage and pain but appearing to be "OK." By age seventeen every situation in my life, by virtue of being a young muscular black man in America, taught me how to bottle everything I felt inside. This brought me acceptance and also made other people feel safe around me. I found that if I expressed being angry or upset that people would respond in fear of me. Even raising my voice brought stares filled with fear. When those in power become fearful it never works out well for those who have none.

I had developed a thick skin from playing team sports. I mostly tuned the yelling out that took place in the military. I also was in pretty good shape from playing both football and running and throwing track. I also purposely trained to enter the military. Push-ups and flutter kicks weren't a problem for me. They were just uncomfortable. Discomfort had long became my best friend. Other people were not so fortunate and they really underwent some mental trauma in the first days of boot camp. We were sleep deprived, marched, and indoctrinated into Army culture. New recruits worlds were shattered as they were reminded that they were now property of the US Army. People broke down crying daily as the fabric of who they knew themselves to be was stripped away. No comforts were afforded us. Our new identities would later be reconstructed to that of competent soldiers and human beings. The hard part was making it through the demolition and renovation process of our psyches. I viewed it as a social experiment.

DISCOVERING WHAT MOVES YOU

One hot Missouri afternoon after doing hundreds of pushups on account of other people fucking up, my thick skin cracked. There were about one hundred of us being corralled on and off of cattle trucks lined up in front of the barracks. They were these white trailers with hay covered floors and no seats. Each person had to carry their duffel bag onto the trailer and stand with our arms wrapped around them at all times. They weighed from fifty to seventy pounds depending on how many personal items you packed. We each held one of these up off the ground while we were crammed into the cattle trucks. We drove for fifteen to twenty minutes, all the while we were holding up these bags, and packed next to each other so close that you could hear the person next to you breathe. Once we arrived we were quickly marched off the trailer and arranged in front of the barracks where we'd stay for Basic Combat Training.

Each one of us was assigned a cement square to stand in. That square was where we had to dump out our personal belongings that we brought from home. For me, this was reminiscent of the dumping of my belongings from a plastic bag when I moved to a new house while in foster care. In the military we had duffle bags though. That was a total upgrade! We were told to stand up hugging them close to our chest. There was no talking and no moving. That sun was hot and we were all in BDU's (Battle Dress Uniforms… Camo uniforms) lined up holding these bags. Our new Army issue uniforms were in there as well. Boots, coats and cold weather gear included. Some of the women only weighed one hundred or so pounds themselves. We stood there for what felt like an eternity. Eventually people started dropping their bags. Some started crying. I felt as though this whole situation was as much mental as it was physical. We were all sleep deprived at this time going on forty eight hours. As duffle-bags were dropped, all of us were sentenced to push-ups, planks, and flutter kicks. Drill sergeants made us unpack and pack these bags four or five times. They were trying to get people to follow instructions to a tee.

You would marvel at how hard that is to get one hundred people to open a bag at the same time and follow commands in unison. People kept fucking up and adding pushups, planks, burpees and other things to the miniscule effort of separating personal things and Army issue uniforms in the blistering sun. This confirmed my hypothesis at the time, that most people were complete and utter idiots. After three times of holding my bag up for five minutes dumping all of the contents out and filling it back up, doing forty push-ups in between my patience ran thin. I got pissed off yelled out loud "This shit is stupid!" I stopped following commands and stood there breathing hard with my fists balled up.

I rarely break but when I do, it's usually pretty ugly! Three big drill sergeants came running over to me and start yelling in my face all at the same time. I remember one was Asian, one was White and one was black. They surrounded me with the brims of their hats touching my head. I was at the point where I was thinking of what order to knock each one of them out in. They were yelling in my face "Where are you from boy?" "Pick your shit up!" "Who the fuck do you think you are?" "Drop and give me twenty!" "Big boy you feel like you're tough huh?". "Eyes Forward!" I was already sweating, tired, and pissed off. I didn't move because physicality and fighting has always been my go to when I am pressed. I knew that it was a bad idea to try to slug it out with the three biggest and meanest drill sergeants but the thought was still in my mind. They violated my personal space. In the environment that I was raised in that was a big no-no. Finally, after what seemed like minutes one of them took me aside. The blonde white one ordered me to follow him and said "I got this one." I was one hundred and ninety three pounds of pure anger. I was breathing hard and never unclenched my fists. We were about the same height but I outweighed him by about twenty pounds. I figured, at the time, that I could take him. (I found out later that I couldn't. He was a badass decorated Special Forces Ranger.) He takes off his hat and leans into me even closer. The look I gave him would have killed four people if looks could kill. He whispers to me "I've seen you before boy! They don't make soldiers in New York." "You're gonna fuck up and fuck up real bad boy." I already see it. I give you two weeks tops boy." "People like you get court marshalled and sent to Leavenworth Maximum security prison. That's where they make big bucks like you, break big rocks into little rocks day in and day out." I slowly began to unclench my fists and breathe normally. I felt my rage subsiding. A few things happened within me in that one sided conversation.

Firstly, I had never stood eye to eye with a grown white man that close. So close that I could see his pores. I hated the smell of his breath too. I later realized that he chewed tobacco. I fearlessly stared back into his green eyes. I hated the language that he used. I hadn't been anyone's "boy" anywhere on this earth since age twelve. By age fourteen I was working and that made me a man. I was also five foot ten and 193lbs of muscle. If I did a crime it was likely that I would be prosecuted as an adult. So, I was definitely a man in my mind. He had a deep southern drawl and accent when he spoke. I could tell from his choice of words that he was racist. Calling a black man a boy is a flagrant foul. Green was supposed to be the only color that we all saw, it wasn't though. He had also inadvertently challenged me. I prided myself on not going to jail. I had grown up seeing so many black boys that I grew up with either end up dead or in jail. When I was about ten I vowed never to go. I carried that solemn oath with me into the military. Ass rape was a great deterrent. I thought of jail as such a waste of potential. I didn't make it from Harlem, to the South Bronx, to Connecticut, to Bed Stuy Brooklyn, to Spotswood New Jersey, to Plainfield, NJ, just to end up in a military prison breaking rocks in Kansas! "Fuck that!" I started obeying the commands again. Boy did I do a record amount of pushups that day. I got really close and familiar with muscle failure and involuntary collapse. I found a reason to handle my anger in a better fashion. I refused to give a racist asshole the pleasure of seeing me fail. I had found my why for the goal of graduating BCT.

Back then if you wanted me to do a thing, the way to get me to do it, was to tell me that I was incapable of doing it. That man not only challenged me, he told me that I was inadequate and that I didn't measure up. I would do everything in my power including die in the effort to prove him wrong. He had made assumptions about me due to the color of my skin, my disposition, and where I was from. He painted a picture of me that was not only negative but stereotypical. All I felt was "Ok Mutherfucka watch me work! I will prove you wrong. Damn your breath stinks!" and "Stop spitting on me." That encounter changed my whole mindset and perception of what I was really there to do in the Army. I knew that as soon as I could I was getting out as well. I made up my mind from that day forward to excel and put forth only my best efforts.

I made a decision to learn me and improve me through all of the hardships that I would encounter. I realized that I had an underlying subconscious inferiority complex. I vaguely noticed it until that point. I got off on proving people wrong and seeking out validation from others. I went to work on amassing accomplishments to prove myself to myself and others that I was different and worthy. It was a hollow patch to how I really felt inside. Being a second class minority citizen living in ghettos that the government and America's citizens created and neglected had done a number on me. Bouncing from home to home as a ward of the state and relying on the charity of strangers giving me a place to live, made me feel less than deserving of good things. I unknowingly spent most of my childhood and adult life trying to prove people wrong. People who doubted my worth and ability were proved wrong time and time again. I spent so many years acting in ways that I believe would earn other people's respect. Proving others wrong is what fueled me to succeed.

What moves you? I consciously had no idea that I was doing this either. The tragedy of the situation was that I wasn't doing anything for my own fulfillment. I earned many accolades but no fulfillment. Being successful was just a suit that I always wore out of habit. Seeking other people's approval and working not to offend or upset those who could help me became my full time job. Proving my worth as a black man became a full time job. This was on top of living and creating an existence, like all of us have to do while being alive. I became fully aware of this while in the military. It was an exhausting effort. I yearned to be spurred forward in life by other purer motivations. I had so much to learn in order to get to that point. Awareness of this mindset and my internal motivations gave me the power to eventually conquer it and be inspired instead of only externally motivated.

In the military every single person in basic combat training lost noticeable amounts of body fat and became more fit within an 8 week period. Both men and women responded very well on a very simple non gender biased training regimen. One program, improved fitness for all! I took these outcomes as evidence of the bottomless power of an unwavering habit. Daily habits shaped all three hundred and fifty soldiers in our company. We simply did pushups, sit-ups, and squats to muscle failure one day followed by a two mile run as fast as you can the next day. That was the entire magical workout program. Simple but not easy. It was done by every single soldier not on medical profile. The internal environment of every person's body was injected with new life. That internal environment was transformed through routine and consistency. Distractions were all but eliminated. There was no room made for excuses. No one cared how you felt about it, or coddled you around failure. There were no other options given and everything that we did and thought about was aligned with becoming strong and tough both mentally and physically.

Basic combat training in the US Army was a shock and the equivalent of being tossed into the frying pan. It was so different and challenged us in so many ways. A profound lesson that I learned was that structure adds efficiency. We were told: when to wake up, how to dress, what to do, how to stand, when to speak, how to wear our hair, when we could shower, when we were good enough etc. There was immediate feedback and instruction on how to become better at the tasks we needed to complete. Everyone needs coaching and instruction while learning. The whole routine shook up everything about who we were, even before we arrived to Basic Combat training. There was seclusion from what was comfortable. The higher expectations set by the Army resulted in people becoming better versions of themselves. While that demand was placed on them they thrived and flourished. Many people became the best version of themselves that they would ever attain in life, while training in the military. Going back into civilian life at the end was essentially a death sentence to the greatness in some people. Without being aware of what really moves you, then deciding that you will set up a way of being and a value system that is authentic and aligned with greatness, it is very asy to slide back into old patterns.

Setting up and living within a strict structure is a good way to begin creating a new habit. Sometimes you need a jolt and some comradery. This may account for the growing popularity of fitness boot camps, adventure racing, and group exercise classes across the country. The only problem is that when boot camp ends, so does the attainment of results. People often avoid altering the mindsets that they carry around areas of struggle. Consistency is near impossible then. The problem with these strict and structured solutions is that they are short termed solutions. It is important to reshuffle our values and priorities as we achieve the results that we want. The strict and structured approach is one that is very hard to hold onto long term. There must be some kind of intentional effort to graduate from simply doing a thing to adopting it and being it. If adoption does not occur then the outcomes will be yo-yo like. The area one wishes to expand needs to rise as a priority on one's list of values. This is essential for long term consistency.

We have yet to fully understand, that without the struggle and temporary failure experienced during the adoption phase of learning we never truly develop the mettle necessary to maintain our hard-fought-for results. Learning about one's self and the tendencies that you have while doing must become a goal. Men lie, women lie, but trends don't lie. Study your trends. You can witness what moves you in a positive or negative direction. You should be able to realize what kind of exercise makes the most sense for you to do and why. Your approach toward your goal will become clear once you know you.

If you hate a task and are not self-motivated to do it in any way, shape, or form you should notice that as well. If the thing that you are aiming to make headway in stretches you in an uncomfortable place you should notice that too. Pay attention to what, if anything comes up for you internally when you are you faced with taking action in order to accomplish a task. You should acknowledge the fear that you overcame by taking action on any goal. There is always an internal situation going on when we take action in the physical world. The euphoric vim and vigor that you feel around accomplishing steps towards a goal should also be noted. Being focused on only getting results as opposed to developing a consistency of eating well, training, and managing stressors is a sure way to fail. Dean Grazziosi a very successful real estate entrepreneur, coach, and author suggest that asking yourself "Why?" can help you to get to your deepest motives around taking a particular action. He believes that it is important to ask yourself "Why?" seven times deep in order to get to the true purpose behind a goal that you set for yourself.

EXAMPLE: I want to get into the best shape of my life!

1. Why? *I want to look and feel better.*
2. Why? *I am planning to live longer, and I want to feel confident, and unstoppable.*
3. Why? *I don't want to get sick and ill like so many in my family do...*
4. Why not? *I've seen the stress and toll that it takes on a family. I don't want that for my family.*

5. Why not? (Now answers get harder to come by. You have to think) *Becoming a burden and being helpless goes against all that I stand for.*

6. Why? *My heart breaks when people I love die prematurely. I lost my biological mother to breast cancer that spread all over her body and killed her. I couldn't help but to think that if she took care of herself and didn't smoke 1-2 packs of cigarettes a day for twenty plus years she'd have lived longer. I felt helpless as her son and I don't want my family to feel that way by losing me early.*

7. Why? *I grew up without my parents and I know how it feels to be prematurely abandoned. I don't want to pass that legacy on.*

From that sixth and seventh answer you know that family is what motivates this person. Getting to the root of why a goal matters to a person in the first place is key. It creates and emotional anchor. It becomes essential to eat better and exercise regularly if holding onto independence for a long time and not being a burden on family is what is really being created by working out. Every mile that is run becomes easier. They are now running towards longevity and legacy. Having a doughnut is now seen as something that will take them towards an early demise and away from dying old, having lived a fulfilled and happy life. It will not be viewed as an innocent escape to be had every night before bed. Becoming focused on who it is that you are becoming (both mentally and spiritually) during the effort to accomplish a goal, is the key. If the goal is worthy it should change who you become. The new person that you become will have new habits. Those new habits will yield an entirely different vision of life.

ACTION ITEM: Accomplishing a really challenging workout is a very good way to become aware of some of the personal thinking and self-talk that hinders you in life. DO ONE ASAP! While panting and rushing to get it done, take the time to listen and become aware of your inner voice when a workout becomes grueling. Take some notes of what you say to you. In that state you cannot lie to you. The truth hangs out whether you like it or not. Our facades drop off during the doing of grueling physical work. Become aware of the "I can't do this.", "They must be crazy", "I have to stop and catch my breath for a little". Pay attention to it all. Also record what you say to yourself mentally, in order not to quit. Or, do you quit? You lose if you are not aware of or have not assessed who you are when challenged in a big way. Without knowing what self-talk inspires you to push through when you want to quit, you risk always having the same mental environment and mindset that you have always had. Subliminal mindsets are the major contributor to us not achieving the goals that we set for ourselves. They fuel most of our breakdowns around discipline.

LIMITING SELF TALK AND STORIES

Without identifying your current mindset and self-talk, around hard-for-you tasks, and then consciously switching it out, you will inevitably experience fleeting or lack-luster results. This goes for fitness, finances, building a business, personal relationships or anywhere else in life. Our minds are very good at keeping us level. Maintaining an even keel is what the brain is great at. It is a survival mechanism. The very real and visceral conversations that you have with yourself in order to keep on going and working through an intense workout will reveal what you really believe about fitness to your subconscious mind. It will also expose ways of thinking that sabotage you elsewhere in life. You will notice that you have tendencies in your thinking. If you are not able to hear that dialog in your head and use what you learn about yourself to make better decisions you are doomed. You can only establish a new way of being if you unearth the default way of thinking that holds you back. Creating a plan of action from what you've noticed about yourself while engaged in intense exercise is smart. Becoming aware of your weaknesses is the first step to acquiring more strength.

When it is raining outside (ie. life comes at you fast), you will always want to run right back to the old comforting habits for shelter. This also happens in our thinking as well. If you haven't become a fit and healthy person by engraining habits into your soul, your body will be the casualty when life gets busy. It is a never ending cycle that happens to far too many. Breaking this cycle begins with admitting your humanity and limitations to yourself. Shine that light of awareness on every dark corner of thinking that sabotages your efforts. Accept all of the blame. Don't blame the class ending or your favorite instructor leaving. Don't blame being too busy or too lazy. Admit to not yet becoming a match for the outcomes that you've desired. That is okay. In order to set the stage to win in an area of life that is historically difficult, it's going to take speaking better to yourself around your abilities in that area of life. Believing that "I have a sweet tooth and it is what it is." will not help you to eat better. Believing that "I am not interesting enough" will never yield you great and meaningful relationships. Start a dialog with yourself about why you quit things when you do. Discover what motivates you and what disempowers you. It will help you build and form new habits. You should write them down. *Writing something down escorts our goals from the land of thought and spirit to our world of tangible reality.* The first time a thing becomes real is when it has been written.

Exerting yourself occasionally during exercise is important. There is pain involved. Doing the hard-to-do-for-you things will also cause pain/feedback and discomfort. Pain has a bad reputation in society and it is usually avoided at all costs. All that pain is, is feedback. Lean into discerning your pain and its cause. Pain is one of the quickest ways to begin to forge a powerful new relationship with yourself that you have never had. Many people feel weak if they admit to themselves that they have moments where they want to quit. Other people are obsessed with "looking good" and they quit before enough action has been taken to succeed. Cool points are hard to come by when we are really working on overcoming old habits and mindsets or making sustained efforts happen. It won't always be pretty. Some are just so oblivious that they aren't aware of any self-talk going on. We all internally speak to ourselves when we are in pain. Pain turns up the volume on what we really believe. Pain is feedback. It is useful feedback.

You will become aware that you also have strengths that you never knew you had. Look deeper than "I'm tired" when coming up with an answer. EX. "Why am I tired? Where else do I suddenly become tired in life? Is being tired something that I resort to when I don't want to do something? Does it get me off the hook? Why don't I want to exercise and I know it's good for me? Am I willing to let "being tired" go in order to enjoy the level of fitness that I desire? So many of us have a default state of being that we run to when hard work is to be done. Don't give in. Move your body, it will shift your state.

ACTION: Answer these after a hard workout

1. What is the first thing that comes to mind when you want to quit during a workout?
2. What mantras or words do you say to yourself to push past discomfort and finish?
3. If you do quit before finishing the program that you set out to do, explain why you stopped, what did you say to yourself right before you stopped?
4. What are some of the strengths you discovered about yourself during training?

Write down the answers to these four questions.

It may take one workout or a week's worth of workouts, where you have to push yourself hard. You will eventually be able to connect. Fill the four questions out after each workout. You will notice that you may use the same words often. Focus on the trends in behavior that you find within yourself. Select challenging workouts with a defined beginning and ending. Find a workout online. You can have a trainer write a workout for you. You could take a class at a gym. Select exercise programs that are a seven or greater on a scale of one to ten as far as intensity goes. One would be being sitting on a couch watching TV and ten would being finishing the last five miles of a marathon. (26.2 mile run).

Shift your awareness internally to answer these four questions. We humans can shine our awareness anywhere that we'd like. If you buy a red Honda, you will notice hundreds of red cars then red Hondas on the road every day. It will be as if they just magically appeared on the road. Our brains work like a Google search box. It will find whatever you populate it with. While working out populate your search box with the four questions above. Don't be afraid to acknowledge your successes. Become familiar with who you are in adversity. You should know when and why you quit as well as what motivates you to keep going. Pay special attention if you find out that you generally hate to exercise. A red flag should go up and an alarm should go off in your mind whenever you find out you have an aversion to something that will serve you well in life. In those cases hiring outside help is a good avenue to take. For years I avoided and hated dealing with my finances. I had some serious subconscious blocks around money. I had to hire a financial specialist to help me to establish new habits and get things in order. The outside perspective of an expert is so necessary sometimes. Even if it is just someone to ask you the right questions it is very important.

Doing hard things informs us of our character and the cloth that we are cut from. It points out alterations that we should make in the fabric of who we be. Those who are providers and look out for others first, usually leave themselves undone. Fitness usually shows up as a problem for these people to engage in for the long term. Subconsciously, they don't feel themselves important enough to spend their finite time on exercising and cooking healthy food for themselves. We all have varying areas of genius. Balancing a family and forging awesome relationships both personal and business may be their areas of genius. Those taught by environment or family to be humble and hide who they are, will also find it hard to find themselves worthy of devoting time to self-care exercise. They (maybe subconsciously) believe that sacrificing their own wellbeing is necessary in order to make room for the thriving of others. This is so far from the truth. Those of us who are self-absorbed and a bit vain may not find it difficult to eat healthily and exercise routinely. They may struggle when it comes to cultivating deep and meaningful relationships. This is where their awareness should be placed. This work will take them far more time effort and energy to find better balance with. Forcing themselves into situations where they have to show genuine interest in others in order to be successful would be wise. Putting ourselves in uncomfortable and beneficial situations is where we grow and gain insight. Growth is a result of mentally wading through uncomfortable waters.

CHAPTER 4

FOOD IS POWER

"Food can be either medicine or poison... It's really your choice"

I studied nutrition to some extent in college and tried just about any sensible (in my opinion) diet program that has come out in recent years. I would like to preface the following opinions by saying that I do not fancy myself to be a nutritionist or registered dietician. I am just a self-researcher who had access to thousands of minds and bodies over a twenty five year career of training and coaching. I have come to the conclusion that food is one of the single most important things to consider when looking to preserve health, become more fit, and live an advancing life. It is also one of the hardest things for many people to control in their lives. A person who controls the quality and quantity of the food that they consume, has access to an exponential amount of potency for living. Once you become an adult and have the means to feed yourself, it is time to eat in a direction that helps you to flourish. Listen for feedback from your body about the foods that you habitually eat. The body has wisdom! Experimentation is the best way to discover what foods work the best for your body's chemistry. Over time you can gain a level of knowing that informs you of what time of year, to eat certain types of foods, for you to optimally show up in life. I cannot stress enough the importance of personal testing when it comes to food. Over time introduce foods and see how your body reacts to it. There is no set in stone right or wrong way to eat outside of eating as much real and natural foods as possible. Balance is different from person to person. You will be consistently eating food for your entire lifetime. Do not rely on the government or the latest fads to instruct you on how to feed you properly. Please do not believe that food manufacturers are there to make food products that optimizes your life. Food is a for profit business. There is not enough food in food these days. Healthy eating is a choice.

THE ART OF EATING

Did I mention that the when, where, and how of your food consumption matters? Well, I am mentioning its importance to our lives again. Scientifically, eating food is what we do to replenish energy reserves in the body. It is how we restore vitamins, minerals, water, protein, carbohydrates, fats, and fiber to the body. It is so much more than that. Food links to our internal worlds of thoughts, feelings and emotions control everything that our bodies do. When looking at the outcomes in life we should also pay a bit of attention to the intangibles that created them. We humans have attached a slew of intangibles to food consumption that underline the problems that we run into with it. Food has become entertainment. Food has is a vice or a drug to quell anxiety and depression in an over-stimulated times. Food is a pacifier. Food is a commodity that generates revenue. Food is fun! Food is power. Food is life. Food is big business. Food is individuality, culture, and memories. Food is and has always been connection, family, and love. Getting to the root intangibles around anything gives you the power to conduct yourself better around it. What has food been for you?

Once you have identified this, then you can ask you "How can I make some real lasting changes in this area of life?" Having a nuanced and deeper perspective of a habit is wonderful. It is the seed of creating lasting change. How we see things determines the actions that we take around said thing. The stories that we attach to eating and food determines how we treat it. Those inner stories that we carry can also magnify the importance we give to the food selections that we make. People who view food as love, family, and connection usually have a harder time navigating healthy eating than someone who only see's food as taking in enough nutrients to live. Someone who religiously counts calories and reads the nutrient profiles on everything they eat because food is scientific to them. Will have very different outcomes from someone who regularly dives head first into a big plate of macaroni and cheese, because it was the favorite dish their mother made them in their childhood. Most of us are both of those people at the same time. Food can be medicine or it can be poison. Food can be a prison and a source of anxiety or it can be freedom, fun, and self-expression. With so many emotional, biological, and societal entanglements to food it should now be clearer as to why there is so much difficulty in this area of life. What role has food historically played in your life? What will you decide for it to be from today?

NUTRITIONAL WARFARE

There is balance to be found with eating and health. You do not have to be the food Nazi and you do not have to be the pleasantly plump, pre-diabetic, family man or woman either. Let's look at some basics. Overeating anything will cause excess fat storage in the body. Undereating certain nutrients can cause deficiencies and cravings. There is a seasonality to eating that is healthy to observe. Food should properly fuel the life that you want to live. There are times when we should be eating more and times when we should be eating less. We need more and denser fuel when times dictate that we will be utilizing a lot of physical and mental energies. Sometimes less food, eaten more often, is what is needed. Maintaining the awareness to know where you are in this cycle is so important. You can intuitively make these shifts after a time, but in the beginning this will be difficult to do. Be quiet and sit still, meditate. Stillness can put you in touch with your own nutritional needs. Studies have shown that exercise also helps with the proper dissemination of nutrients throughout the cells in our body. This helps to neutralize some of the cravings that get us into so much trouble with food. I'd also like to outline the importance of getting sleep as well. Sleep is the only time we ever get to reset and restore ourselves. The way that a tired, stressed out, sleep deprived body, and a well-rested body process the same exact nutrients are very different.

What environment is your food entering when you eat it? What environment have you created through your habits around exercise and prolonged ways of thinking? Is your metabolism primed speedy and efficient? Or is it slow, stressed and ineffective? Resistance training stimulates the metabolism and lean body mass production. Lean body mass is the engine compartment of the metabolism. The more lean body mass you have the faster a metabolism works. A fast metabolism not only affects how we feel, it directly impacts how much fat we carry around on our bodies. We are always focused on the amount of food we eat and what it is comprised of, but the state of our body and its metabolism is also very important to consider. Mental and physical coping tools are necessary for stress filled situations in our lives. When we are stressed and tired the body secretes cortisol, adrenaline, and epinephrine. Our immune system is also temporarily suppressed during times of stress. Things like financial worries, long hard grinds at work, family struggles, big life transitions etc. need to be handled mentally and spiritually. Many of us handle our problems with added consumption of food. Without being able to navigate these things internally the body handles our food differently. Long term periods of being stressed out can lead to bigger problems like depression, fatigue, weight gain, and illnesses. More and more studies are showing that what we are going through in life affects how food is metabolized in our bodies. Exercise and self-care helps to stabilize our internal body environment.

Have you ever experienced being able to eat a lot of food at a time in life and not gaining a single pound? Your metabolic environment was fast. Perhaps you were younger as well. (smile) Have you ever then eaten a fraction of the amount of food you used to eat and then gain weight? It is due to many reasons but the major reason is that we have hormones in our bodies that react to the environmental stressors that we are exposed to. According to Science Directs "Current Opinion In Behavioral Science's Journal" Volume 9 pgs. 71-77 when the human body is placed under stress there is a possibility of two vastly different hormonal responses when food is consumed. When our bodies are exposed to an acute threat in some people, at different times in life, we may experience what is called an anorexigenic effect. There will be weight loss. A cocktail of hormones secreted by the hypothalamus, the pituitary gland and the adrenal glands (namely CRH Corticotropin-Release-Hormone) causes the liver and both white and brown adipose tissue to have a sympathetic (excitatory) response in the body. The sympathetic nervous system is also stimulated. That results in loss of body weight.

Studies further conclude that exposure to chronic stress can also have the exact opposite effect on the body. For some people there is an obesogenic hormonal response associated with long term stress exposure.

Weight gain can occur. Chronic stress exposure can lead to over eating of savory/palatable foods and the increased storage of visceral fat. Visceral fat is not the subcutaneous kind we can easily see, it is the fat that is between our organs. Stressful situations have been shown to activate both systems at once in some people! Weight loss and then weight gain. Finding balance between life and the food that we eat is so important. It is not just as simple as calories in and calories out. We must consider our state of being and who we are as well when looking at weight gain. The jury is still out as to what the stress level thresholds are before experiencing weight gain or the weight loss response. It is interesting to take a look back at life, when we were the leanest and to consider what our stress levels were then. We should look back at what coping activities we used in order to deal with the stress in our lives.

Remaining in touch with your own personal response to stress in life and the foods that we eat is very powerful. Looking back at times when I felt I could eat whatever I wanted and not get fat my responsibilities were a lot less. I worked out as much as I wanted. I was doing work that fed my soul. I also danced a lot every weekend from three to nine hours on top of working out five days a week. The times that I gained large amounts of weight were times when I was depressed and going through hard times with money, family relationships, or work. My internal environment was in such turmoil that everything that I ate had the worst effect possible. The thing is that if you don't remain aware and connected to what's going on within you and around you, hormones can induce changes in eating that will have you out of sorts. I once gained forty pounds in four months! I owned a house that went under water during the 2008 crash. It went into foreclosure. That condo was robbed with so many of my belongings in it. I was having a hard time paying bills as a full time entrepreneur. My savings was diminishing at a rapid rate. Major clients soon began dropping off of my client roster. I ended up joining an elite mobile training group in New York City. Life was being life. Nothing was working in my favor. I lost twenty pounds in a short period of time. My entire identity was wrapped up into my success. I had to mentally separate my self-identity from the happenings in life. Luckily, I had invested thousands of dollars into acquiring tools for coping with my demons and mental hang-ups. It was one of the most painful and necessary processes ever. My ego died!

I never admitted this to myself out loud. I was caught in the washing machine called life and my ego was murdered in the process. I had to move in with my younger brother for a few months. I did so with my fiancé. My mother-in-law to be also fell very ill during this time. We moved across the country to help support her with caregiving. At this time, it wasn't until I checked in on myself internally did I even realize that physically I had gone from having lost twenty pounds hustling and running sixteen hours a day. To gaining nearly forty pounds in a four month period. Initially I lost weight but by the end of this time period I experienced huge and rapid weight gain. I was still working out five to six times a week but the food consumption and cravings were out of control. My outside appearance mirrored the inside undercurrents of a wildly challenging time of transition. It was during a meditation session that I became aware of my imbalance.

It is so important to be aware of the states of your mind and body and then learning ways to manage stress but the quality of our food still matters. Consuming whole and natural foods is your responsibility and yours alone. Uh Oh! I used the "r" word "responsibility". Do some research, not only on which foods to consume, but make time to research the additives inside of your favorite things to eat. A lot of health food has additives. A quick google search can help you differentiate which additives are banned across the globe but present in the American diet. The FDA is very loose with the guidelines in America. There is no way that remaining ignorant is acceptable in this day and age. A world of knowledge is at our finger tips. Literally, thousands of perspectives on food and diet are available to you. Filter them through your mind and body, then apply the ones that serve you best. Acknowledge how you feel before during and after you eat.

As the old adage goes "we are what we eat". Food is such an important thing because we consume it every single waking day. Eating is for some people the only thing that they do multiple times a day every day. Anything you do consistently has a profound effect on your entire being. Consistency is what transforms and creates our solid reality. Some foods contain additives that have effects on our bodies. There are foods that cause us to not be able to focus. Some additives cause us to be agitated. Others even sedate us. Avoid dyes, additives and chemicals that are in so many of our low quality, great tasting foods. People underestimate the power food has on our bodies. A lot of the chemicals in what we eat have even been proven to alter DNA in lab mice. Nowadays, many of our foods are engineered and this engineering is coming at a detriment to the health of humanity across the globe. Eating certain unnatural or fortified foods is just plain silly to me if you want to live a fully optimized life. The bad thing is that these foods taste really good. I would be willing to bet that if a rat spoke our language it would say "That poison that you guys put in those little black boxes do kill us, but DAMN it tastes really good. Plus it's so convenient". We humans say the same thing about the fast food and junk that we eat. We are especially that way about sugar.

The average American eats one hundred and forty seven to one hundred and fifty two pounds of sugar annually. We have shot up one hundred plus percent from eating approximately sixty pounds annually in the early nineteen hundreds. In the same time the amount of health issues that we experience have also skyrocketed. Many experts believe that our latest generation will be the first generation to live shorter and less healthy lives than their parents. People look for convenience when it comes to food preparation. Increasing convenience in the kitchen is often setting oneself up to experience a lack of quality elsewhere in life. Remember the unfathomable power of a habit that I mentioned in the earlier chapter? On all fronts, nature must yield and respond to habit. The human body is a natural thing and therefore it must respond to the flow of current of thought, action, and food taken into it. It is the same with the stone that is worn smooth from the incessant flow of a river over it for hundreds of years. The same is true of the tree that grows moss on the side of it that has the least sun light. (The north side in the northern hemisphere and the south side in the southern hemisphere.) Trends that repeat in nature create the look and feel of our reality.

Many people neglect eating whole and natural foods because they contain carbs, fat or whatever macronutrient society has mentally programmed them to avoid. There is always a new and skewed study that came out last week. Media sensationalism shouldn't control what you put in your mouth. Neglecting a whole and natural food because it contains a single "unhealthy" macronutrient (that has been villainized in the media) isn't wise. Not eating avocados because of the fat content and eating enriched pasta as a low fat food instead is a huge dietary mistake. You should definitely experiment with what works with your body's chemistry. Do your own research. Add awareness to the food that you are eating and note which ones make you feel good and operate at your best. The natural nutrients in the avocado make it a good food choice for many of us. Our bodies instinctively know how to metabolize the fat in it. Up until one hundred years ago, our foods were more natural and less engineered and processed. We lived more disease-free years. Now for the first time in America this latest generation of children has been projected to be outlived by their parents.

For thousands of years humanity consumed lots of grains, veggies, fruit, and far less processed foods- stuffs and enhanced meats. Now it is the exact opposite for so many people. Meat is now cheaper than vegetables? Would you eat less meat if the only way that you could have it, is if you hunted it, killed it and cleaned it yourself? It is cheaper and easier to eat less healthily today than ever before. Less than one hundred years ago the only fat people were rich people. Now, processed foods and meats are readily accessible to all. They are also very cheap. Sweet additive laden foods are manufactured in abundance. We have also enjoyed sharp increases in heart attacks, diabetes, cancer, obesity and premature deaths. People now feverishly dig graves with their forks. The human body has not changed enough in this short evolutionary time period to adjust for recent horrid adjustments in the American diet. It used to be a rarity to see an obese child or a pregnant looking man, but now it is common. The only thing that has truly changed is the way that our food is processed and its ease of accessibility. Healthy eating is now an intentional act. Today it takes mindfulness, time, and intention to make healthy eating happen on a consistent basis. It may even take more money.

Money talks! Spend your money in ways that benefit us all. Spend money on products made by companies that produce whole and natural products. When we buy healthy food we vote to raise food quality for all of us. If the product sits on the shelf and doesn't move, then it is not a viable commodity for food corporations. It will soon be phased out of the marketplace. We need to put our money where our health is. We vote with our dollars. Lobbyist for unhealthy food manufacturers put their bids into the FDA, and other policy makers to fatten their pockets. You should be putting your money behind things that makes us all healthier. I believe the key to a healthy body is eating a variety of whole and complete foods as close to their natural state as possible. I am a firm believer that all things are energy. We are energy and our food is energy. Food is fundamental to our existence and the energy in which our food is created becomes a part of us. The terror an animal feels growing up in a factory does affect our personal energy fields. More and more studies will provide evidence of this reality. People have sustained health and enjoyed longevity for centuries by eating consciously and locally. Whomever controls your food controls your life. Who controls your life?

FOOD FOR THOUGHT

Allow me to introduce you to Cynthia. She was a high level executive at a fortune 100 company. She was loved by so many people both at work and at home. She was someone that I admire to this day. I was honored that she hired me as a guide and mentor on her fitness journey over a decade ago. It was through her that the seed was planted that I should start speaking to executive groups around health/wellness and leadership. She specifically encouraged me to speak about making headway around the consistent doing of hard yet beneficial things. She was only in her mid to late forties and had accomplished so much in life. She had a beautiful family and also climbed the corporate ladder employing hard work, great intelligence, and emotional intelligence while leading. She did so in a very short time period. Many times if I had a problem, professionally or personally, I would bend her ear. She was so wise that by the end of our training sessions she would have a solution figured out. She was able to find these solutions by coming at the problem from an entirely different angle than I would. To this day we check in on each other from time to time on social media.

One issue that plagued her incessantly was that many times she would come into her training sessions battling a cold, congestion, or feeling inexplicably sluggish. The doctors always told her that she was fine. They would give her a clear bill of health and send her on her way with a prescription feeling like crap. Cynthia was somewhat active on her own, but the biggest problem for her was being able to manage her nutrition. Like most of us, she found her time occupied from the moment she woke up to the moment that she fell asleep at night. There were many times that she would not lose as much weight or body fat as she thought she should have in a given time period. Those major stalls had a lot to do with her not having a true and conscious approach to monitoring the foods that she invited to become part of her being. Whether she lost weight or not Cynthia would show up congested with her eyes & nose running or in possession of a slight cold. As seasons changed we ruled out allergies. She almost came to the conclusion of having to settle for a reality that included navigating a chronic cold. It also seemed to be draining her energy.

At that point in my career as a fitness professional working in New York City, I worked with some of the busiest professionals on the planet. I had seen a lot of people work themselves into the ground. This seemed different. I suggested that maybe something in her diet may be throwing her into these spells of discomfort and allergy like symptoms. I had witnessed hundreds of busy successful people ignore eating habits that hampered their health. I asked her to log everything that she ate daily for an entire week. This practice not only gave her a real connection to the amount of food she ate but it also brought a 4K HD level of awareness to the foods that she enjoyed most frequently. In her version of normal one very common food showed up every single day in some way, shape, or form. I suggested that she conduct a small experiment.

Let me point out something. Experimentation and curiosity are two of the keys to long term transformation. You should be running experiments on a regular basis in your life. Experiments give you ownership. It is what personalizes theory. You have to be willing to take inventory of any area of life you want to change. Record with pen and paper, or on your cell phone, how much you spend monthly on nonessential items if finances are you area. Record how many days you went without applying for a job that will pay you more than enough money, if career is the area of focus. If you find that you do not have many good adult friendships, record any weird interpersonal habits that you may have. What habits do you have that may be costing you real connections and healthy relationships? Get it? Ownership is important.

Write out the traits of the kind of people that you want to attract into your life. Contrast them with the types of people who currently occupy your life now. Write out traits that you may not own yet. Take inventory. Maybe track how vulnerable you have been with your partner, if that is one of the things that sabotages your personal relationship. Write out your goals to become a better listener. Write out that you may not have made the time to cultivate any social circles in order to enjoy great friendships. Make clear the hurdles between you and your goals. Writing things down changes a thought that you have imagined into a real and tangible thing that you can work on. You can never work on improving an area of life if you do not have the ability to clearly see where and how your habits have played a role in creating the problem. It is through that clarity that you are granted the power to make things better. You can uncover subconscious thoughts, actions, and beliefs that have held your potentials hostage. You can devise an experiment to isolate the problem and create a solution.

By Cynthia writing out her food diary with integrity and accuracy I was able to pinpoint a possible cause for her congestion and her sluggish feelings. I suggested that she take dairy completely out of her diet for an entire week. I told her to keep everything else the same. Get the same amount of sleep. Eat the same amount of calories. Workout the same times and work the same amount. When I first mentioned it she asked me "Why?" It was way back in two thousand and two or three. There wasn't a lot of layman's literature or studies that pointed out the huge correlation between milk and mucous production in certain individuals. I have an unquenchable thirst for nutritional and health knowledge. I read and experiment to be able to better service my clients. I read about dairy and mucous production. I also took time to experiment on my own body to see how it responded to dairy. I practiced dairy deprivation for a time. My head was clearer and I myself was less congested.

Soon into this process she discovered that she ate far more overall calories than she believed she did. Most of us do! She also discovered that she consumed dairy every day multiple times a day. Every single day she ate cheese or ingested milk in some manner. From her coffee with milk, to eggs and cheese, to sandwiches, string cheese, a daily cup of yogurt, on her salad for lunch. Day in and day out she thought nothing before of eating copious amounts of dairy. It was her normal. She had done this for decades! What you don't know you don't know can cause harm. She cut it all out. In three days she was able to excitedly report that she felt a whole lot better and had nearly no symptoms. She replaced those calories with new vegetables. She lost a lot of weight and the perpetual cold that had plagued her life for many months in just seven days. Anything that we do day in and day out has a profound impact on the quality of our lives. This rule is true whether you consciously know you are doing a thing or not.

Neither I nor Cynthia will totally cut dairy out forever. I love cheese and ice cream. We both know that when we are congested, coming down with a cold, or feeling foggy headed to check on the amount of dairy and sugar in our diets at that time. It's a very valuable practice to stop and evaluate what trends and habits are creating your reality. What familiar habits create your version of "normal?" Tracing the effects that our version of "normal" causes is critical thinking put to great use. Surveying our habits should also include a deeper look into the possible effects of the foods that we love to eat. Our foods become us.

CHAPTER 5

DON'T DIE ON ME YET

"Possibility is all that we are. Never forget it!"

People tend to thrive when they can enjoy some semblance of peace and tranquility. Survival mode is near impossible to create from. Once survival is handled then we are restored to our natural state of being a bundle of possibilities. Most people smile when they see a baby. Everyone experiences happiness when looking into the eyes of that little bundle of possibilities. All humans we encounter are mirrors. Babies reflect the promise of what we could have been. They inspire us to see what the world needs. Many of us see a mirror in a baby's eyes. In that reflection of innocence we get to see the best of humanity. Human beings love possibilities and potentials. We are born as possibilities. America has been such an attractive country for people all over the world to flock to, in order to carve out a better life. Millions come to America to roll their dice. It is "The land of possibilities". When babies begin to grow up things begin to change.

The world starts chipping away at possibility by adding labels to humans as we grow. We add black or white, dumb, smart, stupid, ugly, people add all kinds of labels to the baby as it grows. Labels have connotations attached to them. Before long, these labels and all of the connotations that are associated with them are internalized by that growing human. Critical thinking and self-determination become threatened in a real way unless someone is promoting that in that child's life. People grow up and believe in these labels. We are absorbed by the labels we are given as well as those that we give to others.

Most of us self -identify with the labels and live into the confines of those labels. That is what really stifles possibility. Especially if the labels were handed to us by people that we respect or feared. Life hacks away at our birthright of being possibility. Our potentials become smoothed down by society. We become conditioned to learn which actions will get us in trouble. We then learn which ones get us celebrated. Many times, we learn through shame, and pain not to try out new ideas dictated by the wisdom within. We conform to the rules. We get socialized. We are told what we "should" and shouldn't learn more about. Before we know it, we become fluent in using statements such as "I'll never do_____ again", "I won't ever try_____", "I guess _____ wasn't meant forme.", "I guess I'd better_____" or "I have to do_____ even though I hate it." Our responses to adversity become clichés. Do you realize that all of this is the result of faulty mental programming? Programming that you didn't even ask for. Faulty programming mainly from people you won't think fondly of while laying on your death bed.

There is a part of our mind that revels in the regurgitation of negative thoughts and beliefs of others. Over time, we subconsciously, pick them up, and make them our own. Without shining any awareness from the wisdom within, these thoughts and beliefs become the paradigms that live from. All of these doubt-filled and fear-loaded statements cut numerous possibilities off in our lives. If you do not become aware, you will have whittled away the infinite potential that you exuded as a baby. So many people with dreams and potentials settle into living status-quo inauthentic existences.

Those beliefs make it utterly impossible to take guidance from the highest vibrating parts of who we are. We all came here to this planet with an inner guidance system and a purpose to fulfill in our own unique way. That wise voice in all of us is usually persistent and low in nature. The volume on the limiting thoughts and beliefs drilled into our subconscious minds is super loud! The volume is so loud that it keeps us separated from even having an awareness around what our purpose on the planet is. When our potentials die within our minds and imaginations that is when we age. Not when we start to get gray hair. Some people are sixty at age twenty five possibility wise. What we can be and who we may become is foreign. Living into our purpose becomes improbable. Tapping back into that original power of possibility is necessary in order to unlock and live out dreams and potentials. The expression of our inner greatness is at stake. The higher wisdom in us will always urge us to make lasting changes in various areas of life but we simply can't hear it!

Our inner guidance sounds like a tiny voice behind a live marching band. Over time it can become easy to ignore. Before you even notice, you have participated in a lifetime of cutting off possibilities until you find yourself psychologically residing in a tiny box of your own creation. Some of us become resigned to simply "getting what you get" in life. It is sad if you choose to settle for this state of being.

MIND GAMES

Lots of people survive in life with a mindset that is closed off from possibility. Having a super healthy, fit looking body carrying you through life, is not necessary if you settle for a mediocre or average existence. You can eek by and scurry through life without a very healthy body. It seems that most of the world is more than okay with looking around and feeling that life *"is not that bad"* instead of exploring *"I wonder how amazing I can make my life?"* If life amounts to "it is not that bad", it also means that "it is not so good either." Life can be expanding and inspiring, just as it was when we were children. People tend to lose the excitement for life they once had. Children wake up to life with excitement and possibilities every day. They can barely sleep. Remember how you used to wake up running headfirst into life. Children always look forward to the next experience. If you have children, use their curiosity and thirst for living to fuel you. Fight the urge to quell their excitement and dreams. The world will try to do that. Children are an incarnation of inspiration for adults, a reminder of what being possibility is. How you choose to receive their energy, vitality, and curiosity is everything. A grown-up who loses drive and doesn't hold on to being unlimited possibility becomes cynical. I spent a lot of time as a cynic and that to me, was time wasted. Cynics see little capability of creating a reality that is beyond their eyesight and authentic to who they are. The reason you are holding this book in your hand is because you are not this type of person. You are at the very least, conscious and aware. You are gaining access to manufacturing motivation to achieve all the things that serve the higher and best version of you. Eventually you can harness the power to do it on command, whenever you need it.

Resigning to a "so-so" survival type of existence also translates to the overall state of a person's body. You will feel it in your bones, muscles, and joints. This mindset happens to bleed into other areas of life. Settling in life, makes us older and stiffer spiritually, physically and psychologically. Everybody knows how good the body feels when we exercise regularly and eat properly. People struggle to develop the habits and ways of being that lead to feeling this way. Those same individuals may find it possible to have an advancing mindset and actions to match in other areas of life. If discipline can be had in one area of life it can be accessed and put to work in other areas of life as well. Awareness is everything. It's necessary to expose any current mindset that kills our progress. An awesome byproduct of taking action on creating breakthroughs in areas of life where you have weakness, is that other areas become affected in a positive way.

How we do anything is how we do all things. We do not all start this race called life with the same exact circumstances nor wielding the same gifts. Some people fundamentally start further away from some goals than others do due to who they are personality wise, through societal constructs, their upbringing, and how they were conditioned both mentally and physically. Having a greater distance to cover and also having no awareness around what obstacles may exist on the way to success, is a recipe for great struggle and pain. A huge lever to consider pulling is working to understand how far from a goal you actually are, due to your default way of being. That requires asking yourself a heavy question that sounds a little like "What about who I fundamentally am, (subconscious paradigm) is at odds with me doing what it takes to meet this goal?" When you uncover the answers to that question you will have gained access to increased power and potential.

Understanding where you are starting, in regards to the achievement of a certain goal, and acknowledging the amount of work it is going to take you to get there, will help you to manage expectations. When people start working out they often have a framework of time that they expect to see changes in. It is usually arbitrary or based on how fast they could lose weigh in the past. They have not taken the time to consider who they presently are in the moment, and how far away they actually are from realizing their goal. They have not considered who they have to become in order to achieve the body of their dreams and maintain it.

They haven't accounted for enough variables. This goes for many goals and aspirations in life.

"*Who do I have to become in order to have*_____?" is a question that puts the amount of upcoming work into better perspective. Many times if they do not see the amount of change they expect, in a certain time period, then there is a great urge to give up investing any time at all. They quit prematurely. If you are in the center part of life juggling a family, a career, and aging parents you are in a whole different boat than a single man or woman with no kids looking to get in shape. Especially if they are at the beginning of their career with little responsibilities other than themselves. The balance of health and wellbeing as well as body fat management are different. Due to hormonal responses to stress alone, the single young man or woman will have a head start on achieving his or her goals.

Selecting the right kind of exercise to suit their busy lifestyles will matter more for the family man or woman. The single man or woman can also take a few steps forward in the fitness department, because they have more time to invest. There is also the factor of looking at each person's why? What is their reason for setting the goal of being healthy and fit in the first place? The young and single man or woman may want to exercise to look better and to attract a mate. The family man or woman may be thinking longevity, and increasing energy.

Our beliefs and subconscious paradigms are also partially responsible for creating either more or less distance from our goals. In the example above, what if the young man or woman has never worked out consistently before? What if they believed with all of their might that they inherited the fat gene that no matter what, their body will never respond to exercise? What will their exercise efforts look like? What will their eating habits look like? What if the person who is a parent in the middle part of life was a former athlete? They believe as fact that if they can find a little balance, and make some time, that they can bounce back into great shape. Does that change the distance they each have to cover in order to enjoy great fitness results? Who would you put your money on to get into shape sooner? There are so many variables to consider. Make sure that you do a proper assessment of the distance you must cover when it comes to any goal that you want to achieve.

We are social creatures. What if you wanted to become rich but you grew up in a house where money was always scarce. What if your family was extremely religious and you never discussed money. Furthermore, what if money was portrayed as "the root of all evil?" Would your journey to financial freedom long or short? What if you were fortunate to grow up in a family that lived with an abundance of money, discussed money, wealth, entrepreneurship, and financial strategies around the dinner table? Would you have a long or shorter distance to creating financial freedom? There are so many different starting points for every journey. Depending on the goal, some of us have to run a marathon just to get to the starting line that others take for granted.

Your environment matters. What if you grew up with no financial literacy resources in your community? I mentor young black boys in East Oakland California most Saturdays of the month. I asked that group what the word "abundance" meant. In a group of forty five youth, ages eleven to twenty one, not one knew what the word "abundance" meant. Without having knowledge of a word how likely is it to exist for you? Not likely. What if there were no wealthy role models, no rich uncles, and everything around you was dilapidated and uncared for? What if the color of your skin was weaponized and used against you in the country that you were born in? What if people who look like you were intentionally disenfranchised for centuries? How will your journey towards mastering wealth-building look like? You really would have your work cut out for you as far as wealth creation and money management goes. You should expect that you will have a huge transformation to make spiritually and psychologically before becoming financially free.

You must have patience and compassion with yourself. You have a lot of ground to cover. That takes pacing and a buildup of momentum. The further away that you start from achieving a specific goal, the more you will be asked to change as a person, in order to achieve that goal. If you recognize this, you can learn to manage your expectations around how fast you will achieve something. You become less likely to quit. Don't allow giving up to be an option. Your personal journey may be a marathon instead of a sprint. When it comes to our goals, so many of us strap on sprint spikes when marathon flats are what we should be lacing up.

Patience and compassion are needed along the way for ourselves. Tiny steps moving forward deserve celebration just as much as the monumental wins do along the way. Growing up, I never celebrated my wins. I never rewarded or encouraged myself. This made moving forward harder that it had to be. Instead after every win in my life I always waited for the other foot to drop. I expected my luck to run dry. I cut out all of the enjoyment of the journey. I quickly asked "OK, what's next?" Celebrating hold you to a higher standard. It makes you responsible for doing more things worth celebrating. Don't run from that responsibility, even if it frightens you. You will continue that winning momentum. Celebrating makes you firmly stand in the spotlight and space of being a winner. Accepting the idea that "I am a winner" changed everything. It calls more opportunity your way.

Every time that you try on a new beneficial way of thinking and take action from it celebrate it. The fact that you had the strength to defy the old you is the real gift. Don't wait on achieving the result to celebrate. The shift in thinking is the most commendable part it should be strengthened with a celebration. Acknowledge the courage that goes on full display when someone steps out on a limb, and does something new and foreign to improve themselves or others. We all have races to run in our lives, in various arenas. Knowing that your starting line is different than others is a powerful distinction. Be content with doing things on your own individual time. People will make it out to be true that we all start from the same starting line and are all afforded the same exact opportunities at winning. This is far from the truth. Some of us are advantaged based on the goal. Some of us are simply disadvantaged according to the goal to be achieved. Either way, we all must run our race. If you find yourself disadvantaged in regards to a goal, you don't have the option of being a follower. You must become a leader in order to transform your situation.

Sometimes a spark of anger and frustration is what it takes to get started. You can find a healthier fuel source later. Use it. Get going! Temporarily, you can find access to a defiant fuel and energy. That may be the energy needed to fuel your journey, make sacrifices along the way, and develop discipline is already within you. Be ready to put down that fuel source as you gather momentum. Using anger and frustration to move forward will eventually begin to drain your spirit and leave you unfulfilled.

Blind spots block progress. Things that "you don't know, that you don't know" can hold you back from achieving success. Things outside of our awareness are impossible to detect by ourselves. In order to intentionally make change in those areas, our blind spots must be exposed. Only the perspectives of others can help us shine a light on these situations. Consider that you have, unbeknownst to you, ways of being and thinking that contribute to all of the outcomes that you enjoy and despise in life. Make it a mission to become aware of as many of those kinds of variables as you can. Ask people you respect for their opinions of you often. Achieving a higher level of self-awareness should become a goal. Surround yourself with intelligent people who know you, and want to see you win. Creating a trusted ring of advisors to help you expose blind-spots that you may have is priceless.

CHAPTER 6

MIND OVER MATTER

We are far more than just the sum of our bodily functions. Making necessary surface level changes will only take us part of the way. Our minds, thoughts, and feelings govern the way that our body looks, and functions. Thoughts are extremely powerful forces. Our thoughts attract things into our existence that would have never occur without their presence. Our thoughts are one of the ways that we communicate with the unseen force that creates all that is. It is important to be aware of, and control the overall flow of our thoughts. If you can control the flow of your thoughts then maybe you can live the life of your dreams. Allowing a bunch of random thoughts to run wild in your mind is giving up power. It takes practice, but it is possible to take control of the overall direction of our thinking. A lot of people might not believe that this is possible, but trust me, it surely is. I have been helping people tap into that power for fifteen years now. I had to do it for myself. I am naturally a cynical person. Now I can swiftly change a cynical thought to a better thought in less than a second. Bodies permanently change when the tides of the mind are altered. Lives work the same way.

Weight loss shows on television often promoting unbelievably hard and intense 90 day exercise programs. Sensational shows about winning the lottery and tear jerking family reunions tend to run the entertainment scene. Everything speaks to the sensational, the lucky, and the topical. Those programs, gimmicks, and sensation, sells to the public like cupcakes. Body contouring clothing flourish, and quick laser treatments for cellulite reduction have become common. Record numbers of likes and dollars are awarded to any manner of bull shit posted on social media. Fake gets rewarded. From fitness, to showcasing healthy relationships, to making money to all of the real work is hidden. Superficial fixes aren't the answer.

It is time to go back to being real. Character, communication, grit, integrity, critical thinking, work ethic, collaboration, and confidence were considered softs-kills but they are now vital. Working hard on the right things, with the right mindset, is the key. Nothing is better than being able to apply effort and energy to selecting better thoughts and then taking new and beneficial actions. There was a period of my life where I was always pissed off and angry. I was upset that my biological parents abandoned me. I hated that I didn't have anything to remember them by but a vague memory of a dark skinned woman being my mother. I was upset that where I lived was filthy, forgotten, and that crack heads, and dope fiends lined the streets that I walked on. I hated getting robbed as a little boy in the hood. I constantly had to worry about that every day. I hated ducking bullets during the shootouts at night. I hated having to travel outside of my neighborhood to see walls that didn't have graffiti on them. I hated that every block that I walked on had at least one abandoned building on it. As a community were all abandoned and neglected. I hated that everyone who had any money didn't look like me. Everyone except for the drug dealers on the corner, that is. I hated it when I found out that there were hoods like mine all over the nation filled with poor and disenfranchised people who looked like me. I hated that everyone was mostly angry all of the time, just like I was.

I was a very sensitive little boy with tons of empathy. To this day, I can often feel what others are feeling, without them saying it, in a very real way. Negative emotions, thoughts, and feelings consumed me internally. Externally, they often swirled all around me. At first I made peace with how things were. I felt like I didn't deserve anything better and that I was lucky to have a place to stay at all. Foster care conditioned me. Luckily that conditioning could not stand up to that deep wise voice within me, that told me that I was getting out of foster care soon. After constant prodding by this voice, I found myself able to believe that there had to be life after survival. I was sick and tired of feeling angry and neglected. While living in the foster home before Travis Farnell's home (my adopted mother) I decided that my brother and I would one day land in a loving, safe place to live. I looked forward to that day every day. As a kid I actively believed that we were going to be living in a nice loving home even though we were still living in abusive homes. I created a vision for myself.

I obsessively dreamed of having stable friends and family. I actually got it! Looking back, I can see that I attracted that beautiful outcome my way. I realize that I could feel happier if I reframed how I thought of living in through bad situations. Through repetition of thought, I was able to go from dreading waking up, to knowing that my time living in ghetto foster homes would end. I knew in my bones that living with people fostering children for a check, instead of making an impact in their lives, was temporary. Thinking that we'd be properly placed and adopted helped me to endure many temporarily bad situations. Prior to that, I thought that it was inevitable that I would become a drug dealer, make a lot of money, and get locked up or killed. That is all that I saw around me. Obsessing over being adopted gave me a glimmer of hope. To a kid like me, in a dark world, a glimmer of hope was a floodlight. I stopped getting into so many fights in school. I subconsciously began working hard on being a happier kid. I instinctively knew that carrying so much anger was not good. I grew to hate that darkness in me. It felt like a physical weight on my chest. Thinking better thoughts helped me to take better actions and be a better kid. People love good kids. Good kids get adopted! All of these things led to someone taking a chance on me and my brother. A better situation found us. We were invited to become a part of Travis's beautiful family. Better thinking instead of bitter thinking changed my life! Good thing that I did start thinking and doing differently at age six. My mother still holds to this day, that I was the most serious and angry little boy that she has ever met. I am extremely happy that I didn't stay that way and did the work to move on.

Adopting new habits is hard work. Doing hard work in relationships even with people we love is hard work. You see the divorce rate? It is very popular and glamourized to only entertain relationships that do not require any real work or growth on your part. Easy relationships have a place, but so do difficult ones. A circle full of "yes" men and woman never benefitted anyone. Building the discipline to develop new money management habits is hard work too. It is especially hard if you grew up in poverty and were hard-wired into a scarcity mindset. Until you do the work "There is never enough" will color every decision you will make towards changing your circumstances. Embracing abundance will never be your reality without hard internal rewiring. Much like the algorithms in Netflix, other streaming services, and on the internet, many of us only entertain the things that we already know that we like. What we see and do is only predicted by selections that we have liked in the past. It makes finding more of the same easier. It also stifles our abilities to step outside of the boundaries and experience new things. It lulls us into comfort and complacency. It eliminates challenge, critical thinking, and coincidence. Exploration becomes something that you have to make happen in life. Never allow your real life to be infected by an algorithm that excludes all hardships and critical thinking. Those challenges help us access the "better" that is in us.

It is important that we create our own signals and messages to implant in our own subconscious minds. What are the repetitive signals and directives that you send out into the world on a regular basis? How do you, as a spirit having a human experience, use your own mind for good? Become aware of your thoughts and directives when you take any action. Pay attention when you eat. Pay attention when you entertain the ideas of other people. Your mind is a tool to be used. No way of thinking, or no habitual response is etched in stone. Course correct and adjust the paradigms of the subconscious mind as needed. All of your normal programming can be shifted and manipulated by you. It is not the norm to know this or to even embrace this but it is true. You can upload different programming that is suitable for who you are becoming whenever you want. The mental programming necessary to keep things in life the same is different than that needed to transcend where you are. You have the power to reboot and reload the subconscious CPU any time. Most of the programming there was not consciously placed there by you anyway. Be empowered and Take charge today!

As a whole we give very little thought to our spiritual state of being. Spiritual self-care is important as well. Personal fitness is not taught in public school. You have to figure out what works for you, on your own. As your body and life changes you have to be astute and able to discern what works for the new body that you now inhabit. There are no personal fitness courses offered right on up through our entire educational structure. Our bodies are what house our souls and allows us to make physical impact in this world. More attention should be given to the concerns of all three parts of us mind body and soul.

Physical fitness, spiritual wellness, and often the management of our finances happen outside of our "real" lives. They occur to so many of us as things that we can get to whenever we get to it. There is a rampant notion that our own health is not a matter of personal responsibility. Many of us are relying on the government and food corporations to tell us what is healthy for us. We believe that poisonous foods will be banned to help the population become more fit. Many rely on legislation to be passed to help them select foods. The responsibility is yours and yours alone to do the research. It is our responsibility to take care of ourselves in order to be there to take care of our families. Obesity is now being recognized as a disease by the AMA. The easiest way to lose anywhere from five to fourteen pounds in a day would be to cut off your arm. I don't see a lot of people lining up to do that. Yet, people continue to pick equally inefficient ways to lose weight and become healthier. I believe that there is enough knowledge and information around to empower and arm people to make informed decisions that suit their bodies, their personalities, and their health for as long as they live. The key is awakening people to this responsibility and not absolving them of making choices based off of personal experimentation.

People deprive themselves of necessary nutrition, undergo plastic surgery, and consume great amounts of chemicals in the name of "looking better". Our obsession with "looking better" is one of the reasons that fitness is seen as nonessential. If looking better is all that is considered around fitness it can easily become one of those things that you get to "when everything else is taken care of, in my life." The key to making lasting changes is to assume responsibility for our own thinking.

Be willing to be uncomfortable in order to disturb and alter your own limiting mindsets. Make it a game. There has to be a new way of thinking ushered in that sounds like "Being the very best version of myself is the most important thing to me." "I cannot access my very best thinking, feeling, and experiences in my life if I do not have an exceptional body and health." There has to be a sense of urgency and a priority placed on excellence and purposeful living. Fitness must be positioned as one of the bases to touch in order to make that happen. Education on a constant basis has to be shared around not only what to do to be fit, but how to think broader and differently. Study thinking and concentration. Practice thinking and concentrating. In order to make a dent in the current thinking and create a mental environment conducive to making our best selves happen we have to curate the information that we are exposed to. We have to rival the proliferation of TV's subliminal programming and the programming of others that surround us and pour it on us. Moving fitness from its vanity based roots to a necessity will yield better results.

Deleting limiting mindsets that were unconsciously absorbed and then implanting your own more powerful mindset in its place is the real work. Implant your own mindset that is based on what it is that you want to achieve. You have to create a new powerful story of life to live into. Imagine that until you pick them out, other people's thoughts and beliefs have been subconsciously running your life. You may have made it very far in life already. Imagine what you could accomplish if you decided today to make your own positive and powerful beliefs your subconscious powerhouse. What could you accomplish then? What kind of health would you enjoy? What kind of relationships would you have? What kind of money would you have?

Creating the ability to use new and powerful mindsets that overpowers old mental programming and conditioning is the purpose of this book. I liken the ability to shed a no longer useful mindset and adopt another to having specific shoes for specific activities. You wouldn't wear rock climbing shoes to play basketball. You wouldn't wear construction boots to play beach volleyball or race in the Tour de France. Why painstakingly carry the same mindset through life even when it doesn't fit the situation? Acquiring the skill of shedding and picking up mindsets that serve the situation, will ultimately keep you mentally and physically fit for a lifetime. This ability to surf life is what I will refer to throughout this book as mind-flow. Bringing your attentions to the best possible thinking that you can entertain, at any given moment, is the key to "mindflow".

A VIGILANT NEW BEGINNING

WAKE UP! Become aware of your own most dominant thoughts and actions. Too many people in this fast paced day and age are afraid of thinking. Learning and growing should be something that we all embrace daily. This is especially true when it comes to learning and connecting with yourself on a deeper level. If you have an aversion to critical thinking outside of your job, and you tend to shut down in your real life, turn that critical thinking light back on. Apply it everywhere, apply it to you. Do not make it a normal aim to just kick your feet up and relax when it comes to studying you. Creating excellence is a moment to moment thing. It is the result of making great tiny decisions. Apply being excellent to living. Do not settle. This is your real life so why not play all out? It is difficult to sustain a healthy exercise routine (or do anything difficult and extremely beneficial) if you are not actively paying attention to yourself and what is going on internally. Question your default responses to taking new action. Living all-out and working daily to become a better version of yourself makes that introspect happen. Gauging progress in the direction of your dominant thoughts and actions is a task worth doing. What do you spend the most time thinking about? What habits do you harbor? Where will they lead you?

Many people shine the powerful light of their awareness on only what is going on around them. They only receive signals. They should also be gauging the signals they are sending out as well. Some things that we need to do for ourselves to function optimally are things that we may not necessarily like doing. Fitness falls into that category for many people. It takes extra brain power, structure, and strategy to do the hard and beneficial things in life on a consistent basis. An insane focus or obsession on positively impacting your own future helps. It takes *internal vigilance.* This is how it is starting almost anything new begins. A momentum shift doesn't just happen it takes force of mind. It will be impossible to reap the amazing benefits of enjoying extremely good health and fitness without being aware of your internal justifications for not doing what you need to do to make it happen. It will take internal vigilance to notice when you have settled for not selecting the healthier option for dinner. It takes internal vigilance to know that you have selected the same type of person to date even though it didn't work for you the last time. It also takes internal vigilance to know when you have become complacent.

Life is mundane if all that you pay your attentions to are things and situations that are easy for you to take action on? If all that you do are the things that you are certain that you can win at, you cripple yourself. You place yourself into a small box to live from. The potential left on the table is staggering. Some people have resigned to living lives of attempting to do only the comfortable things. Many people bring this "good enough" and "survival based" mindset to all areas of life. Thinking this way usually stems from an unhealthy fear of loss. A fear of embarrassment or shame kills so much possibility. The pain of shame is unbearable for so many of us, but it is a natural part of an advancing life. Fear is what kills possibility.

There is this pervasive idea that if you don't rock the boat too much, then you can't lose, and things will inevitably "turn out" for you. The problem with playing small is that, though you feel safer, you never have the opportunity to win big. Know that as long as you are a human spinning on a piece of wet dirt through space that safety is an illusion. Fulfillment will always be elusive if you trade possibility for safety. If this is what you have been doing up until this point then choose this way of being no longer. Take the job that you don't quite feel qualified for. Speak to the girl or guy that makes your heart skip a beat when they walk by. Date a totally different kind of person. Try a new exercise class. Do a new activity that kind of scares you and brings you joy and experiential knowledge. Do something that you may fail at. You can unlock an entire world of new outcomes. I used to limit myself at many points in my life. I always limited myself to doing what other people would see as successful for me to accomplish. I always made sure that the task was easy for me to do before I tried it. Deep down inside I knew I could do more. I never really aimed as high as I could possibly have dreamed. This was due to a subconscious fear of failure. I also didn't want to outshine those around me or stand out too much. There is also an unsaid rule in the "black community" that you shouldn't aim too high because it makes others feel bad. It is urged that you "be and remain humble" and never "forget the little people". I also shrunk the size of my dreams because I didn't readily know "how to" achieve them. There was a time that if I didn't clearly see the "how" to doing a thing I wouldn't even aim to take action on it.

I often made "the how" more important than the "what" that I wanted to achieve. I now know that the exact "how" is out of my control. Taking action in the right direction is all that any of us can do. The next step will reveal itself once we get moving. It's logical to think that if you don't know the "how" then the "what" is impossible for you to achieve. People always like to ask you "How?" with folded arms, when you say you want to do something. Not knowing the entire answer can stop you right in your tracks. I also convinced myself that for some things the possibility of failure was too high of a price to pay. I didn't know that temporary failure was a positive thing. I have since learned to push myself and I hang outside of my comfort zone with ease now. Through constantly putting myself in challenging situations and working my way through them I got to believe in my own capabilities again. I practiced stoicism without even knowing what it was.

While living in college dorms in Upper Montclair, New Jersey I decided one day that I was an actor. I used to wake up and go to classes and then scour Backstage Newspapers for acting gigs in New York City. I decided that I was going to be an actor. I took acting classes in New York City at night. I also took acting courses while in college. I actually landed day-player / extra roles, I was on TV quite a few times. I earned two SAG acting waivers. I played background a lot traveling all over the city and shot quite a few pilots for HBO shows that never got picked up and were ahead of their time by decades. One time I ended up as an extra on a shoot for a movie named "Empire" around 2002. That movie starred John Leguizamo, Treach from "Naughty By Nature" rap group fame and Fat Joe. In that moment, between takes of scenes, I realized that all I had done to get to that point was to say to myself that I was an actor and believe it. My word was my bond to myself. Getting myself to believe those words is what made me take action. I got headshots and mailed them all over the city. I went to many, many auditions. I got rejected for so many roles it was crazy. I took public transportation all over the city for over two years in between school, working two or more jobs, and commuting home to see my mom and family. I went to all of the acting, modeling, and networking events. I cultivated so many relationships. I even was a club promoter during the week just to meet new people. The amount of contacts that had filled my cell phone to capacity.

I pursued acting relentlessly and became obsessed with meeting people and telling them what I was up to. Doors opened up after I convinced myself that I was worthy of being who I said I wanted to be. I was a paid actor because I said that I was. My word was the power that got me into the room! I got myself to believe that I was an actor. All of the actions that I took from that point matched my destination. The way that I worked out at that time matched that drive also. What I studied in my free time matched. I mentally became an actor well before I ever landed my first gig. Later on, I allowed myself mentally to become one of the very best fitness experts in America. I have since been regarded as one of the best trainers on the planet in print and online by many major fitness publications. I allowed myself to trust and be trusted and I found and married the woman of my dreams. I also had to give myself permission to spread the messages in this book. I gave me permission to run a knowledge based business. I carve out workshops and speaking engagements in order to share the lessons outlined in this book. Believing the words that you say to yourself takes intentional programming and repetition of thought. You can get there, for sure. You can guide you from the inside out.

I chose to step up and do my part in awakening humanity to unlimited potential through self-mastery. The internal vigilance was most helpful in the moments when I had to ask myself *"Does this course of action match the destination that I have declared for myself?"* This question helped and helps me now to keep my actions aligned with my purpose. Right now, I am creating a reality where my thoughts on leadership and personal growth are being made available the world over. I am doing the work now as I type this book in a library in Walnut Creek, California. Home of the Golden State Warriors. Internal awareness alerts me when I am off track. It alerts you too. Always listen for it. Always listen to it. That feeling in your gut that says "Stop, get back on track." is the internal vigilance that I speak of. When it clicks on to hold you accountable don't override it by justifying that taking of actions that are not aligned with who you are becoming. The more you override your warning system, the more it shuts down. So heed it daily. Surround yourself with people who want to see you win. Keep practicing hearing it and course correcting. Well before attaining a goal you will know that you will accomplish it as soon as you say it. That is power.

Writing this book isn't an easy task for me, but it is in alignment with the mission that I have set for myself. I had to cover a lot of ground in my thinking and being to reach this point in my life. I spent most of my life consumed in warfare of the mind and spirit from my environment and the trauma of being abandoned and abused as a child. I was consumed with survival only. It often takes a very selfish mindset to ensure survival. The traumas that I endured helped me to create a mental and psychological armor to live in and through. Survival mindset was necessary. I had to put that survival mindset down in order to pick up the mantle of authentically helping other people on a large scale. I had to slay the very ego that brought me this far in life. I think all who go through great hardships do in order to fully evolve into who they are destined to be. I had to become vulnerable. A lot of ground had to be covered both mentally and spiritually. After all I was a child from the ghetto with no parents who waited on lines for free food from the government in order to eat. For me to even aspire to helping people find mastery around their bodies and mindsets I had to transform. Internal vigilance was the first step. The initial courage to step into the unknown parts of who I was, is what created the self-belief that has illuminated the way.

CHAPTER 7

WHEN SHIT HITS THE FAN... WHO ARE YOU?

Who do you become when life gets tough? What lens do you automatically see the world through when you fail or struggle? This is the same energy that you will bring to all challenging things. It becomes a default setting. Have you ever heard of the saying *"How you do anything is how you do everything?"* This holds true because we all tend to function off of one predominant default mindset when faced with adversity. That default mindset grants you success in one hand and in the other hand it can leave you stuck in life. Until you become aware of who you become under pressure you will be a victim of something that you don't even know exists.

This is a dangerous proposition. In my youth when I failed or encountered hardship the thinking that permeated my being was. *"Pain is my normal, this always happens, get over it, and move on."* I subconsciously expected pain and adversity to be my outcomes. This lens helped me to pick myself up quickly after let downs and failures. It was a major source of resilience and survival. It also attracted more situations towards me that resulted in pain and failure. Subconsciously, I expected failure and for misfortune to come my way. Even when good things happened I could not enjoy them in fear that they would come to a disastrous end. I wasn't aware that having *"Pain is my normal, get over it, and move on."* was a terrible sentence for achieving happiness. It also had an adverse effect on my self-esteem. Imagine what you really think of yourself, if before you even try to do a thing, the back of your mind is filled with the idea that "you will inevitably fail at whatever you set out to do." How would that underlined directive affect the kind of efforts that you put forward in life? I always did my best but knew that pain would be the outcome.

Becoming a better person and aiming to realize my wildest dreams didn't jive with that sentence. That sentence did however correlate with making failure and pain easier to deal with. Pessimism lightened the blow of rejection, failure and pain, but it also thwarted all of my efforts around making a leap towards better living. It normalized failing. It made me "OK" with negative outcomes. I never really examined the source of the pain to get to know what had caused it. "Getting over it" was paramount. Survival was first and foremost. Learning from my adversity was the furthest thing from my mind. I just believed we lived in a cruel world. That negative lens both helped and hurt me early on in life. One sentence shaped my life. I became aware of it. Then I realized that I had to put down the mindset that had helped me navigate my childhood traumas. That was scary. I had to craft a new operative sentence to live from. I now embrace sentences geared towards me living the life filled with abundance and love.

I will refer to our default settings of thinking as "our sentence." This is a part of our mental paradigm that lingers in our subconscious mind. It secretly controls most of the actions that we take. I have done a lot of research and study courses in the field of human ontology (the study of being a human) and one of the courses that has been transformational in my life was: the Landmark Forum from Landmark education (Landmarkeducation.com) Check it out!

They liken the dominant mindset in our lives as a pair of sunglasses. When you put on a pair of yellow sunglasses, the entire world looks weird for a while. The longer you keep them on, the more ordinary the world begins to look. After a while you don't even remember that you are wearing glasses. Pretty soon everything looks clear and fine. This is the context with which you see the world. This is how our default sentences operates. Every decision and choice you make, or don't make, will be filtered by these "lenses" until you remember to take them off for certain situations that they do not suit. Once they are taken off, you will feel like there is an empty void. That void is where a new possibility can fit. This is a great place to be because you can then choose new and better suited pairs of glasses to wear depending on the situation. The important first step I covered in the last chapter (internal vigilance) is getting to know that you are actually wearing shades.

My hope is that something you read here will help you see what kind of shades (hidden mindset) you currently have on. Then you can trade them out to reap new outcomes. Helping clients see this is something that I love to do most in my life strategy business. One of the first things to do is to acknowledge and surrender to the idea that a hidden mindset may be blocking your progress in a certain area of life. I will pick being fit and eating healthier to use as an example. One mindset that many people have is that the physical activity they get while performing their daily job is enough for them to be fit and healthy. Maybe this was true at a time, but for most of us it is no longer a beneficial mindset to have. Metabolisms usually slow as we age. For most of us, we have reached an age where we have to make a separate and deliberate physical investment in ourselves nearly every day in order to maintain adequate levels of fitness. This includes choosing better foods, learning to relax for recovery, exercising, giving to others, etc.

In order to be able to share and receive everything from living life you cannot be content with fine or mediocre anywhere in life. Working out regularly is an act to ensure excellence. Exceptional living is on the opposite side of the spectrum of fine or average. Embrace the learning processes, setbacks and lessons you will go through by stepping out of your comfort zone. Step forward in all areas of life by doing something out of the ordinary or mundane every day. Defy the lenses that you discover holding you back from progress. Create new sentences that empower you. Put on appropriate shades that light you up after you discover the ones you wear that steal your momentum. Switch them out. Attempt the doing of things that will frighten you but thrill you more. Dare yourself to dream without current and familiar lenses. Watch life open up. Make it a game to challenge yourself to learn something new every day.

ACTION: Get a sheet of paper and write out ten things that you want to accomplish in life. Big or small, it doesn't matter. They should be things that you find challenging. Examine your thinking as you write the ten things out. You will become aware of the sentence that has held you back in the past from taking action and moving forward on these ten things. Identify what lenses you have discovered that hold you back? **Example:** Calling the top person in your field of interest and inviting him/her to lunch; filing a patent for an idea; apologizing to a family member. Anything! **Tackle at least one step to achieving your goals every day of every week. Just one step! When a goal is complete, replace it with another. Keep a tally of the things that you complete.**

After some time, you will accomplish the majority of your goals. Review what it took for you to do it. How was the difficulty? Look at the sentences that you had to live from. Acknowledge the steps that you took internally. Establish new goals armed with knowledge of the sentences and mantras that have propelled you as well as the ones that hindered you. Practice taking off your shades and putting on a new pair when necessary. Weight training only works because varying loads challenges muscles. The weight of your dreams must also challenge you. You may have become complacent in life without even knowing it… A complacent mind will always produce complacent outcomes. The outcomes of complacent thinking will look different on everyone due to genes, due to various natural areas of focus, but we all know deep down inside, if we have been lax in our thinking and doing. We always know if we are not living into a future of our own creation. You will know on the inside where your truth resides. Discover and switch up your sentences as needed. Living from the appropriate sentence is the real work.

Allow yourself to become free and mentally stimulated to explore and try new things. Your body will always be stuck exactly where it is, and becoming worse, unless you switch it up and challenge it consistently. Switch out the workout routine and mode of exercises every six weeks. The human body only changes just enough to make the task at hand easier, nothing more. Make a conscious effort to become alive and mentally stimulated. People are drawn to people who are always doing something new and challenging. It is infectious. You will inspire others by living out your calling in life. First thing in the morning set the intentions for how you want things to turn out. Every single seeable change and transformation takes place in an unseen capacity first. Those morning intentions pave the way for great outcomes. Watch life shift when you challenge how you view it.

WE ARE UNIQUELY THE SAME

> "Only you can choose which perception you will
> live from. Choose wisely because that perception
> will shape your life."

I have been blessed with meeting and working closely with many people in my lifetime. I have worked with people from all walks of life and have also remained open to growing and learning from each person. I believe that everyone is a master of something. I have spoken to homeless people for a few minutes who have given me more useable info and cause for thought than some classes in college have in an entire semester. Every human we encounter provides us with an opportunity to grow and learn. It may take some time to, but put down preconceived notions in order to create room to receive your education.

We each have the ability to do things that others find difficult or cannot do. I have been blessed with having the opportunity to train and coach many different people with many different personalities, strengths, weaknesses, and abilities. I am in love with human beings. I hate to break it to you but human beings are more similar than we think. We are uniquely the same. There is a bell curve that we can all fit into regarding almost every area of life. One of the things that does make us different are the mindsets and perceptions that we hold. You may not have control over your initial perception, but you surely can take a beat to allow room to be able to pivot your thinking if necessary. Responding instead of reacting is a choice that you can make from moment to moment. Responses incorporate both logic and reason. Reactions are knee-jerk, or not well thought out. They are automatic responses. Only you get to choose if you will let an initial perception of a person or circumstance rule and control what you get from a situation and ultimately take action on. You always have the option to choose a perception that will suit you better. Too many people are victims of their minds preset default programming. Reactive people are like those who wear dark shades at night and then wonder why they walk into walls.

How many times have a preordained way of thinking caused you to take an action that you looked back at and regretted? How many times has the way that you "always do something" ended up costing you a win in the long- run? Many times you look back on it and chalk the botched decision up to "not thinking". This is a sign that the subconscious mind went to work without any help from the conscious mind. No conscious thought is needed for us to foolishly spring into action. A lot of people are sitting in jail right now sad because of this fact. Relying on reaction instead of response usually leads to situations where you are going to be sorry in the end. This is true unless you have practiced a desired response to the point of mastery. Practice it the right way and so long that you can't get it wrong unless you try to. This is the point that exceptional athletes practice up to. They practice until they cannot get it wrong. The desired response is practiced to the point of it becoming a reflex. Thought plays a very small role in the very best performances. This is where the difference between an automatic reaction and a well composed response become evident. Reactions are programmed by the past and responses are well thought out and created in the moment. Responses usually tend to fit circumstances better. Responses are better because they are made in the moment, with the conscious mind, taking present factors into account. Responses require that you take a beat to thoughtfully create them.

As a wellness professional, I have sat back for many years and watched people get bombarded with surface level fitness solutions. People gravitate towards easy solutions, elsewhere in life too. "Easy" and fast are regarded as "better" in this era. They're not! That belief is often subconscious. Finding an "easy" solution is a societal norm. Subconsciously, it is conditioned into us. Lacking this awareness is the reason that it can fester and exist without us knowing. Before we get into how to become aware of it let me define a "mindset." *A mindset or perspective is the way that a human being mentally sums up or relates to a person, place, thing, or experience.* You can change the way a situation occurs to yourself by offering up a new and viable perspective, you can then change the actions that you will take when confronted with that situation in the future. Changing the perception held about a person, place, thing, or experience can transform how you take action (or don't take action) around that thing.

We usually sum things up in a split second. Whether that summation is accurate or not really doesn't matter. Our limbic mind or "monkey mind" (which many of us are oblivious to) just loves to categorize everything into boxes. Everything that we encounter in life is placed into mental boxes; Pain or pleasure box, good or bad box, safe or dangerous box, or the ever popular like or dislike boxes. It is the primeval and basic part of our mind that dates back to ancient times as humans. It kept us alive in a world where a human being was vulnerable, weak, and likely to become a meal or a snack for larger more ferocious predators. We had to surmise situations, animals, and other threats in record time. Our survival depended on it. Think of how long it takes to put together a first impression of someone. We can do that in milliseconds, sometimes even before the person opens their mouth. All of this is done from images and mental recollections held in storage in our subconscious minds. Many times that first impression usually sets the tone for how we relate to that person, place, experience, or thing indefinitely. You know how they always say that "you can never have a second chance to make a first impression?" Let's face it, we are all guilty of judging a book by its cover at some point in time. If a negative perception concerning a person is found to be inaccurate, you will find that it truly takes an intentional effort to change your perception of that person to a good one. If you have left no open room in your mind after making your initial assumptions about someone, it will take a lot for that assumption to be changed later. The introduction of new information about that individual, done on a few different occasions may be needed for you to reclassify them

So many people are mentally lazy. They do not want their first impression, or their negative summary of a situation challenged. This is so basic! We can't afford to continue not to evolve our thinking and entertain the idea that the conclusions that we initially jump to are often not true or beneficial. Living into a reality where we expose our hidden beliefs and biases to ourselves, and then challenge them is worth the time. During that quest we will find that an entire different planet and reality will unfold. As it stands, remaining loyal to initial assessments of people, places, and things is a lot easier than challenging our past beliefs and mindsets. Leave room for people to prove you wrong about who you've summed them up to be. Remain fluid.

This is also true when it comes to living an experience. You may have a bad experience at one time. Then you wrote off ever experiencing any variation of that experience for as long as you live. I did this a lot. One time I got really, really, sick drinking Patron tequila. So sick that I woke up the next day from sleeping at a friend's house and still felt super drunk. While I was driving I had to roll down the window and throw up out the window. I had vomit all over my beautiful car! I felt like I was dying. In that moment I swore off tequila for life. I didn't drink any form of tequila for eight years. About a month ago I went on my long awaited honey moon in Puerto Vallarta, Mexico. It is in Jalisco Mexico the home of tequila. I had to confront and erase (the still very vivid) a tequila infused, horrifying night out on the town. At this point is happened ten years ago! I had to make room for a new experience. I loved the tequila that I tasted in Mexico so much. The different flavors and fruit infusions blew my mind. I actually brought back a divine bottle of *"Noble Corazon"* blue agave, tequila. If I held onto my belief about tequila from almost a decade ago I would never have had that chance to traipse through the streets of Jalisco Mexico, hand in hand, honeymooning with the love of my life. I enjoyed a stomach filled with some of the best tequila in the world on the trip of a lifetime.

When you consciously or subconsciously box or label something without revisiting it. Good or bad, you have eliminated possibility around that person, place, or situation. Sometimes you allow yourself to blindly trust a person that you just met, because subconsciously they remind you of a very trustworthy friend. Because of that past relationship you end up getting taken advantage of in this current relationship. Many people determine whether they like or dislike something within the first few seconds of doing it, not giving it a fair chance. Many people may be thinking now: "Why would you do something again that you didn't like immediately?" It's important to revisit things and reassess them often.

Each one of us is constantly changing from moment to moment day to day. You have to give some things time, while looking for the most beneficial perspective for you to assume. Past experiences do not dictate future results or outcomes. We just fear that they will. In the case of a good occurrence the first time, we are likely to repeat that assumption in the future. There is no guarantee that it will be good again. We just hope that it will be. If you categorize a person negatively you have just put on a pair of shades to see them through. Your shades won't allow you to see their best assets.

A person may have hundreds or thousands of perceptions made about them in a day. Those are all different ways of seeing the same person. All of them are valid. If you think a person is stupid, you won't deal with them as if they are intelligent in the future. The mind will always see things the same way until that perception is altered by you intentionally. You will see all of the stupid things that person will do. That will confirm your assumption. You won't get to see their brilliance. Once we have made up our mind we have typed into Google what we will see. Our mind will seek out evidence to confirm the conclusion that we have jumped to. That person can sit down in a lab and create the cure for cancer. The mindset you have toward that person will make it very difficult for you to believe that he/she has accomplished such a feat. Twenty other people may have an entirely different perception of the person and see that same person as a genius. It is not until you relinquish the hold that you have on your initial perception of them, that you will be able to entertain the possibility of their brilliance. If you remain fluid with your assumptions, you can move past them when need be, and have much richer relationships with people.

GIVE UP BEING RIGHT

Once a mindset is set, it takes effort to release it. Repetition, pain, and giving up the idea of having to be "right" will help to change a limiting mindset. Human beings have an obsession with being "right". Many of us will go through all types of hardships and adversity just to prove a point. The funny thing is that the more you look to confirm almost any idea, the more information you will find to support it. In the end, no one perspective is "Right" or "the Truth". We agreed that the world was flat for hundreds of years and we now believe that it is a sphere. Logic dictates that if everything is important, then nothing is. Anyone can find proof to back up just about any conclusion drawn these days. Millions of people are still convinced that the world is flat. They have analytical and empirical data to back their claims up too.

A dominant thought compounds. If you have a single thought, in an instant many similar thoughts come flooding in to bolster it. This is the reason a mother can worry for hours on end until her child returns home. It all starts with "I hope he/she is okay and that nothing went wrong". It then becomes "If he/she was okay, he/she would have called". That escalates to "I hope there wasn't an accident". Soon the mother has locked her son or daughter up in a third world prison all in her mind. They have just been badly beaten and are currently eating saltines for dinner. In reality, the child walks in the door a few minutes after curfew because their friend is a slow driver. Relief washes over the parent. This is the way that all of our minds work. Perception and reality do a captivating dance in our minds. Perception and mindset overlap. Before long our perceptions become our truths. It is extremely important to be aware of the mindsets that you create and not do so blindly or by default. Many times, changing a mindset or clearing one out transforms life.

Keep the possibility alive that the conclusion that you jumped to may be "wrong". It allows you to be objective and gain the most from any experience. For many people, exercising and eating right shows up as a chore. If this is the classification assigned to fitness then how likely are we to do it continuously? Not likely at all. These are the people who need a coach yelling at them to get it done! It is time to play mindset chess. Since I have become aware of this phenomenon in my own life I make the attempt to only adopt mindsets that serve me. I do not allow limiting ones to go unaltered. Once I discover that they are holding me back from success in any area, I get to work on creating and implanting a new one that works. It takes repetition of thought and the uncomfortable taking of new actions to reprogram a mindset.

Early on in my career I trained collegiate athletes. I also worked with soldiers in the US Army. They were my peers. I noticed that both groups had an underlying drive or motivation to succeed. They both possessed a drive to not let their teammates down or to be regarded as the weakest link. Soldiers and athletes have a developed ability to focus on the task at hand with extreme precision. Remember how I spoke about being "in the zone" in life. Focused practice is where the ability to be "in the zone" in sport and battle is created. Repetition, drilling, and constant practice leads to this ability to access the zone without thinking about it. The zone is thoughtless. This is a form of reprogramming. The same practice that soldiers and athletes undergo is needed for the civilian population to tap into desirable ways of being that allow for hard yet beautiful things to get accomplished in their lives. It will take incorporating the mind, body, and soul to establishing a desire that is linked to a purpose. Using all three parts of who we are, to learn (mind, body, soul) makes mastery happen quicker.

LESSONS FROM ATHLETES AND SOLDIERS

If the goal for a soldier is to be able to climb a mountain, he will do *everything* in his power to climb that mountain. He will do everything! Planning, preparation, and execution will happen. The mind is fully absorbed with the objective. They have no room left for excuses and reasons to fail to enter their mind. Athletes will do everything in their power to gain even the slightest edge in competition. Many athletes have what is referred to as intrinsic motivation. Intrinsic motivation is usually derived from the enjoyment of a sport, a feeling of satisfaction, purpose, or the improvement of a skill. An athlete feels this excitement after posting a new personal record. This method of celebrating small wins even in practice builds on itself and keeps them locked into doing all that it takes. A shot of dopamine is pumped into their brains every time an inkling of improvement is experienced. That is what keeps them relentlessly focused. Extrinsic motivations are the medals and trophies. I believe that to the truly great athletes the medals and accolades matter to a far lesser degree. They don't do the required difficult work for medals and stats. They just want to be as great as they can be, and see how far they can take it. They make becoming their best selves in that area of life into a game. Society operates off of achieving surface-level results and only gives credence to the outcomes. It totally misses out on the sweetness and personal development that occurs during the journey.

I was a first squad leader and part time platoon guide in charge of physical training for 70 soldiers in the US Army. I was asked to help a lot of soldiers to pass the physical training tests who were in danger of failing. Failure was not an option in their minds, but many times their bodies were untrained and not able to do the work that the drill sergeants set forth. The determination and fight to achieve their goals were at an all-time high. I was able to push some of these soldiers to places they had never gone to mentally and physically. The desire to pass was very high. They were being conditioned to have a "do whatever it takes" mindset by myself and the drill instructors. I have yet to see that kind of perseverance and drive in any other setting. Soldiers worked to the point where they would uncontrollably throw up, or even pass out from exertion. They would go to the latrine clean off and then come back and continue training. I held physical training catch-up sessions right before bed, at night, to further train those that needed it. Many times this would be after sixteen hours of drilling and training in the field during boot camp. There was a lot at stake for a soldier if they didn't satisfy the physical training aptitude test. If they failed, he/she would be held back and not allowed to graduate with the rest of their class. That meant spending a longer time in the basic combat training barracks, repeating training drills, and sometimes losing rank. Extrinsic Motivation was very present in this situation as well. I do not believe that it was the "negative reinforcement" or the many shame tactics that helped the majority of the soldiers pass their PT tests. I believe that it was an overall shift in their mindset: They found a "failure is not an option and I will do whatever it takes to progress" mindset that propelled each soldier down their course. They also had me every night drilling into their minds and bodies that no matter what it took that they could pass the tests. Their normal standards of "Ok" were no longer acceptable. Their standards of "normal" were raised to only accepting "exceptional" as their standard when it came to giving effort. This is a mindset instilled early on in training in the military and also in many high-level team sports. Your best efforts and beyond are all that is acceptable.

Athletes and soldiers were deprogrammed away from mediocrity in the beginning of their training. The concept of self is stripped away. The first few days or even weeks are focused around being stripped of "normal civilian" ways of thinking that would prove weak in the military or on the field of play. Whatever mindset they carried before entering the process of becoming either a high level athlete or soldier was simply erased. At the same time, they gained a different level of self-belief. This was accomplished by being pushed passed the brink of what they physically thought possible. Being exceptional became the only option. Regular and even reasonable excuses begin to hold no weight. When aiming to be exceptional and achieving the very best in life becomes the only option it is amazing to see what humans can accomplish. We shatter standards!

The first two weeks in the military is used to psychologically and emotionally break you down. The objective is to wipe away any limiting mindsets, perspectives, and ego that you may have brought in with you and erase weakness from both mind and body. The US Army really values the creation of a soldier from the ground up. The best way to create the world's best soldier is from a clean slate. There are all types of drills and exercises geared towards cracking your personality. Stretching you further than you have gone before is the goal.

The process begins at the welcome Battalion. You are constantly placed in situations that challenge who you know yourself to be and yanks you out of your comfort zone. Sleep is the first thing to go. The mental and physical rigors that you undergo force you to face yourself head on. Through great pain and adversity you get to see the real you eye to eye. During this process you are the most honorable and truthful to yourself. For most of us this is the hardest push to look at yourself that you may have experienced, in your entire life, up until that point. This is when you get to witness other people's true colors show as well. All of the pleasantries go out of the window. Out of the corner of your eye you can witness others confront who they are when their back is against the wall. You also see people learning to release limiting mindsets and perspectives in an instant when they do not work. You get the best and sometimes the worst out of people. Those who survive become people they would have never become without making it through the US Army Basic Combat Training. Observing this is when I fell in love with coaching people to shed limiting beliefs and become their best selves. I was seventeen years old. I thought it was witchcraft. I imagined a world where everyone on the planet had the nerve to face themselves and live purposeful lives that positively affected everyone they met.

Every single soldier is put through this rigorous elite program: limiting mindset extraction in its rawest form. It is also known as a rite of passage for any military personnel. Most soldiers do not consider you a full-fledged equal regardless of your rank until you have passed BCT. You are given coaches called drill sergeants who guide you to follow orders to the letter and only deliver to the best of your ability, without any questions asked. It doesn't matter who you were before you got there, your mindset and outlook on life will change drastically after the first two weeks of basic combat training. The physical challenges are just as tough as the mental challenges of being away from home in a foreign environment. You get a very intimate look at yourself while navigating pain and pressure. You fight sleep deprivation. You are constantly barked at a lined up. You are exercised to new uncharted boundaries, and you are forced to consume and memorize an entire military handbook. Your physical limitations are exceeded every single day, multiple times in a day. Your character and integrity gets a makeover as you are held to high standards only. You forge a new relationship with your inner being. Just as steel is hardened with fire, so are the people make it to the end.

I also watched people crumble under pressure as the masks that they showed themselves to be in the world were stripped away. I watched them then walk through fire and come out expressing the best in their personalities and being. Trials and challenges can help to create a super focused mindset. Getting in touch with who you have been on a mental level around anything you want to accomplish is illuminating. You can then make adjustments. You don't have to join a high level sports team or be in the military to do this. You just need desire and a will to become exceptionally real with yourself. You must also build in enduring some pain (that you control) into the process. Doing something difficult builds great character.

Become aware and conscious enough to pay attention to the directives that your soul and inner self gives you. Read on for tips to understand how to do this better. Be willing to admit your humanity or weaknesses to yourself. Push past your personal hurdles, likes and dislikes, and limiting mindsets and make progress. Erase that limiting perspective and replace it with a new one that serves you. Do this continuously until you feel that you own the new mindset and it becomes second nature to you to say to yourself. First and foremost, draw up a contract with yourself. Honor it. The contract that we signed while entering the military was referred to daily. Writing things down is a very good way to hold yourself accountable. Writing makes things real. Make yourself open to taking new and drastic but exceptional actions. You can't have normal thoughts and take normal actions and expect to win. Exceptional must become your new normal. Document your pledge to be so regarding your goals.

Just like an athlete learning a new sport for the first time, the mindset you have outside of the sport will carry into the sport. The mindset you maintain will either be threatened or empowered by the mechanical learning of the sport. If you have a personality that was conducive to playing the sport at a high level, you will likely continue. If not, you will inevitably quit or choose another sport play. In the military, opting out and choosing to do something else is not possible. New soldiers have to march whether they like it or not, eat when they are told to, exercise whether they like it or not and sleep whenever they are allowed to. Through various drills and confidence building activities while in the military, each soldier develops the mindset of being able to do whatever is set in front of them to be accomplished. An athlete forges a very similar mindset. They archive positive performances or breakthroughs that they have. Self-belief is also fostered through hard work, and dedication. Both the soldier and the athlete experience times in training when they are "in the zone" thanks to their focus and intensity. The more time you spend living "in the zone" and at peace, the better everything in life will work for you as a whole. Imagine living "in the zone" at all times, like Neo in the movie "The Matrix". Everything slows down and he realizes that he possesses the power to control everything in his surroundings. We have all experienced times being in the zone while doing something that we were well prepared to do, or doing something that we love. Being able to be in the zone with things your mind doesn't particularly like to do is also possible. We just have to reframe it in our minds as a task that is part of us achieving a greater purpose.

The ability to push through adversity, even overcoming injuries, creates a certain powerful mindset that is only activated when confronted with the possibility of failure or adversity. It is no wonder that in the military, every single soldier loses weight, becomes stronger, leaner and more defined. There is absolutely no rocket science involved in the training methods used in the military. First, there is running, and then alternate days there are various callisthenic exercises done until muscle failure occurs. That's it, there are no other options at all. The same exact exercises and measures are done day in and day out and the regimen is repeated over and over and over again. They are done by the young and the old. They are done by males and females alike and everyone sees results. A person's mindset is sculpted by the measure of discipline and structure in their movements. Consistency and conquering pain is what changes bodies and minds. That type of mental environment makes nothing else possible other than the steady progression for the body. The ability to push though pain and embrace failure is also a key ingredient that is trained into each soldier. Powerfully navigating failure is as necessary for any advancing human as oxygen is for our planet to live.

CHAPTER 8

FAILURES AND SETBACKS ARE NECESSARY

A soldier or athlete mindset is created first from a clean slate, then the trial by fire and rebuilding. In the process of creating a clean slate, the military or high level athletics enhances or erases the original mindset and replaces it with a brand new one. Adversity and hardship make you or break you. Either way, there is a lot to learn by enduring adversity. The action of going through adversity and setbacks is not enough, it's important to take note of lessons gained from each obstacle that you pass through. Becoming familiar with the mindset you have towards exercise would be key to making it a habit. Becoming aware of your overall mindset around money can be the first step to changing how much of it you have. Noticing who you are and how you show up in relationships can put you in a position to have better ones.

Look back at life. If you have ever accomplished anything you have overcome obstacles and setbacks. The beginning of anything is always hard. Your desire to achieve your goal was stronger than the failures you encountered along the way. In fitness, if you want to transform your body, failure is tool. It's through failure that muscles and physical strength grow. Try on the idea that failures and setbacks are good things. They're indications that you are living a life that is moving towards an ideal you have set for yourself. Failure is the opportunity to learn and make adjustments. Innovation, wisdom, expansion, and creativity can all be bi-products of experiencing failure. All successful people experience failure. Failure is inevitable when reaching for something foreign, new, and exponentially better than what you have.

Failures and setbacks are great teachers. View and handle them favorably. Be disappointed, pick up the lesson, and then continue on. Most times in life, we are taught from very young to avoid failure at all costs. Fear of failure is one of the most powerful oppositions to progress and human evolution. This type of mindset leads to a resigned and complacent existence. Many people do participate in health and fitness regimens and their bodies never change because they feel this way. Being afraid to strive will put you in a comfortable prison. Body environments adapt rapidly when the threshold for what the body is capable of doing is tested, visited, and redefined with challenging movement. People who are afraid of failure never dare to break the comfortable boundaries of what they know they can accomplish. False sense of safety and little to no results will be the outcome.

I urge all people to redefine what they see as possible in their lives. Exercising is not a chore when you see it as an opportunity to expand possibilities and options. It becomes an investment. Let's say that you barely squeaked out eleven squats with a hundred and fifty pounds the last time you lifted weights. You almost failed on the eleventh rep but you powered through and got it. You got eleven but the goal was twelve. That should be seen as a failure. How will you negotiate this? Will you aim for twelve again on the next set? Many people will never ever attempt to reach for that twelfth squat on the next set. They may cut their sets back to ten reps in order to be "safe". (to ensure that they do not fail) Most will entertain mindsets that sound like: "That was hard, and scary, I will never do that again." "If eleven were that hard, there is no way I can ever do twelve". "I'm going to hurt myself." "I'm having a bad day." Will any of those mindsets or questions help? Very few will say "Let me take a longer break to make sure that I recover and then I am going after that full set of twelve." Fewer will ask someone to spot them in order to safely step outside of their comfort zone and attempt the twelfth squat. The effort exerted in the eleventh and twelfth reps are what make the entire set worthwhile. They promote the most growth on a spiritual and physiological level. Successful or not, in the very attempt of those hard reps, the effort hints to your soul how resilient and badass you really are. It can shift what you believe possible in the future.

What you believe to be possible will always dictate the quality of the actions you take. The absolute biggest obstacle for so many is their disbelief deep down inside that they will never be fit, never be wealthy, never find love etc. Disbelief in receiving success kills efforts. People literally eat themselves into oblivion because in their minds, "it doesn't matter anyway". They are subliminally convinced they will never lose the weight. Attempting to complete those two last unfathomable reps doesn't even make sense to do. Holding a static training pose for ten seconds longer, while all of your muscles are burning and trembling is not worth it. Sprinting for five seconds longer than you believe possible, to the point your lungs feel like they are going to explode won't even cross their mind as something to do. They will quit. Rev the engine on occasion to bring your best self to the surface. Those very moments define who you are becoming!

Give the middle finger to every way of being that you engaged in in the past that hasn't served you to this point in life. Turn your back on who you were and make a new declaration of who you are and who you are becoming. Do this on a physical and mental level. Trust me, the person who pushes past perceived limitations regularly, in many areas of life, and the person who never does, have very different experiences when shit hits the fan. In life there inevitably will be tests and adversity. Personal development gives you a better chance at weathering those storms and experiencing less of them.

Having a mindset of optimism and possibility is tapping into a powerful state of consciousness. It is what makes the imagination run wild in a good way. You will discover new ways to work out and new foods that resonate with your body. A mind-state of possibility is the opposite of a mindset of fear and pessimism. Be honest with yourself. Write out some fears and limiting ways of thinking that may be holding you back from achieving a goal that you desire. Expose them! Become intrigued by finding solutions. Cultivating a possibility based consciousness will make it possible to overcome life's circumstances. Failure is the breakfast of champions and because they never stop, success is what they get to have for desert. Trying on new ways of thinking may make you feel uncomfortable. Good! Good pain is weakness leaving the body during exercise. Bad pain is an injury. Work to be able to tell the difference. In over twenty three years of being a personal trainer and life-strategist the biggest cause of unrealized dreams has been faulty mental programming.

BE PATIENT GRASSHOPPER

Defeat is when failure has been accepted as a final outcome and intentional action towards a goal permanently ceases. All changes occur first in the unseen and then materialize. There is always a lag time before the outcomes that we desire manifest. This is why patience is a required virtue when we look to transform our lives. That surge of feel good hormones that travels through your body after the initial discomfort of beginning an exercise routine is an indication of the body starting to adapt. These changes happen far before any of the visible changes manifest.

Despite how good exercise and movement feel, many still quit and chalk their lack of visible success up to "I don't know, I worked out hard and nothing much happened, it's a complete waste of time". They have a skewed idea of how fast their aesthetic results should show up. Many also have strong opinions around how much effort they put forth. I have heard "I am working so hard. I should see more results." My first question is "According to who?" When it comes to making any huge change in our lives we have to understand that we are also manipulating energy momentums. These are unseen levers.

If for the last decade a person has been gaining weight year after year, that momentum must first be halted and then reversed. That takes time and tremendous energy. Many people feel that they know exactly what to do to become fit and refuse to let their old methodology go when it no longer works. It is so important to be adaptable in our approaches to do anything. It also take time and thought to find what works right now. Our bodies are constantly changing. Its needs and responses to stimulus also change. What we eat and how we train should suit the season that the body is in right now. The approaches to making it better must also change. The lessons gained mentally and spiritually while becoming a regular exerciser are the true reward. It will take time for new actions to become habitual enough to garner mirror worthy results. They will undoubtedly develop in the new momentum. Let go of preconceived notions and allow a new reality to form and materialize. Be a blank slate. Remain willing to make the necessary course corrections along the journey.

In order to illustrate the concept of needing patience when shifting a mindset, I will expose some mindsets that many people hold about money. I will show you how they create a reality. Some people believe that they will never have more than enough money and that money is very hard to come by. They take actions, consciously or not, that will guarantee that this perception remain true. Every individual has a money thermostat and a level of wealth consciousness. Every family has one. Every community has one. Every city, every state, and each country has a level of wealth consciousness. This is all energy. Momentums take intention and repetition to shift. The momentum is selected by an underlying set of stories/perceptions around money. You can find evidence of the "money being scarce" mindset manifested in many ways in our nation's ghettos. You can see the opposite in various zip codes around the country as well. Either way, people have populated the Google search bar in their minds with either "scarcity" or abundance. If people believe money is limited or always in short supply, they will never give it away freely. They will never invest in vehicles that make it grow. Money has a flow to it. They will never be on the positive side of it. They will struggle to invest or take any high-risk high-reward opportunities. Money likes to be used and put into motion. All of their actions will be saturated in lack. Consequently, they will never have more than enough. Working from a mindset of fear & scarcity will only bring about more scarcity.

It is true that "The rich get richer and the poor get poorer." This is because the unseen beliefs of the rich and poor create two different operating systems. Changing an operating system takes time and effort. Example: A position opens up at work. The position pays fifty percent more then you currently make and will allow the possibility of savings, investment, and abundance. People who operate from limiting mindsets or stories of lack will never apply for the position. They will disqualify themselves or find a way to miss or botch the first interview. They may show up to the interview unprepared. They may say to themselves "I am not ready, I will apply next year." They will procrastinate around getting to know the people involved in the hiring process. The quality of all of the actions they take towards securing the job will be very low. When the first hurdle appears they will stop efforts altogether. They will not put their best foot forward. There won't be a lot of expectant, eager, and exciting effort put towards getting the job. They will find logical and sensible reasons to justify not applying instead of looking for ways to match their experiences with the qualifications of the job.

This is self-sabotage. Most people are not even aware of it. The momentum can be shifted. Other people believe they will be affluent and abundant a hundred percent of the time. They feel entitled to being prosperous and have more than enough at all times. They take all actions to make it their reality. Even when they lose everything they bounce back quickly. These people believe money flows freely in and out of their lives. They study or know a lot about wealth creation. They will have a different stance when it comes to taking calculated financial risks. Applying for that new job will happen naturally for them. Even if they are underqualified they throw their hats in the ring. These people usually seize opportunities to make money by the horns. What you say in your head becomes reality in the world. "Whether you believe you can or cannot, you are right." Many people are unaware of their self-talk. They are unaware of their current mindset when it comes to doing hard but extremely beneficial things. If you are doing "all of the right things" but the mind is subconsciously aligned with a faulty story and mindset, your results will falter. Invest the time and energy in exposing a limiting mindset and transplanting a better one. Seeking out the mindset that doesn't serve you is the first step. Increase your knowledge base in areas of struggle. You gain options when you cultivate knowledge.

CHAPTER 9

MIND FLOW

I refer to mind-flow as the ability for people to fluidly select suitable mindsets as needed. Think of performing a mindset transplant in order to adapt to circumstances or reach goals that you want to accomplish in life. The ability to discard an old mindset that doesn't serve you is critical for success. This ability is a major ingredient that allows for people to be able to be very successful in multiple areas of their lives. So many of us develop unhealthy attachments to ways of thinking that helped us before but hurt us now. You should not take an axe to do the work of the scalpel or vice versa. It is important to be able to adapt and change the perceptions in your head. Mind-flow is the oil that keeps a successful life functioning optimally. You will experience less stress. This is good for immune function and body fat levels.

The ability to establish different mindsets to suit various situations and areas of your life is challenging in the beginning. This is a very difficult practice because, in order to get through and survive life, we have adopted one primary mindset that is weaved into the very fabric of our personalities. This predominant mindset has shaped everything from the clothes that you wear, your hair style, to the kind of car you drive. Even who you choose as your life partner is shaped by this hidden mindset. Many times, we don't even know that this predominant sentence exists. One of the craziest things that I noticed while working with various people is that it is so hard to let go of their dominant sentence even after they discover that it is killing their progress in life. I will get more into the importance of the hidden sentence etc. A sinking ship is more comfortable for them to stay on than it is for them to take a chance leaping into the unknown.

ROGUE MINDSETS

How many times has the same exact undesirable outcome happened over and over again in your life? Have you ever been caught up in a negative loop? I have. What does it take for you to finally do something drastically new and break free of it? People date the same type of person over and over again, wondering why their personal life is in shambles. People continue to do the same things at work and wonder why they get passed over for promotions continually. People get sick then go to the hospital and get treated. Then they go home and eat the same foods and do the same activities and live the same exact lives that got them sick in the first place. Scientists use mice in labs for experiments. What we do in life is the equivalent of a mouse running into the same wall over and over and over again when placed in a maze. Even mice learn they will have to take another route and switch their gears in order to get to the cheese. Mice simply choose a different path. People often don't even know how to change course because they are unaware of the current mindset that drives them repeatedly into walls. They can't discern what makes it impossible for them to get to the cheese. Good news is, once the awareness is turned on, you are then able to access new courses of action. Anyone can turn that spotlight of awareness on.

The example above about mice running into walls less than humans do is not funny it's pretty tragic. People spend priceless years being stuck. Life is too short to stay suck. I spent years and years stuck due to unchecked stories that I clung to around the idea of trust. Batterers of their wives or girlfriends have subconscious beliefs and mindsets that lead to that kind of behavior. A certain mindset when it comes to food results in obesity, sickness, and premature death. A certain type of mindset will render a person with many resources all around them, to suffer in poverty.

Let me illustrate this point further: A very determined and strong mindset is great in business, the military and professional sports. It is not always the best mindset to have when dealing with people and matters of the heart. The approach I had while training athletes and soldiers is not the same tact I'd use to train regular people just looking to gain a better handle on their fitness levels. Using the same tact no matter who is involved isn't smart. I most likely would have been dealing with numerous lawsuits and client injuries as well. People are simply different in the civilian world. They have different things are on their plates. They have varying values and focuses and should be dealt with differently. Ignoring their stresses and the loads they have elsewhere in life is a way to cause more harm than good.

I do see some trainers who don't have a grasp on this concept out here pushing people with cookie-cutter techniques and reckless abandon. I always say "good luck" to them. I pray for their clients. When it comes to exercising and doing it on a continuous basis, the mindset you carry through life matters. I will go as far as to say that many people's mindsets are not conducive to exercising and eating right on a regular basis. This is the real reason why the world is becoming sicker and more obese. Exercise and healthier eating are acts of self-love and preservation. When most people become busy and chaotic in their lives the first person that they will neglect is themselves. In doing that, they give less to everyone that they love. "I am too busy to take care of myself. I have to do and be less so that the others that I love can be more." is a tough story to break away from. Is this something that you have had to navigate? Do a lot of people depend on you? I was the oldest in my household. I was expected to help my mother raise the younger kids. I also had to show any foster kids who came to stay for a whole, what the rules were. I placed no importance on my own self-care growing up. I actually never got my first massage unto I turned forty.

JESSICA

Jessica was either thirty pounds overweight or thin on a yoyo roller coaster around her weight for her entire life. There were a few times when she lost thirty pounds and adopted a healthy lifestyle. She reported that the longest time that she could maintain this weight loss was about three years. She actually made health and fitness a priority for three years and did everything she knew to get in shape. She ate well, exercised every day and made it a practice to take time out of each day for herself.

When I met her, she touted those days as some of the best days in her life. They were long gone. It had been seven years since she lived that way, and since that time, she had gained forty six pounds. When I asked her "What happened? "Why she stopped?" She said that she simply lost the momentum as life got busier and time sped by.

Jessica was one of those people who would start new projects with great strength and ability. She was not a natural finisher. We all have one of these superpowers. Are you a natural starter or a finisher? She was very successful. Jessica had a beautiful family, made a good living and enjoyed her life. Her ability to succeed was attached to the doing of things where a strong start to get the ball rolling was necessary. She relied on others to finish. She stated that in her job, she was called to work with teams in early stages of project development to get them kick started. She actually was able to trace back many times where she had gotten fulfillment from getting projects off of the ground. That was her sweet spot. After experiencing success, she usually stopped putting forth that same kind of effort and moved onto the next project. This same exact approach bled into her very own health and fitness. Are you a gifted starter of big projects or are you a better executer and/or finisher? You should know this about yourself! It is so powerful. You can then become aware of where you need support and how to keep yourself motivated. Do you need support starting or do you need it during execution and completion?

Who we are in one area of life is who we are everywhere. Jessica naturally lost interest in things when things took longer periods of time to accomplish or establish. The mindset at play was "I did my part, I can always start over again." Can you see how that mindset played a part in her yoyo relationship with fitness all her life? She flourished on teams at work as a spark plug. This didn't serve her while working on her health. She put forth efforts to get into shape on numerous occasions but always quit at some point. There is absolutely nothing wrong with this mindset in certain situations but it sucked in her fitness life. As a project manager in research and development in a huge company, she developed new initiatives and business structures. She did not necessarily have to participate in the long term implementation of the project. She supervised it. She was there for the initial push but another team member further cultivated and implemented the ideas.

Creativity and power are needed in fitness to start a success, but continuity is a measure of success as well. All fitness regimens will eventually fail with the mindset *"I did my part, I can always start over again."* In order to make a lasting change in her life, she needed a new fitness mindset: We chose *"Being fit is my responsibility, now is the only time that there is."* With this mindset she took responsibility of the entire process, not just the starting point. Her new fitness mindset led her to continuity and the ability to sustain healthy habits over time. Working from this new and conscious mindset changed the manner in which she took action to becoming fit. Over time she made healthy choices that coincided with treating herself like a healthy person consistently. We even used short term races to keep her motivated in the beginning. We selected back to back runs for her to have to get ready for. This way she had to continuously train to be in shape for them.

Her old mindset would always be engraved in her and show up from time to time but with practice, integrity and some other processes outlined in this book, she was able to notice when the old thinking pattern was back in play. After more than a decade she is still in great shape and healthily enjoying her grandchildren today. We fortified her ability to stick with a project to completion and be able to foster maintenance.

DON'T DO IT ALONE

A very popular mindset that I have encountered many times is the idea that we must do everything on their own. We are conditioned in school to "keep our eyes on our own tests." We are celebrated for doing things ourselves without help. I embraced this mindset of solitude for a long, long time in my existence. Who we become in the face of failure is "I've got this". Gyms are full of people just like this. They have no clue about what they are doing and at the same time, they refuse to ask for help. They often end up quitting fitness efforts due to getting little results, or worse yet, getting more injuries than results. The only good thing about quitting for them is that they have reduced the risk of getting hurt worse due to improperly exercising. We all need help. The sooner you realize this fact, the more successful you will become in areas of struggle.

This is one of the main reasons why January resolution makers quit mid to late February. Some people do the same thing every year without recruiting a professional or recruiting friends to workout with. When what you do does not work, seek help. Too many people embark on "hard for them" adventures and do not seek assistance. If something is difficult and beneficial, it makes sense to partner with someone for whom that action is fun. It is a really great idea to work with someone who enjoys doing what you struggle with. I still struggle with empowering other to help me in business, to this day. I am aware of this and working on it every day.

There is no such thing in life as self-help or self-made. You may have thought that this book was a self-help book up until this point. It is not. My hopes are that it serves as a spark to activate critical thinking by the reader, for the reader. You are exactly the best you that will ever be right now. All of the materials needed to create a smart phone were here on earth back in the thirteen century. Think on this a bit. No miraculous element fell from space to enable us to create smart phones. The ingredients were all here in the thirteenth century. Our thinking just evolved on how to use the materials on this planet to create a smart phone. You and I can facetime like they did on the Jetsons due to transformations in thinking. Books like this one, can only stimulate that which is already within you to be expressed. Seeds of greatness are already within you. It often takes the insights and perspectives of other people to help you to realize and awaken to what is already here within you. It took breakthroughs and technological advances to be able to take the raw materials of the earth and fashion them into a smart phone. Those seeds needed water. I hope that this book is water and nurturing for people. All good teachers know that their job is to make you aware of abilities that you already possess. They are there to spark critical thinking and help you to find the components within you that you need for success. There's nothing foreign that can be added to you to make you better than you already are. You can either be dormant or alive and well watered.

Knowledge grants you a greater awareness of things. That awareness grants you access to more facets of who you can become. Another person's perspectives can make visible to you potentials that you previously could not see. Training with another person can make you aware of hindrances and gifts that you were not aware of. A good mentor can condense years of pain filled learning into short periods of time. Most believe that changes in belief take years. It doesn't have to. They can happen in an instant. Being a very independent type of person who never wanted help, I had to really challenge myself to learn this principal. I used to see asking for help as a weakness. Once I began to challenge this mindset my life began to transform. I have cut a considerable amount of time off of all of my endeavors and work more effectively by incorporating the help of mentors today. I am now able to help even more people and express myself even better. My mentors have done amazing things for my mindset. They have shaved years of struggle off of my progress in business, finance, my health, and in dealing with personal relationships. One of the greatest and most rewarding things about what I do as a life strategist and fitness expert is that I get to learn while teaching and instructing. Each one of my clients has helped me to grow. Learning is definitely a two-way street, everyone you meet can add to your being. When you have exhausted all of your immediate knowledge, go out and meet people who can help you to expand. Meet and interact with some new people that are already where you want to be in certain areas of life.

YOU ARE MORE THAN WORTHY

One of humanity's prevalent mindsets has been that we are fundamentally flawed from birth. For some reason, from the time we were young, the ethos (air around us) says that we are not good enough or perfect the way that we are. We can all point to times when life confirmed this statement and many of us unfortunately have come to believe it as truth. Religions informs us of our imperfections and unworthiness. People often love to tell other people what they can and cannot do or achieve. There are so many ideals set up in society and so many measures reminding you of how poorly you measure up to these ideals. Capitalism is founded on pointing out a flaw and selling you a solution to help you cope with it. We all have felt this and we all have different responses. There is an overwhelming and ugly feeling among many of us, that something is inherently wrong with us.

Some people run around, trying to prove to the world that they are worthy and that they are good enough. I did this for so many years. They feel the need to hoard up on accolades and education in order to measure their success. Other people crawl up into a corner and basically shut down. They resign to the idea that they will never be able to have it all so they may as well settle for securing the little that they do have. Above all else they have a need to feel and remain safe and secure. They seek comfort in aiming low and playing small in life. They do everything in their power to ensure stability, feel safe, and not lose what they have. They deny any risky and authentic urges to do or be more. They deny the larger dreams that they may have. The bury them. Some people are just angry and frustrated and don't even know why. Some prove their worth by taking care of all other people and never themselves. Being unworthy or somehow flawed from the beginning is incorrect thinking. Loving yourself and those who depend on you, is the beginning of making fitness, financial wellbeing, & self-care happen indefinitely. Think of doing the hard things as a way of showing love to all whom matter.

The human subconscious mind is very suggestable. Repetitively hearing the same thing over and over will program it. Developing an inferiority complex or claiming fear, leads us away from accessing the greatness that lies within us. Everything great and unique about you is already inside of you. We all come well prepared for life from the creator. Great coaches, teachers, parents share and learn how to reunite you with the dormant tools inside of you. You can create the life you want to live and succeed in whatever it is that you want to accomplish. The addition of outside things to who you are never really makes any lasting and meaningful transformation. Using outside things to access your inner gifts is a different story. This means that the best workout in the world and the most properly balanced diet tailored for you will ultimately fail until you consciously choose to use these practices to tap into great qualities that are already within you. Discovering you and finding self-expression is what makes progress addictive and perpetual. More money, more friends, more anything cannot make you *more* than who you already are. Nothing in life truly transforms forever until you do the real work on the inside. Make a pact with yourself to remain vigilant and aware around your thoughts and your surroundings or backsliding is inevitable.

Your conscious mind is the unruly, reasonable, and uncontrollable voice in your head that talks to you over and over as you encounter new people, places, and things. It is a source of confusion for too many people and stops many from achieving their goals and making their ultimate donation to humanity by becoming the best version of themselves. The goal of this part of our mind is to keep things the same at all costs. It is the birthplace of our fears and doubts. It has also saved our lives a few hundred times. We tend to believe and trust it. People who don't have mastery of the mental tools needed to calm it down try to dull the noise in the mind with drugs, alcohol, or other destructive behaviors. We figure if we shut it up temporarily then we are better off. Some people are. There is a healthier way to shut up the mind and then use it to access inner power. The mind is a very powerful tool. I would like to introduce you to the powerful idea that your mind is not you and you don't have to believe everything that it concocts.

YOU ARE NOT YOUR MIND

"You have the power of choice"

You are not that wild, unruly, untamable force that we refer to as our mind. In reality, you are quite the opposite. At the core of who most humans are, we are a lot more tame and peaceful than our minds are. The times that you feel "in the zone", totally relaxed after a deep tissue massage, or lying in a hammock by the pool while on vacation are times you return to your natural state. In that state we are all able to make decisions without second-guessing ourselves or experiencing much anxiety. It seems like everything that we do while in this state turns out absolutely great! The decisions you make are always the right ones. The people who you meet, add value to you and everything seems to come together better than you could have thought. If you play a game or a sport, you just cannot lose, your focus is great and your timing is impeccable. The noise taking place in the head is what causes us the biggest problems.

"What if this happens?" What if that happens?" "I can't do it." The human mind manufactures a minimum of six thousands thoughts every day. If you were your mind, you would be all over the place with no rhyme or reason. You'd be certifiably insane if our minds were all that we are. If you function like all that you are is your mind then maybe you are insane. If you buy into the concept that you are your mind then you will undoubtedly feel lost in a storm and unable to function without stress. I have definitely been here before. We have all felt overwhelmed in life. Do you feel like you are all over the place? How did it happen? Somewhere along the line, you got mixed up and you fell into the trap of feeling that your mind is you. Your mind is something that you have the ability to use in your own favor. It is a tool. Quit it and control it. It is a very powerful tool that your "Self" (higher being) can utilize to create sustained action that can help you to accomplish big things in your life. Through repetition around using your mind to your own advantage, you will find that you can take initially difficult actions with greater ease.

Consider the possibility that "what you want", "what you like", "what you dislike" are not the essence of who you are. They are just evidence of your higher self. The awareness inside that observes all of these things about you is the real you. Let me explain: This chatterbox in your head that until now has made it difficult for you to exercise consistently is not truly you. The small voice that says "I don't want to work out today", "I don't feel like eating this again" or "it is okay to break your promise around your health just this once." is not you. The part of you that sums up strangers who approach you, and decides whether you want to speak to them or not, is your mind. In ancient times, when human beings lived on the face of the earth as small mammals that were being hunted by larger animals, our minds saved our lives multiple times. It said "Run up that tree NOW! A saber tooth tiger is coming!" Last week, it said "Watch out, don't step off that curb or you will be run over!" You listened and now you can read this book. It has helped you avoid pain in the past. The survivalist thoughts manufactured in your mind have even brought you success through avoidance. It helped you to solve great problems in life and avoid calamity. This chattering (fearful) voice in your head is also the voice that leads to all confusion, self-doubt and anxiety. This is often referred to as the "monkey mind" or our limbic mind. It is ancient and necessary for survival. Use it, but don't allow it to take over the prime directives of your soul today.

Your mind is a tool that if allowed to take over will hold you back from realizing your potential. In Buddhism the "Monkey mind" refers to the wild chaotic, limiting, and irrational thought patterns of the untrained mind. Unfortunately, this is not known by many people. They think that they are their minds. They think that this voice is the real version of them. It is not. How many times did you desire to try something new and you noticed your mind tried to deter you from taking that new action? The action can feel right and you know in your heart that it is right but the chattering in your mind makes you feel anxious and doubtful. This brand new thought that beautifully entered your mind may be from your higher "Self", the deeper wise voice within. If the urge is in accordance with your current mindset, you will get a "go ahead" and if it challenges what you regularly do, the mind makes alarms sound. You will be reminded about how risky the new road could be. This takes place even if the new activity or thought process is super beneficial. Actions that get the go ahead are usually actions that will not shake up the boat too much and are well within your comfort zone. Nowadays when this happens I pay extra attention to taking the new action as soon as possible. It is time you recognize that your mind is not you, time to realize that you are the combination of mind, body and soul (Self). You have the power to qualify and disqualify the many thoughts that control the actions you take or don't take.

The mind will use all manners of fear, doubt, and good reasons to convince you of why you can't accomplish what you want. This is referred to by many as negative self-talk. You ultimately have the power to control that. Knowing that your mind is not you gives you the power to operate outside of what it says is possible. You can do things that were historically hard for you to accomplish when you work outside of the perimeters of your mind's chatter. Now that you are aware, you are responsible. You are responsible from this moment not to be run by your mind. When the mind freaks out due to you wanting to do something new. You can override the chatter by saying aloud "Thank you for your input but I will be doing this anyway." Make it a game! When your mind creates excuses and reasons for you not to do the workout, or reasons you should be eating foods that you love but fluff you up, Say "I know this tastes awesome and we love it, but today we will be eating this healthy food_____ instead. We are committed to better health."

Over time, when you feel fear welling up in you around doing something totally aligned with your best interest, you will graciously thank your "monkey mind" for its input and then intentionally do what you need to do. Instant reframing! It's important that you celebrate the times that you decisively take new action where you normally would have been stalled. These are the real wins that matter the most. These are evidence of a transformation in progress. Even if you have not achieved the goal yet, celebrate the shift in thinking. This is the root of all success. Shifting long held mindsets are no easy feat. No one points this out as a win, but I will. Know that once you shift your mindset you open the gate for success to walk through.

Poverty and lack marked my childhood heavily. As a foster kid being passed around the poorest areas of the New York City tristate area I eventually developed a sense of comfort in not having anything. I subconsciously adapted to not having what I wanted. I became accustomed to living in a perpetual state of wanting. I felt like I had no intrinsic value as a human. Going to sleep with my stomach grumbling was my normal in many of the homes that I lived in. Having nice things was a pipe dream for a kid like me who's Christmas celebration was governed by the toys donated through toy drives at local businesses. Today I now get to donate thousands of dollars and facilitate leadership workshops across the country to foster and disadvantaged youth. I also now comfortably live in the beautiful San Francisco Bay area which has the highest cost of living in the country. In order for me to have made this jump I had to overcome a lot of mental baggage. You can too. I had to defy my monkey mind hundreds of thousands of times. I hunted for "better" in every possible way because my reality was so ugly everywhere I turned. Over the course of many years of work I adopted the idea of abundance and that there was more than enough in this world. I still powerfully work on living into this liberating mindset as much as possible. I decided to develop habits that those who had wealth and opportunity enjoyed. I had to embrace new and scary habits that run opposite of the thoughts that my mind was conditioned for. Prevalent thinking conditioned by the ghettos that I was brought up in had to be tossed aside. I had to convince myself that the disadvantaged reality that I had come to embrace didn't have to be my reality forever.

The deepest wisest part of me said "Hey Dre, despite what you are experiencing, you can have something better. You deserve more and you can help more. LEAVE THE HOOD!" I was immediately hit with my monkey mind asking "How are you going to do that?" "How many people from this neighborhood go on to have wealthy and beautiful lives?" "Are you smart enough?" "What makes you so special?" "You don't even have any parents to help you." "You are the wrong color, sex, and wrong demographic to win." "Black men are targets" As a kid younger that ten I decided that I would embrace a different reality. I was totally fed up with settling for living a low class life. My adopted mother Travis Farnell also instilled in me that I must create the vision of life that I wanted. She said if I was willing to work towards it with an attitude of "no matter what" I could have it. I developed a staunch and defiant attitude. I began to detest mediocrity and wasted potential in myself and others. I began to seek out new knowledge about making money and then investing it. In elementary school I used to sell the medals that I won in track meets to kids for a few dollars. I would then take that money and put it with the money that I earned for doing my chores each week. At the end of an entire year my mother would double our money. If we hit fifty dollars saved in a year she would triple it. After a few years of hitting this goal and buying things that I wanted with my own money I began to believe that if I used my talents and found people who wanted what I had to offer I could one day be wealthy. I am still working from that operative mindset and it serves me well. Through saving, working hard and investing, by age twenty three a little black orphan had served in the US Army, graduated college, bought my first condo and owned my own brand new car outright.

By defying my default settings of lack around money and the probability of me living a good life, I was able to create a life that I loved against all odds. A lot of luck and timing was also involved but I believe we create luck. I created so much luck in my life by seeking to know exactly what it took to make my desires a reality and then doing it. Actively learning what it took to live my vision of a plush, fun, and abundant version of my life was also very powerful. Defiance of my naturally murky soup of thinking was the first step. I was born into that soup. I hated it and said "fuck it" in order to move forward.

The belief that I could create a better life was fostered in me by my new found mom. She provided me a little stability in life. That stability allowed for me to breathe and dream. The power of belief and the defiant "by any means necessary" mindset is what made seeking knowledge the next natural step. I had to not only defy my old and well grooved ways of thinking I had to learn many new things. I asked my mother so many questions. I helped her renovate homes that she owned over the years. I leapt at the chance to read documentaries and explore the life journey of people that I admired. I already knew how to delay gratification because poverty is a great teacher of that principal. I just had to work, sacrifice and hunt for knowledge to make my dreams come true. The hardest part of all of it was going against the mindsets that were painfully conditioned into my psyche. I had to also conquer the ideation that the odds were insurmountably stacked against me, and that I was destined to lose and be trashed by reality. This single mental win is responsible for all of the wins that can be tangibly witnessed in my life. Overcoming any obstacle in my way became a thing that I knew on a cellular level would be done. I would be in better circumstances one day or not alive. Seeking knowledge exposed me to so many of the tools necessary for me to transform my mind and ultimately my life.

Many people subconsciously despise knowledge because of the immense responsibility that comes attached to it. When you know better, there is an unconscious covenant within our DNA to do better. That responsibility is a threat to the monkey mind running loose. The monkey mind in us all will manufacture reasons and excuses as to why we shouldn't take new actions. New knowledge makes the monkey mind uncomfortable, it dislodges what is so. Don't believe the lies. They will be extremely convincing and real. Consider yourself informed by me. Choose to do the new and scary actions commensurate with the knowledge that you have been exposed to. You can either feed the wild monkey or the quiet wisdom within you. Feeding both is ill advised. It creates imbalance everywhere in life

Change happens in an instant. Imagine if someone had a gun to your head and told you to do the hard yet beneficial thing that you've been procrastinating on. How many seconds would it take you to do it? It does not have to take years of painstaking slow steady changes to begin to create a momentum around turning dreams into a reality. We are just more comfortable with letting things stay the same, even if they are terrible, than we are with jumping into the unknown. Taking full responsibility for life, being aware, and holding yourself accountable for what happens in your life helps us to put knowledge to use. Fighting our natural predisposition to create stories that stop us from using the knowledge we have acquired is key.

When you have thoughts of cheating yourself by not living out a commitment that you have made to yourself, a slew of red lights and sirens should begin going off in your head. Practice telling your mind "Thank you for your input but I will do this instead". After practicing this technique and living this distinction for a while, you will become an expert at discerning between mind's chattering and your inner wisdom. Directives from your higher self (inner wisdom), insights, creativity and the chatter of the mind begin to sound very different after a while once your awareness is shined on it. The real you has a slow deep and insistent voice that rings with truth and is backed by love. Thoughts manufactured by the monkey mind are usually backed by fears. Notice ASAP how the monkey mind begins to make certain circumstances insurmountable. Practice being able to choose who you will be in that moment and consciously map out actions that you will take. Do something immediately that acknowledges your higher self. You are not your mind, you must become the user of your mind. Become the boss and CEO of your mind. Override what the "monkey mind" tells you if it holds you back from progress and successful living. Repeatedly override it!

ACTION ACTIVITY

- Get a sheet of paper and write "**My New Reality**" at the top.
- Divide the sheet of paper into three sections: Column 1: "**Higher Self**"; Column 2: "**Monkey Mind**"; Column 3: "**Solution**".
- Listen within then write down five new actions you know you should take in column 1. "My Higher Self"
- Write down the first hindrance that pops into your mind next to the action in the "**Monkey Mind**" column.
- **Say out loud** "Thank you for your input but I will achieve my goal by taking _____ new action instead.
- Think about and then write a new powerful and doable *action* that you believe that you can take to make the "**Higher Self**" Goal happen. Once again, be honest with yourself.

EXAMPLE:

Column1 (far left): Lift weights twice a week
Column2 (center): You know you hate the gym after work.
Column3 (right side): buy dumbbells and lift at home one of those two days.

Once you create new actions, the initial objections are banned with the "Monkey Mind" column. Make it happen, take action and then be committed to living your objectives!

CHAPTER 10

FACING YOUR OWN BULLSHIT

> "A challenge ceases to have power over you the
> moment you choose to face it head on."

I wrote an article for Men's Health MVP Network a few years ago about facing demons. The gist was that facing things in life head-on gives you power regarding it. In recent history, we have come to see many scandals play out for our celebrities: Kobe Bryant, David Letterman, Charles Barkley, Bill Cosby, Anthony Wiener, Tiger Woods, Bill Clinton, and many more, have had to deal with legacy altering scandals. Those who confronted their public accusations truthfully were able to move on with their careers pretty much intact. The people who lied or took longer times to fess up have paid dearly. Of the celebrities listed above, those who admitted their humanity and their sexual indiscretions, right away, were able to get over the damage it caused a lot faster. Charles Barkley is America's "Tell it straight" NBA correspondent on our TV's every day during basketball season and almost no one remembers that he had a whopper of a sex scandal. His candor in admitting what he'd done took all of the fire power out of the media. David Letterman has retired an iconic comedian and talk show host and his legacy is virtually untarnished. He publically apologized to his fans and his wife for the affair that he admitted to. Bill Clinton got caught in a lie publicly and was impeached. Even in 2020 we still talk about Monica Lewinski from time to time. Kobe could have been even bigger than Michael Jordan.

In normal life, we should always look for our fault in any bad circumstance or outcome and own up to it as soon as possible. If it affects you and happens to you, then it is very likely that you have played some role in its creation. Even if it is only a miniscule role you should own it. I am sure that as you read this, you can trace through your life and see when facing the fallout from a mistake has helped you to move quickly past it. You can also trace back times when you decided to take no responsibility and how a mistake can haunt you for a longer time than necessary. The sooner you face up to a failure or a bad move that you made, the sooner you can get to making things right again. Doing this gives you the upper hand over your mind as well. Facing your flaws takes the emotional charge out of the situation for other people as well. What can "they" say when you already said it and owned it? When you point out your own humanity you take the wind out of their sails. It's never fun to make fun of people who already make fun of themselves. Something happens internally when you face up to your mistakes. It says to you that you are responsible and in charge. It means that you are not hiding and that you are willing to face up to the consequences of your actions. That is leadership. You begin to see yourself as a leader. You are already a leader if you are considering living an intentional life of your own creation. Only leaders are internally called to do this. Not confronting yourself is giving your power away. Nobody's got time for that!

OWNING LIMITING BELIEFS

When your mind is holding you back from creating the life you desire, confront it. Own your procrastination. Own your acts of self-sabotage. Shine some awareness on it! Doing this quickly makes sure that your next move is your best move. At some point, you have to say to your mind: "Yes, I hear you, but I am going to do things this way!" Defy and declare what it will be, regardless of what it has ever been. This takes vision and strength. You can also order your mind to be quiet and to get out of the way. The reason many people are not able to tell that their mind is not all that they are is because their mind is cluttered and racing with unchecked thoughts. There is so much going on around them that they literally cannot hear themselves think.

Care about less things and put greater time, effort, and energy into them. Make quality the priority. Prioritize forming a social circle that values being well and enjoying peace. Start to pay attention to the things that really matter in life. Ask yourself: "What is really important to me?"; "Why are these things important to me?" "What are my unique talents?"; "What am I being called to share with the world?" If you still find yourself procrastinating or self-sabotaging, remember that a mindset created some time in the past is to blame. Find it, expose it, extract it, and then implant your purpose. You must be able to hear your self-talk and limiting mindsets. This may call for you to stop and be still. You won't be able to hear the directives given from your soul unless you meditate. Meditation puts you in touch with your higher self and de-clutters the mind. You get tuned into your own stream of consciousness. A clear mind is a super powerful tool that puts you in touch with accomplishing things that you may have once thought impossible

QUIETING YOUR MIND

"A clear mind is the clean canvas that we create the art of life on."

We all have things that we love to do. When we do these things, time passes quickly but in slow motion at the same time. These are the things that we could do forever. Most of us have abandoned consistently doing these things. We have also lost the peace that comes along with the doing of these activities. Take time to think of three things that you thoroughly enjoy. It could be running, coloring, writing, exercising, or drawing for some people. For other people it is being in the presence of good friends or a pet. Think of how peaceful your state of being is when you are doing your thing. It is an amazing time of clarity when you are focused on doing only one thing that you love doing. This peace and clarity can be the state of your entire life, every day. Imagine that! Peace and clarity without turning to alcohol, weed, or other substances. There are other ways to calm the mind. I urge you to make time for doing these activities on a regular basis at any cost. I have made a good living and built a career working with some of the busiest type "A" personalities on the planet. They could not fathom sitting still with their legs crossed, in one place, trying to clear their minds in the traditional sense of the word "meditation. A moving meditation such as jogging or hitting a speed bag has been the answer for so many of them, myself included. Over time it graduated to me being able to sit still and meditate. Peace is the natural state of a human being. We create the best things on the planet from that place. Workouts have been my therapy and my access to a greater life. They bring me to a place of stillness.

If you cannot pursue old activities that used to take you into a zone of peace, then make it a priority to discover a new hobby. Try new activities with an eye to add them to your moving meditation portfolio. My personal favorite activity is lifting weights. I love the challenge, the burn, the sweat and the focus that it takes to make it through a grueling workout. I also love reading and writing. I love getting lost in the world of words. My mind enjoys peace while doing these activities. In very recent years I have discovered hiking and being out in nature. I was introduced to meditation twelve years ago and it changed my life tremendously. It is now another one of my favorite past times. There are times when life renders sheer will, discipline, and desire useless for achieving peace. They will not keep the mind from becoming cluttered and chaotic. You will feel lost. This is usually the time to reach for a still meditation. Different times call for different tools. For me, overwhelm tries to creep in when I have not been diligent in setting aside twenty minutes daily.

When I get out of a good session, there is nothing else in the world that can create such clarity, peace and drive for me. Other people spend time praying, running, sewing, getting massages, drawing etc. They are all the same. Meditation puts you in contact with your purpose and your natural state of being. It can be done anywhere and for as short as five minutes. It also makes it a lot easier to hear the instructions and directions from your higher self. Remember that meditation is not necessarily about erasing all thoughts. It is about stopping in order to slow thoughts down to be witnessed.

Answering our calling in life goes hand in hand with the state of health of the physical vehicle that we control. A better body of sound mind and clear soul will lead to your best existence and have the greatest impact on the world. Being guided by purpose will wring the very best out of your existence. Meditation clears your mind and gives you a clean slate to work with. You will find that routinely you are able to tap into elusive answers to questions that have lingered for a long time. You may find new energy to take on new and exciting projects. You can only create a permanent and effective approach to being in the best shape of your life from a clean slate. The clean slate and centered feeling is what meditation provides for me. I have seen it soothe and clear out some of the most cluttered minds. There have been shifts in less than five minutes.

A very quick and easy meditation strategy I still use to this day is to sit down in a quiet room with my eyes closed. It can be anywhere, a car, a room in your house, anywhere you can find time to be alone. I close my eyes and pay close attention to the three parts of my breathing: I first observe the inhale, then I notice the exhale. Then I acknowledge the natural pause before the start of the next breath. I slow my breathing down until all three parts are discernible.

MAKE IT A GAME

ACTION: Clear your mind for a few seconds. Close your eyes and begin:

- Inhale, exhale and count the number "1" on the pause
- inhale, exhale and count "2" on the pause
- Count 3 for the natural pause between breaths.
- Repeat until you get up to ten breaths totally uninterrupted by any other thoughts.
- If a thought does come to you while you breathe you must go back to the number "1"

If you have a foreign thought before you reach ten, you must go back to one. Imagine each thought free breath carrying away thoughts out of your mind, leaving it clearer each time. Each time you make it up to ten without any foreign thoughts coming to mind it counts as one set. When you complete three sets without any thoughts coming into mind, you have really accomplished something awesome. When I started I couldn't get to 3 breaths without thought. Be patient with yourself. There is no right or wrong and if your competitive nature and the numbers throw you off then take them out of the process. I now get three to five whole sets of ten on a regular basis.

It definitely takes practice to make it to the first ten. Noticing the failure is a thought and automatically brings you back to zero again as well. It takes daily practice to be able to make it work for long periods of time. Start with just five minutes and then progress up to half an hour. Your life will totally change for the better. Your mind will feel a lot less cluttered. You will find that you are way less stressed and think with even more clarity. This should be looked at as "Your time" to get reacquainted with yourself. Your goal is to slow down the traffic of your mind so that you can pay attentions to the important communications that you receive from within. Many good things come from this exercise. Peace and clarity is a priceless outcome that comes with the mastery of this practice. Soon numbers will not be necessary. Look into transcendental meditation as well. Keep a pen next to you for when you are done. Record any excellent ideas that you may have encountered. Every great human creation comes from peace of mind. Each one of us is an artist aiming to create a masterpiece of a life. A clear mind is our clan canvas.

MAKING YOU A PRIORITY

"Our Top Three Priorities Always Get done."

The real reason that people are not in shape is not lack of time or information. The real reason people are broke is not because there is a lack of money circulating in the world. The real reason that we may not enjoy many really good friendships or fulfilling relationships is not because people don't like us. We all have twenty-four hours in one day and not everyone is out of shape, broke, or lacking great family connection and companionship. Chances are that each one of us has one or two of these areas of life just the way we want it. Getting to the root of why the other areas are in disarray is important.

Let's look at exercise and nutrition as an example. Why don't people like eating healthy food? It's boring and hard? That answer is a start, but the question and the answer aren't deep enough yet. "Why is food a source of entertainment that people indulge in so much?" "Is there a different way to see food, so that it is not the first form of entertainment that I gravitate towards?" "What fun things can you do instead of eating unhealthy foods?" Can you adopt a view of food as medicine instead of entertainment? Can eating food become something mindful that adds life and quality to the years that you live? Life is only as good as the quality of the question that we ask ourselves.

External motivation is all around us. People die prematurely, of heart-related diseases and cancer at alarming rates due to the foods that they consume. Obesity is at an all-time high. I highly doubt that if you have this book in your hand, you are the type of person who is unaware of the epidemic happening worldwide. If this is not inspirational, I don't know what is. Learning from other people's failures is a must and it is often pain free. Do you lack discipline? No, that can't be the answer either. You wake up every single day, without wavering, and do work that makes you money. Many of us also brush our teeth every day to ensure that they don't turn brown and eventually rot and drop out of our heads. That stuff takes a lot of discipline. The truth is that the majority of people haven't made wellness and fitness a priority?

SEVEN WHY'S DEEP

If you do exercise from time to time, why can't you make it stick as a habit? Why can't we stop eating the things we know ultimately harm us and keep us away from our desired goals? We know that a healthy diet and exercise helps our bodies, minds, and souls to be well. Let's begin to hold ourselves accountable for our own health. It is not entirely your fault though. Society has a level of importance placed on fitness and nutrition. Is your personal level of value on fitness and nutrition in alignment with the rest of America? Are you being defiant enough? Do your actions fly in the face of what the country thinks? Your health and wellbeing comes down to your personal context of what fitness and nutrition means. How important is accessing your healthiest self to you? The truest answer to this is also seven "whys" deep into the question "Why don't I eat healthily and exercise on a regular basis?" Ask "why" again once you have the answer to that question. Continue doing this five more times until you get to the root of why it is such a struggle. Once you are conscious of it you can elect to change it. Be truthful and vulnerable with your answers.

What has been drummed into our subconscious minds and disseminated to us around "fitness" in society? Why is regular exercise a thing that a select few people do, when we all need it? Why is fitness marketed as the 3 minute six pack and the next super food supplement to take? Why are we so focused on creating more workout programs and building gyms that people do not use frequent enough? Why do fast food and prescription drug commercials run more frequently than healthy food commercials? Where are the healthy government campaigns promoting exercise, fruit, vegetables, or better nutrition on air? They used to run in the 70's and 80's? What happened? Healthy humans are not profitable in the sense of money but a society full of healthy vibrant people is better for all of us and the planet. The overall tint of the word "fitness" today doesn't have a context that makes it show up as a fun powerful priority at all. (Hence the name of the book) It takes independent and driven effort to focus on better. Change the context of any area of struggle and you can change the habitual actions that you take in that area of living. Awareness is the first step. Intentionally changing the prevalent mindset that you function from is next.

You are your first and best doctor. You are your only patient. Practice preventive medicine. You spend twenty four hours a day and seven days a week with the patient. Most importantly you should be in love with the patient. You have invested into the patient in the past. You will invest into you in the future as well. The patient's best interest should be one of your greatest concerns. You depend on the patient. When the patient no longer exists you cease to exist as well. Exercise and a healthy natural diet are your first line of preventative medicines. Your first line of defense against illness is your food and how you treat your body. Own the health of your own body.

If you find something especially hard to achieve there is always an internal blockage. Use all seven "whys" to get to the root of what is holding you back. You can apply this line of self-questioning for any new outcome that you struggle to be consistent around taking action on. You will likely have a breakthrough or an epiphany. Most importantly, be willing to let go of what you have previously learned if they prove obsolete. Old beliefs, lessons and solutions are comfortable to cling onto but they often lose their usefulness, and over time, they can become roadblocks to progress. Select a new tact around what it mentally takes for you to adopt the habits that mean transformation in life. You can't apply old formulas to achieving new levels. You may have to move your ego out of the way to do it. Be open. Admit your humanity. Be willing to admit where you fall short. You are not alone in hustling backwards. Inversely, give yourself props for moving beyond old limiting mindsets and taking a new action towards a goal. Even if you deem your new actions small celebrate them as huge wins. They truly are!

THE EGO BELOW

Our egos is an amazing force. Sometimes it pushes us to take action when nothing else will. The ego also blinds us and often limit us to only seeing what we want to see about our lives. It lies to us and paints a personal picture of who we are that is not totally accurate. This phenomenon is common in all humanity. The funny thing is that it is much easier to see another person's ego at work than it is to see our own at play. You can see egos in "Gone Wild" on Instagram, Twitter, reality television and all manners of living. The persona we share with the world is often far removed from who we truly are on the inside. If you are not careful you can die to provide for the survival of the persona that our ego constructs. Company advertisers and marketers know this and make billions by pandering to our egos and the cracks in our self-images.

The lavish luxury brands appeal to our egos and sense of vanity, using words such as opulence, VIP, excitement, elegance, lifestyle, premier, elite, and the list goes on. We, consumers, have personas that we subconsciously reinforce at all costs. We buy brands and products that align with the idea of who we have created ourselves to be. Before long, one item is obsolete and a new shinier and upgraded thing comes out. We have to get that one too. After some time, you've gathered a bunch of things that are the ego's symbols of who you are. I use this analogy just to paint a picture. There is nothing wrong with having the newest and nicest things as long as your happiness isn't dependent on it. Egoism gets in the way of discovering what changes you must make on the inside. Buying contraptions and making new attempts at moving forward in life without admitting to yourself what is going on within you will not work. When the ego is checked and we no longer work for it, the simple but not easy solutions for removing stagnation are easier to see. Caring about yourself and serving those that you love is fuel enough for making your own health and fitness a top three priority for a lifetime.

Many times, in the race to collect things and experiences that align with our egos, we lose our health and wellbeing. Gathering things on top of a fundamentally damaged premise for living is futile. Make sure the ego is not the lone thing moving you onward and upward. All actions will feel empty if that is the case. There are real issues that must be dealt with properly. Whether you are aware of them or not they cost you to carry. They should be brought up for judgement by your mind's eye if this is the case. It is like a wound with a scab that is infected with pus festering just under the surface. We can survive like this, but only for a while. The truth of the matter will always come to the surface and manifest as a complete and total meltdown. Fever and disease will always return. Living powerless and totally unfulfilled is terrible. Here is a case where a person's self-image and unresolved issues hurt more than just their six pack.

ELGIN

A former client of mine took time to explain to me why it was time for him to secure my services. My clients come from all walks of life but this client stood out. He was a very affluent middle-aged man. He traveled the world and partied with the most exciting people. He had pictures all over his house with many celebrities and politicians. He had a home gym the size of my entire apartment. He owned cars that cost more than most people's homes. He was a very successful venture capitalist who invested in many startup tech companies all over the world, before it was a popular thing to do. He told me that deep inside he was unfulfilled.

All of the things he had and all the people that surrounded him did not fulfill the gap that he found in himself. He was in his mid to late forties and had a thirteen-year-old daughter he had not seen for ten years. He explained that when the relationship with his daughter's mother went south that she moved out of the country. In response he decided to throw himself into his business and career a hundred and ten percent. He was depressed and aimed to subconsciously fix himself and regain his idea of self-worth by becoming successful and acquiring things and experiences. He relied on his ego to get out of bed every day. To the world he looked like a huge success. He told me that he experienced only a glazed over and short term feeling of happiness. He blamed his ex-wife entirely for the split.

One day with a planned workout session underway we shifted gears into an impromptu life coaching session after he stated the following: "I miss my daughter so much. She was taken from me and I did everything right." I asked him if I could share a perspective with him. I told him that is was precisely that mindset that had possibly cost him a relationship his ex-wife and definitely cost him a relationship with his daughter. He always thought that he was "right". His language over months of exercise tipped me off to him believing that he was always "right" in every situation. I hipped him to this observation and told him to try on the possibility that if he is always right then he possibly made everyone else wrong in their dealings with him. Elgin looked at me puzzled.

Elgin gained a lot of weight and hadn't felt his best in years. In the back of his mind he wanted to rebuild the relationship with his daughter. As he stacked on the pounds as he built up a mental wall to keep people on the outskirts of his life. He didn't want anyone to know how unhappy he truly was. He subconsciously punished himself for losing contact with his daughter. By the time he caught himself in the spiral of defeat he was ashamed of how he looked and didn't want to meet his daughter again being overweight and unfit. All of this happened with a complete gym in-house. Eating on the road during business ventures, high alcohol consumption for business and self-medication, all added up to many sleepless nights. It all caught up to him and he was disgusted with himself. I helped him to remember that taking care of himself would add value to the relationship he wanted most to one day start with his daughter. I helped him to see that his inconsistency around fitness was due to how hurt he was about the death of the best relationship in his life. I asked him to try on the idea of every rep being a step towards mending his relationship with his ex. Together we actually were able to find that he actually did play a part in the demise of his marriage. I urged him to reach out to his ex and tell her what he discovered and how he really felt. He gathered up the courage and put down the anger and resentment long enough to hire a private investigator to find his ex-wife. He found her! He contacted her with no ego, no blame, and he ultimately requested visitation with his daughter. His ex-wife was shocked! She hadn't known him as capable of admitting fault and taking responsibility. She only knew arrogant ego filled Elgin. After a decade apart she expressed to him that it had become important to her that their daughter knew him. His ex-wife shared with him, that it hurt her to have to tell her daughter that she had lost track of her father. She was open to her daughter getting to know him.

It was at this moment that he had finally realized that after all these years, he was lying to himself and settling for unhealthy living as a result of his need to prove his worth to himself. He valued the outward trappings of success over his health. His ego created a negative self-image. He had a self-image that labeled him as the least important thing in his own life. He saw himself as a failure as a father and worked really hard in business to prove to himself that he wasn't. He was also bitter and angry after being left by the woman that he loved. He saw himself as a faultless father being victimized and he totally lost himself.

His daughter needing him woke him up from that egocentric stupor. He told me he would trade all of his money to have a meaningful and healthy relationship with his lost daughter. It may have taken a decade but it is a short time compared time wasted by others before they wake up to what is really important to them in life. He was finally ready to allow his ego to put the malice he felt in his heart to death. It takes time for people to de-clutter the mind and to stop believing the stories that we have built up around what happens in life. Better yet, it takes time for many to allow themselves to do the work it takes to truly enjoy what is important to them. Life always has a way of sporadically reminding you of what is truly important, no matter how hard you try to ignore it. He used the love of his daughter to pull himself out of a lavish ego driven cycle of accumulation and excess. He eventually got over himself and began forging a real relationship with his teenage daughter and ex-wife. Also last I checked on him six years after we worked together on mental and physical strength he has an awesome relationship with is daughter and he looks awesome. He works out three to five days a week as a way of being. More pain than can be quantified is caused when we give into the whims of the ego.

On the other hand, some of us have created lives depriving ourselves of anything that could bolster their egos and autonomous personas. They are martyrs. They don't feel right if everything in their lives is working out for better. They deprive themselves of all luxury and relief. Many people are resigned to never acknowledge the greatness within themselves. They relinquished the right that they have to create and enjoy lives full of blessings. They hate attention being placed on them in any form or fashion. They have become content with being less than. They are the backbone for everyone else. People do this with their bodies as well. They turn away and sabotage every opportunity that comes their way for better health. They are in some ways comforted by being uncomfortable and left undone. They feel the void and know that something is missing but they rather stay broken than to indulge in self-care. It is as if they have resigned to the idea that they must sacrifice happiness and their wellbeing because of something that took place in their past. They are those who live with less so that others can have more. It is important that we each thrive individually and as part of a whole.

The sacrificial lambs serve their persona and ego the same as the overachievers do. They just do it in a different way. Everyone is more important to them than they are to themselves. Somehow, by sacrificing their comfort, progress, and authentic self-expression, and giving all of their self to others, they feel it is noble. That noble feeling is ego driven. These people make do with less and justify doing so for a plethora of reasons. I was this kind of shepherd and leader for a long time. There are many underlying reasons leading to people self-sabotaging every time they are on the brink of a breakthrough for themselves. These issues should be exposed and replaced with new found purpose for living. I had to do this work as well. I had to give me permission to be me and understand that by taking care of myself I was not harming anyone else.

I love being a catalyst for people awakening and then jumping into doing things that allow the light in them to shine. I had to do this same work for myself. I had many shackles to break free of having been an orphan. Self-expression is so necessary and so powerful for us all.

It is time to get your ego out of the way and allow for some soul searching to take place. We have to slay the stories that we make up about life that hold us back. Ask you some hard questions. Do you feel guilty from something that happened in the past? Is procrastination your answer to any difficult problem? Is being a victim of circumstances and living a life by default now a comfortable thing to you? Do you make yourself busy with trivial tasks to avoid taking major steps towards progress? Do you not feel worth the time needed to invest in your own wellbeing? Are you simply too busy taking care of others and leave you undone? Do you always break the promises you make to yourself and therefore you no longer believe in you? Are you low-key depressed and are not thrilled about anything anymore? Do you live a life smaller than the big spirit inside of you should? Are you subconsciously afraid to become fit because you are simply used to being out of shape? Have you recently been attracted to the easy way out? Have you simply never completed a truly difficult thing in your life, and fitness is no different? Whatever mindset blockage you have uncovered make up your mind to release it. Let the story go. Take off the sunshades. Get as deep as you possibly can to find the answers and admit them to yourself. Below is an activity that can help you erase blockages caused by stories we've created around relationships with others. Sometimes a story that you've lived into steals your power and costs you a great relationship.

ACHIEVING CLOSURE & PEACE

ACTION: Write a letter to one person who you no longer have a good relationship with. One that you may still be mourning. Write it looking to admit any role you played in the demise of the relationship. Admit any failure around integrity on your part. Feel what negativity you must, let it go, and then write the letter. Make sure that it only admits your faults in the relationship. No blame should be tossed their way. Share how you currently feel about the relationship's death. It should address how you see any mistake or action that you made. Write out what you would do differently. **You can choose to send it to the person or to destroy it at the end.** Writing is what makes it real.

This is not to make amends with the other person per-say, but to give yourself peace and help you take responsibility for your part and how you currently feel. You can then move past the story. Include everything that you want to say to the person, let it all out. After sending it or tearing it up into little pieces, or burning it, do not allow yourself to burden yourself with the weight of that relationship any longer. Leave it in the garbage. If it is a current situation and you choose to send it, trust me things will turn out how they turn out. You can do whatever you want with the letter but it is liberating simply to get it all out on paper. Become free by admitting your mistakes! Doing this allows you to create a clean slate in your mind, a level of peace and closure. It frees you from the story of the relationship. You can also do this with people who have passed away too so that you do not have to actively carry past hurts into your future. You can have, do and be anything when you are start from a clean slate.

WHAT YOU DON'T KNOW... YOU DON'T KNOW.

Knowing is just not enough for some people to make lasting changes. Just like the law of attraction doesn't work without taking action. Taking new and repeated actions takes spiritual buy-in and ownership of your blockages around not being as successful as you'd like in the past. How many times have you known in your head that you probably should do a thing, and for absolutely no logical reason at all you do not do it? A lot of times you are held back from taking action by things that you *don't know you don't know* about yourself. Hindrances that you are not aware are buried in your subconscious. Thoughts taking place in your subconscious actually run the show. Hopefully, you have become aware of some of those thoughts as you have read this book. Every time something you don't know you don't know is brought into the conscious realm, you have a sort of Aha moment! This new information about yourself can lead to solid changes towards a new outcome. Once you know what holds you back within you, then you can choose to change it. It is really important to look within and allow yourself to have Aha! Moments. With each of the stories I share in this book, make sure you look inside to see how they can apply and benefit you.

VICKIE

Vickie was 5 foot 4 and 220 pounds, the heaviest she had ever been in her life. She was a 48-year-old mother of three. Her kids were young adults in college so it was only her and her husband in the house most of the time. This was the time they should have both been enjoying a rebirth together! It was time to live it up and spend time together. They worked really hard to set things up for themselves financially. She told me they often did not spend a lot of intimate time together and she believed her weight was a factor that caused the distance between them. By the time she reached out to me, she no longer had the self-esteem, power and satisfaction in her life that she once had. She spent her days taking care of the house and working in her business. Vicki was an incredibly nice woman and had a great spirit. She was the kind of woman who always had a smile for the people she met. She donated her time to charity, spent a lot of time helping others and she was an amazing cook.

As I trained with her, it became obvious that Vickie did not feel beautiful, attractive, or sought after by her husband any longer. She was very self-conscious about her legs and stomach. She tried the Atkins diet and lost sixty pounds but she was not able to maintain that weight loss when she started eating carbs again. She gained back sixty eight pounds of the sixty that she lost. Do the math. They had an entire gym in their basement gathering dust and holding up clothing from the laundry. Vickie and her husband financially lived a very comfortable life. Vickie did not look or feel the way she wanted and she knew a lot of it had to do with her inability to exercise and eat right consistently. She wasn't pouring into herself. She was not living the life she wanted to live, something was missing. After working out with Vicky for approximately three weeks, I chose to test her.

At this point I pretty much knew her physical limitations and her mindset towards exercise: "I don't have time, I have to take care of everyone else." I really wanted to know who she was in her own mind. I wanted a glimpse of her self-mage. People lie to themselves all of the time. They never consider or even decide to specifically take a look at what is behind the curtain. I set out to triple the volume of her daily workout routine. I pushed her to hell and drew her back from the edge before she threw up. Everywhere we normally did ten reps, we did fifteen to twenty. Everywhere she usually did fifteen, we moved up to twenty or twenty five. I cut her rests and sped up her rep speed. There was extra sweat, complaining, and colorful wordplay everywhere! This normally nice woman had turned into a sweaty, panting evil woman. I never knew what I expected to see revealed in her as I asked her to do things that she believed that she could not do, but I never expected to see that kind of fire. That was the beast within her that she kept locked away behind bars in the prison of her mind. She spent her whole life wanting to be liked. Being pleasant and liked by the world was important to her. It took so much background bandwidth to hide that hard and powerful side from herself and the world. *Who you truly are comes out in the face of great adversity.* You never really know people until you have seen them stripped of the façade they share with the world. Training hard and to the point of exhaustion brings that out. I get to see what people are fundamentally made of from every walk of life as a physical trainer. I get to see the fabric that people really are made of. *Who you become in the face of total failure, adversity, and pain gives true indication of your hidden mindset.* Vicki revealed a hidden strength, energy, and a fight that was nowhere evident in the rest of her life. I concluded from that display that she suppressed all of this vibrant energy every single day for many, many years. The energy it takes to be that inauthentic for so long is a monumental waste. Think of a phone that is constantly running background programs and being drained by behind-the-scene apps. She had put everyone else's feelings ahead of her own. She curbed who she was inside to make others comfortable. With that type of mindset, you will never invest the time and energy to take care of you. Let's face it: some of the nicest people we know, some of the most giving people we come in contact with, are out of shape. They take care of the world and leave themselves out of the equation.

There is no possible way you can give the best of yourself to your family, your friends and the people who depend on you, if you are not the best you. That is exactly why they tell you to put on your oxygen mask first and then help the person next to you in an airplane. You can give great quality assistance after you have secured and taken care of yourself. She had it backwards. Every effort her soul made to get her into great shape was self-sabotaged. Your soul always guides you from deep down inside. Many people ignore the guidance or intentionally override it because it is more comfortable not to answer the call. Vickie had become too comfortable taking care of everything else and never accessing her true self. This is just easier to do since we are conditioned not to look for adversity as a tool to elevate thinking and capability. Once you become quiet and enjoy peace through meditation, introspection, or somebody else pointing out something you didn't know about yourself, you can then face your shortcomings and then change them. You can never change the dynamic and take new continuous actions if you have no idea that there is an underlying blockage taking place. Every single person who has trouble eating right and exercising, even though they are well aware of the magnificent benefits, has an unconscious blockage of some sort. This goes for anything that you struggle with in life. Your current programming is not in alignment with what you want to manifest. This discomfort or clash is referred to by psychologists as cognitive dissonance. Without using the mental tools outlined in this book the real you can stay locked up forever. The outcomes aligned with that version of you will be elusive.

At the end of the painful session that she barely survived I asked

Vickie if I could share what I saw within her from my perch as her coach. She said yes. I told her that I saw a lion locked away in a cage. I told her that keeping the real Vickie locked away was the real reason that she was tired all of the time. She locked away the spicy, fiery, and vivacious side of herself to make life comfortable for others instead of being fully self-expressed. I informed her of the crazy amount of energy that had to have been drained from her doing so. Being tired all of the time makes it hard to train or make good eating decisions. I could see things from my vantage point as a coach that she could not.

I began to show her how everything was connected. I even pointed out that her relationship with her husband could be affected by her locking away who she really was on the inside. I showed her how shutting down who she was and always putting other people's needs, perceptions, and well-being ahead of her could be costly. I urged her to be free! Mentally, spiritually, and emotionally step into a different place. I asked her if she thought that any of what I saw was true. She was silent for a long while. Then she said quietly whispered "Yes". She reminisced of her young free and fit self. She did prioritize herself at some point in her life. She was strong, assertive and spirited. She said "Somewhere along the way I lost me." How many times have you lost you? I sure have lost the essence of who I am a few times in life. I can identify with shutting down parts of myself to make other people feel comfortable. Then, I mentioned to her to evaluate what it may have cost her to become comfortable with not being her own priority. I could see the wheels churning in her mind as she gathered her things to leave. Sometimes it takes the insights of someone else to wake you up.

Once we made the subliminal struggle visible to her conscious mind Vicki was able to take charge. She agreed the idea that being authentic with herself was a worthy pursuit. Living a life of quiet pain-filled sacrifice for years would no longer be her reality. She was sick and tired of it. We also concluded that her reaching out to coach with me was a cry from her soul to make herself a priority in her life once again! There are absolutely no coincidences in life. Everything happens for a reason. That was a breakthrough she would carry with her for the rest of her life! She finally had the power over making herself a priority in her own life forever. There was a new awareness awakened. Everything showed up differently for her in her life. All of her workouts became actions geared towards her snatching back who she really was. She was on fire to reclaim flavor in her life. She gave herself permission to be spontaneous and joyous around life. She reconnected with an adventurous side of herself that went dormant over two decades ago before she was a parent. Children meant sacrifice in her mind and over time she shut down any possibility of her own self-care and expression. She hadn't even recognized that this happened. She vowed to change her focus drastically and worked daily towards living a life that thrilled her. Over time she lost all of the extra weight she put on. Vickie even dressed differently. It was like someone took the emergency brake off of her entire life. I know that her husband, was happy to have her back. That was who he fell in love with! She even took the leap into owning her own hair salon which was a dream that she always had but never imagined would make it into a reality.

What unconsidered baggage could be holding you back from taking the necessary steps? Really think on it. What can you live towards that thrills you and makes you smile inside? Always ask you "What is holding you back from discovering what will work for you and then doing what it takes?" A repetitive cycle of discovering a new answer, making a plan, using it short term, and falling back off the wagon will continue until you do the real work of discovering what you don't know about you that is in the way. Never justify living on a lower vibration than who you really are. Some people have chalked up their inability to attain their goals to genes or circumstance. Too many people chalk up holding extra fat to just having bad genes. I'm here to say that everybody on this planet must have bad genes. We are the descendants of human beings who are able to store fat. They had to live through famine and endure the hardships of not having apps to ensure that hot food is delivered to your door while they watch Netflix.

I will get into the process for cementing or forming a particular mindset a little later on. Many people have simply become settled and complacent. You are not on this earth just to pay bills, and live a life full of regret and foggy visions of a time long ago where you were winning. You are fluid and here for a greater purpose. You are here to do, be, and share something unique. What will you add to the world? As I stated before, human beings are amazing creatures! No one knows exactly why we are conscious, but we are. Whether you believe in God or not, you do have a unique function to perform. Follow your instincts, maintain your inner peace and integrity and heed the prodding wisdom from your soul. Cut out anything that adds to the clutter in your mind. Make sure to fine tune the static in your mind. It is easy to gain clarity and then lose it in an instant. Make decluttering a practice. You will bump into more hindrances that you didn't know that you didn't know existed. Peace will paint a way.

CHAPTER 11

ABANDON WORRY

Do not waste time worrying. When you worry about anything, you consensually have granted power of a psychological, physical, and life-changing variety to a negative happening that has not even taken place in reality. It's a poor use of our intangible powers. It also attracts that which you are worried about into your life. My advice is to stop living in an unreal world. It serves no purpose at all. Spiritually, it causes stress; stress causes the secretion of cortisol and a cocktail of hormones that stimulate appetite and stores belly fat. I have never seen unwarranted stress cause anything good to happen. Recently, I have discovered that you can make insane progress in your life without enduring the pain of worry and extreme adversity. Never speak aloud the worries that you may encounter inside. Don't give them life.

Graduate surviving as soon as possible and start living. When people spend all their energy, time and effort on survival, their life flame is stifled. It is impossible to share to take good aim on a dream while sitting in a dingy on choppy seas. Have faith that you will not be homeless, destitute or ill. Someone in this world loves you enough to help you prevent that from happening if all things that you attempt create fail. Someone who was born with far less things than you and with less intellectual capital, is living the life of their dreams. The life that you dream about will also be yours. Dreams are hard to focus on when survival is not secure. Get to the level where survival is guaranteed. We live in the age of cell phones, computers, and booty enhancing panties. In this day and age, the worst case scenario like losing your job or getting a divorce will not end your life. Opportunity is abundant. Declare what you want your life to become and take unrelenting steps to that end. Putting forth your best effort should give you peace. Create the life that you want to live intentionally. Live towards it every moment of each day. There is no "Someday" on the calendar. Today, in this moment, begin living your real life.

Fear sucks, do what you have to do anyway. Too many people let fear hold them back from sharing and displaying their greatness. Fear is pumped into society. The news constantly reminds us of the latest crazy study proving that strawberries may cause cancer. It conveniently reminds us that the world is coming to an end. It always shows you the worst of humanity. There is every type of insurance on every single thing sold, just in case an accident happens. The worst case scenario is put on front Street for everybody to see and to be aware of. This is how the masses perceptions are hijacked. The people that we encounter daily and on social media also regurgitate all that negative scariness that they hear. Don't allow them to contaminate your thoughts. We are programmed to expect the worst and of course it happens. Many very successful people purposely do not spend time watching the news or reality TV. They don't dwell on things occurring that are not empowering or somehow adding to their beings. Things you put into your mind subconsciously affect the things that you do. Guard your mind and watch out for negative things seeping into it. Have you ever listened to a song you didn't like, and couldn't stop singing it for the entire day? This is a sample of something seeping into your subconscious mind and running a muck. This is how corporations and agencies program our minds. McDonald's never has to tell you where they are or what they serve again in life, but they do and they will continue to tell you. They know that repetition will implant their products into your subconscious and that if you see enough advertisements that you will unconsciously reach for their food stuffs the next time that you are busy and hungry. They use visual and auditory ques to program cravings. What thoughts cyclically run around in your mind? Who put them there? What are you programming yourself with? Curate your mental input and stifle fear.

Spend time around people that support you and add to you. Run away from people who drain you or poison you with who they are. Preserve your sanity and yourself at all costs. You are the director of the movie that is your life and you get to choose all supporting cast members. Whether it be physical or emotional support look for what you need from people who have shown up to support you time and time again. Stop looking for those who have abandoned you to give you what you need. They simply don't have it. People dry up like wells. We expect people to remain assets in our lives just because they once were. Everything changes and people do too. This is a major cause of pain. It is up to you to recruit and hold onto individuals who love you, support you, and want to see you win. If a goal of yours is to be fit and you do not know any fit people the road ahead of you will be long and harsh. If you want to be wealthy and know only poverty you will suffer. It always takes more work, bandwidth, & willpower on your part to maintain the drive to take actions that no one else in your environment is doing. Environment trumps will because it is ruthlessly consistent. Willpower ebbs and flows. The people in our lives become part of our environments. Environment will inevitably trump even the most resilient human's willpower. Losing people and leaving old neighborhoods can be outstanding ways to grow forward. Do the people in your life fuel you? The consistent input from our surroundings often becomes louder than the wise prodding from within. Don't allow this to happen in your life. Remain aware that you are the awareness that runs the show. Surrounding yourself with other people who value and have what you want to create will bolsters your efforts.

Add value to other people's lives. Giving is one of the quickest ways to raise your spirits and feel great about living. When you help someone else, you actually help yourself. Always strive to make an impact in someone else's life. Subconsciously it says to you and the world that you are valuable. You must know that you are valuable in this world. If you don't have much to give, a smile or kind words can mean the world for someone else. Small giving on your part can be huge for someone who needs it. When you look at depressed parts of the country and the inner cities. You witness people who have lost a sense of value as a whole. Many of these poor and disenfranchised people have given up on being of value in the world. Systemically, they are told that they don't matter. Scarcity kills giving in so many minds. Anger and depression has grown into a second skin to many people in ghettos. No value is added to the country at-large and ultimately, these people are forgotten in their own land. Even if living in the ghetto find a way to give and be of value to other humans.

Take the time to understand other people are responsible for their lives and you are only responsible for yours. You can never live another person's life for them. Even your children will grow up one day to be one hundred percent responsible for the choices they make. Do not spend your time making decisions for other people's lives. Don't spend your time hurting over decisions that those around you have made for their life. This may sound callous but I assure you that doing this is a total waste of time. All that you can do is make suggestions and hope to influence them in selecting the best options for themselves. Too many good people mentally and spiritually kill themselves time and time again because someone who they were rooting for failed. There is someone in this world right now losing sleep over the choices that another person has wholeheartedly chosen for themselves. This is a quick way to lose your peace and lose touch with who you are in your own life. Be *"committed"* to helping others, but not *"attached"* to outcomes that they create. Understand that life is a delicate balance of autonomy and community. Peace is a non-negotiable for the creation of your best life. Allow people to live their own lives. Give them grace. It will give you great peace. No one does anything in their life before they are ready to.

THE POWER OF "I AM"

Take your time to pay attention to the language that you use. The words "I am" refers to the choice of who the spirit within the body has chosen to be, in any given moment. The words following "I am" in any sentence you utter is extremely powerful. The phrase "I am" has tremendous power because it gives a direct view into a person's internal environment. It gives a telescopic view into how a person views themselves and their capabilities. By speaking to a person for ninety seconds. I am able to see what thinking is holding them back and how it is that I can help them. What gives me the insight is the words following the phrase "I am" in every sentence that they utter. "I am lazy"... "I am so busy"... "I am stuck"... "I am not able to keep up the effort"..." I am tired and unmotivated to exercise..." "I am such an idiot." "I am" gives me a window into their "truth" or what they subconsciously believe to be "the truth". A person's "truth" and the results that they create are never ever misaligned. They will always match. When you become aware of your own "truths" you will know your own results... even before they materialize in reality. You can also change the course of your thinking. Check into the quality of your go-to "I ams'". Take inventory of the "I am..." phrases that you say to yourself and others without even thinking. The ones that you use daily run your life. The outcomes in your life will always match them. *"I am fit", "I am valuable", "I am a priority", "I am valuable", "I am living into the very best version of myself"* should all be staples in your mindset toolkit. These are affirmations. Affirmations are one way to reprogram the mind. Repetition with feeling can transform mental connections.

It is very difficult to affect and transform only the physical shape of your body and no other aspect of your life. Our physicality, our psychology, and our personality are all linked and interwoven together. Changes come quicker to a person whos' psychology plays in the land of possibility and creation. Purpose driving living is tedious and dreadful without the clarity of a greater purpose attached to it. Living in a world of survival is usually synonymous of living in the world of lack, not a world of constant expansion, progress, and growth. Discomfort made comfortable and little progress, line the streets of fear and survival. If exercise and choosing foods based on nutritional value and not only taste is counterintuitive it will take some mental work to make it a new habit. It is very important that you attach the taking of those actions to a powerful purpose, something bigger than you. Ensure that it is something that shows up as a need to do in your life. Consider linking it to what you have decided is your purpose for living. Define something that is really important to you. Make yourself aware of the connection between your health and well-being & the true reason why you feel you are here on this planet. Link exercise and healthy eating to your ability to do the special thing that only you can add to this planet. What cause bigger than you can you attach your exercise efforts to? What is each rep taking you closer towards? Use the idea of being part of something bigger than yourself to help make taking the best care of you a habit. Allow being significant to others to keep you on task with your fitness efforts.

ACTION: Purpose finder Find your purpose, make time to figure it out daily. Be still and ask yourself. Take time daily to focus on what it is that you would do for free. What pursuits bring you great joy in life? Focus on your strengths.

ANSWER THE FOLLOWING QUESTIONS

1. What are the things that you loved doing as a child? Can you tap into doing it now? Can you make money at it today?
2. What do you do easily that others find difficult?
3. What have others thanked you for that took very little effort for you to do for them?
4. What things are you naturally good at?
5. What is really important to you? What must you achieve in this lifetime?
6. What is unique about you that only you can contribute to the world?
7. What can you do forever that others find tiresome or difficult? What so you have inner passion for?
8. What are some of the ways perfect health and a higher level of fitness will facilitate those things happening?

DO THIS Write out how being physically fit will aid you in doing what you've discovered by doing this exercise? Write out clearly what your purpose is for living or a list based on your answers to the 8 questions above. **What action can you take within 24hrs towards becoming more fit? Write it out & make it happen.** It's no longer about sweating and doing painful exercises to look good in the mirror. This is about healthfully living the possibilities of your life.

You can determine that you are here to support your family. Your purpose may be to help others in various ways with your gifts. You may be called to support a cause or movement. A fit and healthy body is what will enable you to do that longer and more effectively. You are in control of setting the ceilings for your health, fitness, finances, and relationships. You also get to set the ceilings for living a version of life that thrills you. Your imagination is the only limit. Perfect sustainable health and fitness is best created from thinking in the field of abundance. Start taking steps towards living a life of intentional creation and growth versus a life of survival.

Most times when you leave your house you can sanely conclude that you will make it back home in one piece. This is very different from prehistoric times when man was at the bottom of the food chain. Even though we now sit atop the food chain many of us are still locked in on finding ways to simply survive life with the least resistance. Many of us live with a great aversion to risk taking. That mental wiring dates back to a prehistoric era in humanity. Seeking comfort has become intertwined with modern society. We have become deathly afraid to do more, think more, fail forward, and be more. People now lean on technology more and more between work, school, and even fun. Complacency has seeped into almost every area of modern day living. It has not been implanted in many of our heads to embrace the idea of doing the uncomfortable yet rewarding things that help us realize what we desire in life. We've become content with simply "making it through the day", "trying to survive", "taking it one day at a time" instead of living all-out & being the best versions of ourselves that we can possibly be. Every human being should be up to more than simply surviving to see another day. A yearning in every heart calls us to thrive, & more importantly, regain the knowing that we can express who we really are to the world. It takes mental self-conditioning to shed the prevalent mindset of not deliberately creating one's life. It takes work to avoid falling into the prevalent pattern of simply surviving. Fitness is taking action on intentionally creating a purpose-filled life. Thriving should be the goal lived towards each day. It took me almost three decades to embody this truth in my cells. I didn't have a blueprint like this book to consult.

I spent most of my childhood in survival mode. I couldn't mindlessly play video games or play for hours with toys. I had to worry about who in the foster home that I moved into with my younger brother was our ally and who was an enemy. I had to determine if the home that we were moved into was a safe environment. I had to judge the intentions of adults as well as the other children. I did things to get kicked out of certain abusive homes. I fought, I broke things, I acted out to save us on many occasions. I also made sure that my brother and I were on our best behavior in homes that felt safe. That was a full time job in and of itself. I had no time or bandwidth as a child to do anything else. I had to be the protector on standby for most of my childhood. When we were adopted by a loving and supportive woman I had to learn for the first time how to trust. How can you build an intentional life if you can't trust anyone else to help you? I had to learn to let go of barely surviving and work towards believing that I deserved and could enjoy a future that flourished. Years after I was adopted, and caught my breath, for the first time, I could contemplate what I wanted in life.

I got the opportunity to create a vision bigger than survival around age twelve. In that effort as a kid I created the seeds of a future vision that I now enjoy and love as an adult. The things that I get to do now are insane when considering where I started from. Last year I went racing Ferrari's at one hundred and sixty miles per hour in Las Vegas. This abandoned and abused kid who was born in Harlem in the 70's, and raised in foster homes in the Bronx, Connecticut, and Brooklyn during the 80's drug era, has literally climbed mountains. Mountains made of granite stone. I have jumped out of airplanes at fourteen thousand feet. I have traveled around the world coaching, training, and teaching. I have given time, energy and resources to children growing up in the same corrupt and racist system as I did. I have been part of raising millions of dollars for kids not afforded the luxury of starting at the same starting line as most people. By arming youth with mental tools that took me years to acquire, I now get to directly help at-risk youth onto a shuttle to take them to the starting line of life that most people take for granted. They ultimately get a better shot at running their race of life because I dreamed and decided to become more than I was. It is so humbling to be used. Being used for the betterment of others is my purpose. Coming full circle from receiving my only Christmas gift from children's charities to donating thousands for at-risk youth to go to college is me living out my dream and embracing possibility. Allowing myself to dream bigger and imagine better was the spark.

Worrying is one of the greatest things that detract from people's ability to achieve goals and dreams. Worrying is fear going to town with a paintbrush in your mind. A person constantly thinking of being fat will never be thin. Remember, once again, that you control your thoughts and your prevalent mindsets. Sustained thoughts are very powerful because they are the preview of things to come. You will start to notice once you take time to reflect on life that what you think about the most usually manifests. In order to change the pictures of your life, change the thoughts you entertain and the *words that you give breath to*. Direct your own energies on purpose.

Science is starting to prove that there are indeed links between our thoughts, feelings, and emotions and the world around us. We have powerful but subtle energies that we use to shape our bodies and our lives. Our minds play a major role in the responses that our bodies have to various stimuli. Our minds even control the secretion of various hormones in our body that affect body fat levels. See yourself in the shape that you want to be and know that you have what it takes to make it show up in reality. One of the mantras that I have chosen to live by is "If there is one other human on the planet that can do it, then I can too". Be thankful and grateful for who you are becoming even before you arrive at the destination. There is no possible way that your mindset and subconscious mind will allow you to become wealthy if they are both cemented around you never having enough. Creating a positive consciousness around money and abundance is necessary. Mentally anchor living in wealth and abundance to living your purpose just like we talked about with fitness.

IT'S MUCH DEEPER THAN YOU THINK

"It takes repeated efforts to change the shape of your world."

It actually takes a long time for someone to get out of shape enough to become "unhealthy". The human body is resilient. Everything in this realm takes time to materialize. Even things that appear to have happened in an instant, have a lag time. Think about a time you were the most unfit in your life and review the events that took place to help you reach that point. It took some time. There is rarely one circumstance that happens in people's life for them to become fat in a day, a week, or even a month. It is rare that any ailment or affliction is absolutely acute. Something intangible leads to that occurrence. Most results are cumulative. It usually takes a long time for the body to manifest the symptoms that correspond with something going on within. If you keep abusing a body, it will eventually respond. If you keep properly training, nurturing, and feeding a body, it will eventually respond. It also takes repeated messaging to get the body healthy and fit because it is very resilient. It takes a lot of thought and physical processes in order to get to the point where you feel very uncomfortable with the way you look due to excess weight as well. Most times we are not aware of those processes. Due to our awareness being elsewhere the weight sneaks up on us. It usually takes quite some time for us to get "sick and tired of being sick and tired." The sooner that you get fed up with how things are the better.

Take a look at your response to your first experience with fitness. What is your current relationship with fitness and exercise now? Do you like it? If not, what do you hate about it? Do you like it but don't make time to do it? Maybe it was at recess in elementary school when you were last to be picked to be on a team. Maybe it started with a very aggressive weight training program or a running program and you decided that the sweat, pain, and burn did not work for you. Many people do not like the sweat and exertion aspect of working out. If you do not like to exercise, it is something that can be changed. Remember "you are not your mind", you are the awareness that is in control of it. If exercise is something you do not like, it can happen in a different way and become bearable when weighed with the benefits it brings. You may have to explore various new ways of exercising to find something new that suits you. Doing new things helps us to release former negative connotations that we once held. By finding areas of fitness that you enjoy you then have the power to alter how you currently relate to exercise. You can find your perfect blend. Right now exercising and eating right may occur to you as a chore. Anything occurring to you as a chore will be hard for you to do on a regular basis. The way things occur to us (our perceptions) dictated the actions that we take around that subject. You actually can control what perception and mindset you develop around any action or situation.

Your default (off the rack, go-to) feelings are not always the ones that you should allow to become set in stone. To gain the most out of life critical thinking is important. Hoping and wishing, while on autopilot, is no way to purposefully live.

Let's take a look at the possibility that you may genuinely not like to exercise (or the doing of some other beneficial act) for whatever reason. If you don't like something, it is usually based on a past experience or currently held perception. One of the things we seem to forget is that past experiences have already happened. They are over. It is strange, but we mentally relive painful circumstances and events over and over again. It is so important to become aware that if we put events from the past on instant replay, in our minds, that we become vulnerable to experiencing blockages and stoppages in life. Take some time to look around and see if any events from the past still shape what you like and dislike. What stories keep playing over and over? What will you not try again due to past experience? Realize that the unpleasant experience you had with _____ is over. Can't create a brand new experience with the debris from the past mucking up the place. You have the mental capacity to take action on beneficial and unpleasant things if you reframe them in your mind. Mentally frame exercise as sipping from the fountain of youth. Healthy food can be reframed as medicine in your mind's eye. Chores can become the rent that you pay to enjoy your beautiful family. Turn the beneficial things that you really hated doing into practices and investments that add substance, vitality, and longevity to your life.

Visualization is everything. Maintaining a clear vision of where you are going is epic. Decide to work on the vision in your mind first. Lasting new actions can be taken on a physical level when a new mental vision is established. Consciously choose to be healthy and fit every day because it will materialize your greatest whys in life. See yourself fit and healthy before the mirror agrees. See the millions in the account before you even have a single comma in your bank balance. Visualize your grandkids as adults, enjoying a legacy that you set in motion. The best piece of "Good News" that I can share with you is that intangible changes happen instantly as soon as you believe. Permanent change occurs when there is an inner shift in a person's being due to a newly attached passionate vision. We all have really felt a time when we learned something new and that knowledge changed a perception in our minds forever. You knew from that moment on, that regarding that topic, things would never be the same. Aim to have these kinds of shifts around areas of struggle in life. Knowledge alone grants us options and potentials. Knowledge paired with the taking of new actions is power!

BUILDING FAITH

Many times, people only acknowledge change when the outcome they would like to see has manifested. This is one way to look at things but not a complete perspective. You must realize that in this realm that we call reality, everything that happens has a gestational period. The visual change takes time to materialize but the change has already occurred as possibility in a realm that we cannot see. Babies take time to come out into our world from the womb. Their presence is already here before they are born. A baby exists as a possibility in a chance meeting between male and female strangers. It takes time for a caterpillar to become a butterfly. The butterfly is there before it emerges from the cocoon. An acorn takes time to become an oak tree, but the possibility of the mighty oak lay within the acorn etc. Hold onto the idea that change occurs in the moment that you make up your mind to commit to do "whatever it takes" to make the possibility materialize.

Make a sincere promise: "like the human body needs oxygen, to get it done". Once the agreement is made between the inner being and the mind we must add action. Action is the bridge from our inner desires and possibility to material manifestation. Know that once the necessary action is underway, the desired outcome is already created. As long as you work continuously, feel the certainty. That is faith! Do not step out of the line for receiving the desired outcome, by quitting. Simply make sure that your actions remain pointed in the right direction. If actions remain aligned with the desired outcomes you have earned the right to enjoy faith. Faith should be made even bolder when looking back at the track record of what consistency has caused in other areas of life. Consistency has moved so much in each of our lives for the better and for the worst. Trace what consistency has created in your life. Look at what consistent inaction broke. Reflect on the outcomes of consistent ways of being that you have. Notice any callouses on your body. What consistent actions have caused them? Notice your consistent shortcomings and the various outcomes they cause in life. Notice your strengths. Consistency equals an outcome always. You can harness it. That alone should furnish faith.

This is the type of bond that you can forge with yourself and regain both faith and power. Faith over time develops into a "knowing". When you declare that fitness is a priority in your life that is the instant that change is underway. When you say it, go write it down, with an unreasonable commitment to the result. When your resolve is strong and unreasonable the task is energetically done. Consistent action will usher that energy into a new physical reality. When people successfully quit smoking, the change they made happened in the instant that they decided to embark upon the successful attempt. It needed to occur in their mind first. Something clicked, forever changing their lives for the better. The same thing has to occur in order for you to do what it takes to live an intentional life. There are many reasons why people take so long to make changes they deem necessary. One of the main reasons is that people hold onto old misaligned behaviors in fear. Deep down comfort in familiar failure is easier than facing possible failure while making a change. Consistent aligned action can help people truly trust themselves again. Eventually results bolster the faith that they have in themselves again.

Dreams are simply dreams and nothing more if you do not believe or trust yourself to make them happen. Lift off takes belief in ones' ability to achieve. This is called self-efficacy. It is not enough just to dream, the world is full of dreamers. Trust yourself to be able to realize your goals. You have a one hundred percent track record in figuring things out and staying alive so far. How many people still smoke every day even though they know that it contributes to bad health? How many people are told to exercise because of possible heart complications and death and don't? Even then that switch has not flipped to make exercise a regular habit. Sometimes a hard reset is in order.

CHAPTER 12

THE SENTENCE

*"Failure is never final until you choose for it to
be so."*

I can remember feeling the feelings of failing very early on. I realized
that something was wrong with me early in life. I registered the loss of
something vital in my life when I realized that I was being raised in foster
care. Not having my biological mother or father in the picture really had
a powerful impact on the formation of who I became as a human. Not
having any parents that looked like me to identify with, to watch over
me, or to shelter me, led me to dig deep and find my own solutions in life.
I wasn't nurtured much as a child and I was a pretty serious and angry
young boy. My childhood was filled with hunger and anger. I was hangry
all of the time. I had no control over where my brother and I would end
up. I had no control over what happened to us while at the houses we
were sent to live in. I hated being at the mercy of others.

We bounced from home to home for the first part of our lives. I also
noticed that the areas that I lived in were the ugliest, dirtiest, and most
dangerous ones in New York City. I hated navigating the crackheads and
drug dealers just to go to and from school. I hated having to run from
older kids who tried to rob us for our lunch money and whatever nice
clothes we had. Growing up in a chaotic unstable environment created a
yearning in me for control. I really hated people for a long time. All I ever
wanted was stability and some control in my life. I soon became those
two things to survive mentally and physically. Always being responsible
and in control is not fun. I forfeit my childhood for our survival. I was
growing up with a younger brother I felt very responsible for. I felt that
no matter what, I had to be strong and manage our situation. I turned
to building my body as a coping mechanism. I had to be hard to handle
the hard circumstances that we navigated. I sought out opportunities for
me to be in control, no matter how difficult. I always emerged as a leader

because of that. I took care of my body always because it was one of the few things that was mine to control. Control shaped my personality. It took me the next twenty-five years to figure out that the context of the mindset I lived by was *"I am in control"*. That single statement shaped the next thirty years of my life.

Everything I have done since then can be traced to this single four-word statement. This was part of my sentence. It shaped the way my house is decorated, my personality, the friends I picked, the way I shape my beard up and cut my hair. It made me an entrepreneur. Who I was from situation to situation and who I was becoming by default was run by a single mindset that I developed when I was very young. *"I'm in control"* also silently and sneakily dictated who I was in romantic relationships as well. Woman who looked as if they were in control but were really chaotic were like catnip to me. They presented well and gave me a project to tame and work on. I was lost and unaware why.

The same is true for most human beings before they become aware of their sentence. Much of who you are and what happens in life can be attributed to one simple sentence! If you are unaware of it, you are bound by it. It blows my mind that a simple three to five word sentence can make and break us. I have noticed that many people's sentence is one of the powerful variables that keeps them from becoming fit, wealthy, or enjoying happiness. These powerful and hidden three to five word sentences are writing people's lives today without them even knowing. Some sentences I came across while training were: "It is not my fault", "Someone else did it", "I'll do it when I'm ready", "Do not mess with me", "I do not care", "I did it well enough", "It's not that important", "I am confused?", "I am the victim".

In order to uncover your sentence answer the following powerful question. *Who are you in the face of failure?* You will find that the answer is illusive. It is not easy to put a finger on. When you do find it your world can shift. It is not easy to find when you look for it. Be truthful, open and honest. There is no wrong answer. Your sentence is not right or wrong. It is just something really good to be aware of. All of your habitual wins and losses come from it. If you have a hard time identifying it ask somebody who knows you the following questions. Ask a few people to truthfully answer the questions below in order to give you some insight. Ask people who know you *"Who do they believe you to be in the face of failure"*. Interview family members and friends who are not afraid to give you the truth. Ensure them that you are willing to hear their truth and that you value their perspectives.

ACTION: Interview at least six friends or family members and ask them:

---

1. What can you count on me for?
2. What can you not count on me to do?
3. Who do you believe I am in the face of failure?
4. What are my top three strengths?
5. What are my top three weaknesses?

Make sure to thank the people you interview. Review the answers. They may vary from how you see you. That is a good thing. Look for what repeats. The answers should give you good enough insight to come up with a three to five word sentence that pretty much sums up who you are in the face of failure. You may not like what you hear at first. I hated finding out that I was a control freak. My girlfriend at the time, now my wife hit the nail on the head when I asked her. You know truth when you hear it. It has a certain ring to it. Remember that none of these answers are negative or positive. They are simply perspectives. Take all perspectives at face value. These are all various perspectives of one single person... You. Notice what repeats. They will give you guidance to discover something profound about yourself. Who you are in the face of failure will have a direct correlation to your ability or inability to regularly exercise. Who you are in the face of failure was created long ago. It has both saved you in times of hardship and limited you in times of great opportunity.

Fortunately for me and my personal fitness levels, "I am in control" is a perfect fit when it comes to getting into shape and exercising. What shows more control than consistency around exercise? For a person who looks for control, it makes sense for them to first take care of their own bodies. There are other sentences that make regular exercise easy like *"I am strong"*, *"I will get better"* or *"I will show you"*. At the same time none of them will serve anyone well in all life situations. An advancing person will switch them out in orders to fit life's circumstances or situations. If you hold onto a single way of being and act from it in all situations, it will definitely hinder your progress. The mindset "I'm in control" is perfect for exercising in order to control my body. As a young newly adopted child, my body was one of the few things I had control of. Around the age of twelve I chose to take charge of what my body look and felt like. This mindset even shaped how I chose the activities that I participated in. Honestly, I only chose to do things I knew I would be very good at doing in school. I played sports. It gave me a further sense of control. I did not give much effort to anything that could possibly be outside of my realm of comfort. I loved individual sports the most because I didn't have to rely on others. Under the circumstances, survival and being accepted by my mom, kids at school, drug dealers on the block, and adults was more important to me than risking failure in order to grow on a personal level. It was natural to pick doing only the things I excelled at.

It felt great to always win, please others, and never fail. There were so many things in life that I was missing out on though. When I dug deep down inside, I felt like a professional baseball player playing in a little league park. I was always a big fish in a small pond. I grew up with *"I'm in control"* running my life. It picked my career path. It got me promoted in the military. Being a personal fitness trainer and constructing exercise prescriptions that told people exactly how many reps and how many sets to do to get the body of their dreams was obviously an excellent fit. The ideal fit for you career wise are occupations that run parallel with your sentence. I am a world class trainer and life strategist coach today because my sentence is *"I am in control"*. The power of this four word directive has been immeasurable in my life. Coping mechanisms often stay in place unless you intentionally take the "shades" off and replace them.

We all have coping mechanisms. Many of our deepest rooted ones were created to deal with the first time we failed as a child. "I am in control" was created by the toddler version of me. It was my coping mechanism for becoming aware that I was an abandoned child raising another abandoned kid. It secretly moved me until I became aware of it at age twenty nine. What is yours? It is so easy to have a coping mechanism manufactured by a four-year-old running your entire life. If you are unaware of what yours is, this is exactly what is happening to you. Remember that your current sentence works for both good and bad. It was developed to deal with absolute failure. It is not negative or positive. It is just what we choose in order to get through various situations of life.

Give it some real thought: Who do you resort to being in the face of failure? What underlying mindset moves you? If you unlock that secret, you unlock a huge insight to the reason why you do what you do. You can see why you don't save and invest as you should. You will understand why trust takes effort for you. You also uncover why procrastination kicks in when you do certain things. It explains why you will thrive at others endeavors. The greatest thing in the world is that you can snatch the driver's wheel from the four-year-old you that created it. You can replace it with a new sentence that is going to serve you better. You will be able to do things that have historically been impossible to do consistently. Imagine the upside and what kind of new contexts and mindsets you can create using the knowledge that you have just read. This is something you can take to anything in your life. It doesn't only have to be fitness and exercise. If your default sentence in the face of failure is "I don't care", most likely you will tend to quit efforts in any area of your life that doesn't yield immediate results or is tough for you to deal with. Trace where in life your default response to failure has taken over your actions. Check yourself. This will be a traceable trend that you can see in many facets of your life. It is quietly behind many of the failures as well as triumphs that you have had.

GET OFF OF MY BACK

Who you are in the face of failure is only one part of the equation of self-discovery. Another three to five word sentence actually running the show in conjunction with that first distinction is the answer to the question; *"How do I get people off of my back after experiencing failure?"* What phrase automatically pops into mind when you fail and have to respond to authority about it? What words do you use to get people off your back after you failed and you are confronted? Think of what you would say to your boss when you ruin something at work and you are called out on it. What I say to get people off my back is *"I will fix it"*. It shuts people up right away. Some say *"I can do it again."*, *"I will pray on it"*, *"I will do better next time"*, *"Get somebody else to do it"*, *"I quit"*, *"I need a break"* or *"I don't know what happened"*. The reason this sentence is so important is because it will bring you awareness to how you internally justify not doing what you said you would do in order to win. It points out how you justified to yourself failing to maintain healthy habits and promises to yourself. It pops up when you miss the gym. When you don't make that contribution to your financial freedom account. It pops up when you fail to keep a promise to someone else. So my full sentence is *"I am in control and I will fix it."* This full sentence lays out my relationship with fitness. "I am in control" always keeps me involved in a workout routine because I know that it helps give me control over my body's environment. "I can fix it" keeps me adjusting workouts and looking for new ways to challenge my body. This combination can be traced all throughout my life in so many decisions I have made.

Even the decor of my house now is sparse neat and controllable. I tend to only have things that serve a purpose in my possession. I don't have a lot of decorative items in my home. They make for less control. I don't have any pets because I perceive them to take a lot of effort to control. The conflict between your sentence and your job makes you very good at it. People choose jobs in constant opposition with their sentence so they can continue to solve problems over and over again and remain intrigued. I am surrounded by people who don't have total control over their bodies and lives. People seek me out when they are in the throes of chaos. Control and structure gets to play in my work life and makes me great at what I do. I had very little control and structure as a boy growing up. Now I teach these things. This was bred during the chaos of my childhood. A great prosecution lawyer may function from the sentence "It's their fault, What are the facts." In order to prove a crime was someone else's fault, this type of mindset will serve him greatly as a lawyer. "What are the facts." will also serve efforts as a lawyer. When it comes to exercise and fitness, this sentence may not serve so well: "It is their fault" will hinder him from accepting responsibility for his body.

"What are the facts?" Can lead to he/she knowing everything about exercise and nutrition but not actually taking action until they have done adequate research in their opinion. How many people do we know in that boat? Always hunting knowledge and never executing? They are well read and informed but don't do what they know. They actually don't have a problem with working out and working hard but still do not take full ownership of their health in all aspects. Seeking evidence takes precedents over doing what's necessary. Their efforts will not be effective or sustained until that sentence changes.

THE PROCESS

Many times, romantic relationships crash and burn with someone who has a sentence opposite of yours. My own full sentence playing was why it was so hard for me to have a full and substantial relationship with anyone. I was a charming lady's man all through my twenties. I think that the same was true of my father. He was a super handsome man from USVI. I inherited some of his looks and from what I hear a lot of his charm. I also learned about the power of "what you don't know you don't know can hurt you." Things that you are oblivious to really can cost you. As far as romantic relationships went I had on colored "shades" and didn't even know that I was wearing any at all. I thought that I had clear reading glasses on. Not trusting people to be themselves and trying to control and fix them is not conducive to having a great long-term relationships with anyone. Once I had this revelation, I could do something about it immediately. My wife is the one I'd credit with opening my eyes to my controlling ways. Awareness is everything. Turns out that her sentence is allergic to being controlled by anyone. I share all of this personal information to help trigger the awareness you have within yourself. When you discover your sentence for yourself, or someone else shares it with you (this is how I found mine) you will see that it affects many areas of life. Being aware makes it easier for you to make changes that resonate with your inner being and will not be very difficult for you to maintain or remember.

In order to help you define your sentence if you haven't discovered it already, here is one of the most common full sentences that I have encountered while training people across all lines: *"I'll do it when I want, I will delegate it."* This sentence might be an excellent sentence running a fortune 100 business, but when it comes to just managing your personal health, it does not work so well. Many executives I have trained have this mindset. Unless they have decided the time for them to get in shape is right now, it is very difficult to get them started on a program to do it consistently. In order for them to even take action, they must deem it to be a major priority that was set before they even met me. The "I will delegate it." Is detrimental for them giving their very best. This is especially true for the workouts they do alone at home without the push of a coach. Seventy-five percent of what it takes to make a transformation is done outside of the workouts with a coach. We must work together to create a brand new sentence. We create one that can be leaned on when I am not around. This sometimes takes the most time. What you dislike about exercise usually has its roots in the sentence that has been running your life.

Change your sentence and you can totally alter the relationship you have with exercise. What do you dislike about exercise? If you actually like exercise but don't do it regularly, you have to become a person who takes action as soon as you feel or notice you are becoming complacent. Things you deem hard to do should become the things you tackle first. Taking action first in order to stimulate inner motivation is a great trick to use when creating change. You have to be vigilant because complacency and stagnation can sneak up on you. As soon as your mind creates excuses and reasons to miss a workout, a fire alarm should go off in your head to "Get Moving!" Chances are that if you find yourself adamantly disliking something that will benefit you tremendously, it is a long standing position that you have taken. The mindset around that action has taken root. A way to conquer them forever is to work towards experiencing the activity in a new way. Try as many novel ways to experience that difficult and great habit as possible. Let's say that you despise running and traditional cardio but you know that the benefits of running are tremendous, it would behoove you to try the various versions of cardio available. You can try various types of interval training, walking on an incline, running on a treadmill, other pieces of equipment, dance, road running, competing in a walk or run, speed walking, etc. If you don't like any of these options, you have sports, Plyos, aerobics, functional training, dance, agility training, kettle bells and other forms of cardio training. Chances are that along your journey, you will find one or two that you can tolerate or even may like. Action taking will change the shades you wear around cardio, and you will start to relate to it differently. You can reap the benefits of cardiovascular training without hating it. All of this is created in the "Doing" and not writing it off. You should be very hesitant to write something off forever. Doing varied new actions this way can change the context surrounding anything in your life.

You hopefully took the time to really explore some things about yourself from the inside out to explore which sentence that has controlled your life to this point. Hopefully took the time to mentally explore some things about yourself from the inside out. Celebrate finding the sentence that has controlled your life to this point. This entire book is written to help people take a deeper look inside of themselves and to make themselves responsible and accountable for who they are being. When we, human beings, make a distinction about ourselves and become aware of a facet of our personality that we did not know we did not know we can take charge of it. "Better" becomes possible when you add a new level of mental connectedness to your life. With practice, you begin to foster a brand new sense of awareness and new way of listening to the world. You no longer have to be confined by your mind. You get to use your mind as a tool for creativity instead, that makes things happen that you believed were impossible. You can expand the realm of what you believe is possible in this short lifetime. Now that you are aware of the origin of how you get what you get in life, you can realize new possibilities. You do this by making new choices that defy your current mindset.

Remain open to being adaptable and listening to your own thoughts through a different filter. We human beings are very complex yet simple at the same time. The sentence running our lives are immensely powerful. It is ironic that a single mindset or coping mechanism has so much control over so many facets of a person's life. Being unaware that it even exists, until it is pointed out, is even crazier! It can be devastating at times. Remain aware of the idea that "We are not our minds". If we are not the fear filled voice in our head rambling all day, who are we? I have noticed that people, myself included, are simply possibilities. We are the possibilities of who we say we are or choose to become. We are whomever we have the guts and consistency to become.

The language, inaction, and actions that we give life, right now, are responsible for futures that we will either dread or enjoy. You are not simply what you like, you are not what you want, and you are not what you feel, you are who and what you decide to be. What you like and what you don't like are many times based on past experiences. How many things have you not liked initially? How many things have you tried out at a later date and enjoyed? How many times have you wanted something, then you got it, then wished you didn't have at all? People are a combination of what they have the courage to take consistent actions around and who they've personally defined themselves to be in the now. Until they have awakened to this reality, things like past experiences and what the mind likes and dislikes will run the show. The default setting will just continue looping over and over like the menu screen of a Netflix show. The same things will continue to happen over and over in various versions until you intentionally turn the program off and pick a new program/ sentence to live from. People who grasp this concept and make the effort to transform their lives by transforming their sentences can become brand new people.

STRENGTH & PAIN

Another reason why it is imperative for you to be aware of your sentence is that there will be a certain amount of fear, pain, and discomfort associated with change. It is a lot easier to sit down and not take any action. In fact, I joke with a lot of people who say "I wish I could work out", save everything on a flash drive, load it on computer and hook electrodes up to people and transfer the physical information from my last workout over to them. They would get results without lifting a finger. I would be a multibillionaire. I am happy there is no mainstream technological way to do that yet because exercise is a rare opportunity for people to learn about themselves.

What you go through physically can peel away layers of faulty mental programming like an onion. The self-talk that helps a person make it through a tough workout can afford a connection to their inner wisdom and resilience unlike any other activity. The mindset that can be developed through exercise can transfer over to other areas of life and result in unbelievable success. In order to get past your discomfort and make it through the pain it takes to get fit, your relationship to the pain will have to change. You have to become able to tell the difference between good pain and bad pain. Pain is feedback. There are people who relate to the pain of soreness as a hated unnecessary pain. Pain shouldn't deter you from exertion. There is no transformation anywhere in life without exertion past what is comfortable to you. Allow this chart to help you create a different context of pain for you. Below is another way to relate to healthy pain during exercise and life.

RPE CHART

0	**Nothing at all**	Sitting down watching Netflix
0.5	**Very, very weak**	Stand up while on the phone
1	**Very weak**	Daily activities your body is used to
2	**Weak**	Going for a walk
3	**Moderate**	Brisk walk or jog (able to talk but not sing)
4	**Somewhat strong**	It takes some exertion to continue
5	**Strong**	Able to talk but not without pauses
6	**Moderate to difficult**	Begin to feel the burn of fatigue.
7	**Very strong**	Feel the exertion (fragmented speech)
8	**Very difficult**	Putting forth great effort to continue Can't Speak)
9	**Extreme**	Very high level of effort/fatigue
10	**Very, very strong**	Impossible to continue, physically taxed, last .5 mile of a 26.2mile, total fatigue imminent any second.

Source: Borg, G.V. (1982) Psychological basis of perceived exertion. Medicine and Science in Sports and Exercise, 14, 377-381. American College of Sports Medicine. Exercise References by Andre Van Lun CSCS, HFS

This is a Rate of Perceived Exertion chart. What RPE are you living at now? Trainers and coaches use it to monitor individuals that don't have normal physical responses (those on blood pressure medication etc.) to physical exertion due to taking medications that hinder the body's natural response to exercise. We rely on gauging their mental connection to pain and discomfort. When you begin a new exercise, expect a brief period in the beginning where you will feel like you have already reached an eight or higher on this scale. Exertion is high in the beginning of any undertaking. It takes more effort to get something moving from a standstill than it does to maintain momentum. One of the things to keep in mind is that the level of perceived exertion will go down to about a four once your body recognizes and acknowledges that there is a new level of physical stimulation occurring. This is called "steady state". Provided that the level of intensity of your exercise has not changed as time progressed during your bout of exercise, you will progress through the numbers in the exertion chart at a much slower rate.

You will reach a *steady state* during each exercise where the activity seems more manageable to continue. This happens *everywhere in life* that you decide to change course and keep efforts alive. Fight past the initial discomfort. Many runners report a runners high two to three miles into their run. That steady state will usually occur when the body has adapted to the new exercise stimulus. Feelings are feedback. Pain and discomfort are also feedback. They will not last forever. Too many people give too much focus to the period of discomfort where they drastically shoot up to an eight in the beginning. They quit before reaching steady state. They don't keep up effort long enough to experience exertion and pain drop down to an RPE of five. There are often feelings of discomfort in the beginning of doing anything outside of your comfort zone. Saving and investing forty percent of your income and living off of sixty percent becomes easier over time. Don't quit on forming new habits and taking new actions. You will become stronger. When exercise intensity is lower than a four no adaptations have to be made by the body. The thing I love about using this chart is that regardless of the activity done, it is specific to the individual. Two people can be doing one exercise and interpret their RPE levels entirely differently. Depending on their fitness levels, one person can be at a seven and the other at a three. This chart can be applied to any beneficial human activity. I had to include this chart here as a point of reference.

If you know what to expect when you want to make a change in life, it will be harder to quit while going through the paces. Hopefully, when that eight comes storming out at you in the first few minutes of making a change in life, you now have what it takes mentally to push through and continue. In fitness the eight will show up as soreness days after you start working out. If it is finances that eight will show up as not being able to go out to eat as much as you want to. It may show up as unrequited interest after being vulnerable in a new relationship. Expect it. Do not allow it to be a deterrent to your continued action. You may feel like an eight or even a nine the first times that you step outside for a run, and those lungs and muscles start burning. You may feel it while beginning to lift weights. This is normal. You will soon be able to do the activity and feel like a three or a four when your body adapts.

This same adaptation happens when you step out on a limb and dare to go back to school after age forty. The same thing will happen when getting back on the horse and dating. You will feel the same way when you embrace the feedback given to you by a lover or a spouse. You will notice the drop in needed exertion to make things work. Another final thing to keep in mind during your use of the RPE chart is that you should not start any sustained workout regimen at super high intensity (nine or ten) because it will not be sustainable. Don't bite off more than you can chew. Start with smaller bites and digest them along the way. In strength and conditioning we call it the progressive overload principal. Start at the point of mild discomfort (a seven or an eight) Wait for the adaptation (two to three minutes) to occur. The RPE will fall to a four or five. Then in small increments add a little more intensity to your efforts. This should be repeated until a good portion of the exercise bout is spent at a level six or seven. No one who exercises on a consistent basis can maintain every single workout at a nine or ten. This leads to burnout, fatigue, inflammation, and injury. Think of this RPE chart whenever you start something new and difficult. Expect the beginning to suck. Expect to level out and "steady state." Then finally, expect a tipping point where you begin to see noticeable changes. Expect your efforts to meet a threshold and for there to be a powerful shift in your progress.

SHIFT

"The illiterate of the twenty-first century will not be those who cannot read and write, but those who cannot learn, unlearn, and relearn." Alvin Toffler

First and foremost once you discover your sentence write it out on paper. Writing something down immediately graduates a whim into a tangible thing in this world. It brings tangible form to a thought. It exposes the atmosphere of our inside worlds. When things are plain, concrete, and simple, they are easier to be aware of.

Write out who you are in the face of failure. Also write out what do you say to get someone off of your back after it is clear that you have failed? The answer to either question cannot be longer than five words. Both answers must begin with "I". The very first time I discovered my sentence, *"I'm in control, I can fix it"*, I felt a little uneasy about it. I never saw myself as a person who was a control freak. I spent my whole life up until that point, not even knowing that that sentence was present. Not only was it present. That sentence was silently running my life. After asking a few close friends and family that all had different perceptions of me, I began to realize that this could be my sentence. It struck a chord and I was able to trace how this sentence had shaped many super important decisions in my life. My then girlfriend and now wife, was the one who truly shined the flashlight and helped me uncover this sentence.

She had a unique perspective into who I was. The way I dressed was an expression of control. How I groomed my beard. Where I sat in restaurants always facing the door. How I treated her was as well. Once you write down your sentence, write down three times this sentence has benefited you in your life. Then write down three times this sentence kept you back from reaching a desired result. Let's get specific: Write down three times you believe your sentence has held you back from winning. You can recall as many situations as possible on both ends. Recall times when you were unknowingly functioning from the sentence. Remember this sentence is neither good nor bad, it is both. This hidden sentence, just *is*. Do not condemn yourself.

MY THREE WINS

1. For me, this sentence served me well in my career as an entrepreneur and personal trainer. **2.** It made me an excellent and responsible older brother to foster children that lived with us growing up as well as my adopted siblings. **3.** It made me a lot of money as an employee and served me as a leader and soldier.

MY THREE LOSSES

The three things that *"I am in control, I can fix it."* cost me were. **1.** I never aimed for any objective bigger than the ones that I believed I could control. I subconsciously capped my dreams. I couldn't dream enormously big. **2.** It ended all of my romantic relationships with quality women. I hurt those who didn't seek to be controlled or fixed. **3.** I was always uptight and overall unhappy for thirty years of my life. Trying to control and fix everything will drain your battery dry.

You can only alter your sentence in the present. This game is only played in real time. I change mine daily from situation to situation. I am also just like you. I had a blind spot running my life. Once it was uncovered I felt obligated to shift it as needed. I decided to snatch back my power. Take a look at the power of this one sentence. It is a part of you. It was formed in your formative years. It has shaped your personality. It is something that you will never totally get rid of. You will be able in time to control whether or not you live from it though. That is extraordinary.

The exercise that I hope you just completed, was meant to dig up and till the flowerbed of you mind. Much like a garden, you have to maintain the minds flower bed. Lifting the soil prepares the soil for new plants that can take root. You now have it identified, written down, and have traced the power of your sentence in your life. With time, you should be able to notice your default sentence and when it sneaks up to play in the areas where you find it difficult to succeed. Your awareness should trigger alarms for you to take notice. It should scream! "You may want to change that right away, select a new one that will serve you better in this moment."

Repetitively taking immediate action from the new mindset and sentence, is what makes it stick. The lens that you bring to any situation is absolutely decisive. How you see a situation will determine exactly what you do in regards to that situation. I have witnessed many mothers who have the context and belief that their children can do no wrong and therefore never ever correct them. Kids without boundaries grow up to become convicts as adults. Many people never see themselves becoming more abundant or having more than what they have now. They certainly will never attain more, and if they do they will squander it all returning themselves back to the paradoxical comfort of being broke. Many people never feel they will ever get in shape. They do not believe it possible or imagine it. They workout and sabotage themselves through food choice simultaneously. This aligns with their subconscious sentence. It is sad but human. Here are some examples of sentences that were limiting results in life for some of my clients. By changing the sentences we were able to transform lives. As you read this, think of your own sentence and how you can powerfully change it. Which words can you choose that inspire you and grant new meaning to living life? What new mantra can you use to help create a brilliant and healthy lifestyle?

NEW CONSCIOUSNESS

Let's start with my own personal sentence. By the way, when I discovered this sentence it rocked me to the core. It explained so much! It exposed the root of why I was stuck in transition in my business. It explained why I had to sit facing the door at every restaurant that I ever went to. It also explained why no matter what woman I dated, we always came to the point where I lingered on some flaw that I perceived in her, and fixated on trying to change it. It was behind the scenes like a puppet master pulling all of the strings. This sentence shaped my existence. A sentence that I created in response to failure as a young boy navigating the foster care system, ran my life for over twenty years. I discovered it while at a conference at age twenty nine. In that moment, I knew that my life would be drastically different. I felt liberated. I could finally create my life as I saw fit. In any situation, I had the power to lean into the use of my default sentence or defy it, and choose a more appropriate one to live from.

Pertaining to my romantic relationship with Nicole, my then girlfriend, now current wife and mother of my twins, *"I am in control, I can fix you"* had to be swapped out for→ *"I am a team mate, We will find the solution"*.

My default sentence is very good for exercise and fitness. Taking control of my body and finding new ways to fix it by various methods of training was, and still is, working nicely for myself and my clients. When it came to intimate relationships and building a successful business, this sentence had to change. I adopted *"I am a team mate, We will find the solution."* I had to consciously give up the need to control every aspect of our relationship and allow Nicole to give input. This new mindset has led my company to grow through three reiterations. It has relieved a lot of the pain of being an entrepreneur. Collaboration means growth. It also has me enjoying a successful and loving relationship greater than any I could have ever dreamed of. I have pledged to be a teammate and enjoy collaboration and connection with my wife for a lifetime. One of my greatest accomplishments was becoming a match for the extremely beautiful human being that she is.

I had to make my sentence known to me. Then I consciously choose to override my subconscious default sentence when I deemed it unsuitable for my goals. It was hard in the beginning, but with practice it becomes easier to see the old you. You will gain foresight into the decisions that the old you would have made. Then defy the old you and make a new selection. I have a far more collaborative life now that I made the decision to do so. I still find that at times I take action from my former default mindset but it is no longer my "normal" to work from it unchecked. I can actually sense my internal motivation to do selfish and controlling things and gauge its effectiveness before I do them now. I had to practice consciously, discarding the old one and bringing in the new. Vigilance is the key. It is a skill that you build with practice. Every time that you defy that default sentence, and create a new and awesome outcome, allow your soul and your body to feel bliss down into your toes. Regardless of the size of the situation, celebrate. You have done what only a few of us humans do. You have intentionally elevated your levels of awareness and thinking. Imagine what this skill can do for your life! Living life from a new level of consciousness makes you your better you. Dare I say it? It makes you God like. This is no easy feat. You will have to relentlessly practice the awareness and then reprogramming yourself. Repetition is key to accessing the subconscious mind. At first it will be like riding one of those mechanical bulls at a bar. Just like anything else you practice, you do get better at it. At some point it will become second nature.

SENTENCE #2: "I need help, I will do better next time" ➔ **"I will take action, I'll do my best now."**

The first sentence strangles ownership and responsibility in tough-for-them situations. It is necessary for this person to seek assistance to become fit and exercise on a regular basis. Once they shift this sentence they can become independent. Until then they will be waiting for the right person or outside influence to inspire them before they move on their own. Just going for a walk by yourself is enough to get the ball moving in the right direction around fitness. Some people won't do anything until help or support arrives. Sometimes it never comes. Then what? Doing their very best every workout eliminates quality control issues. Too many people work out and do a little something that ends up being minutely better than doing absolutely nothing at all. It is pretty easy to see how the revamped second sentence is a way better fit. This sentence becomes a mantra when it gets tough to exercise. *"I'll do my very best"* should be replayed in the mind over, and over, again during exercise and in life. It should pop up when you are prompted to quit or not to start a thing. *"I will do my very best"* holds you to a higher level of responsibility. Many times, we shy away from responsibility as if it is the plague. No responsibility leads to no growth. *"I will do better next time"* always insinuates that one has not done their best in their previous effort.

SENTENCE # 3: *"I shut down, it is not my fault"* → **"I will seek to learn, I've got this."**

This is the sentence for people who walk away when things do not go their way and never face failure head on. They quit exercise cold when it gets tough and when they decide that the results are not enough for the amount of perceived pain that they go through. They avoid confrontation throughout life. They never stick around long enough to learn anything from a situation they feel has become unfavorable. When confronted with the slightest discomfort or adversity during the workout they usually quit. There are many things to be learned from your mind when you push your body. If we are seeking to learn through fitness, we can become aware of a whole new world. We can discover and experience what best suits us as we train. We can also find effective exercise methods that do not lead to very high levels of pain and soreness. The second half of the revised sentence is to empower the focus on what it is most important on the inside. No more running! A sense of power and self-belief is needed to circumvent circumstances, reasons and excuses. It is easy to become so focused on the actions of others and outside circumstances that it takes precedent over what we really want. Blaming everything and everyone else for your own lack of results may be steeped in truth, but it doesn't help to move forward.

If we are living intentionally, outside circumstances, and other people should have less sway than what we do when it comes to living our lives. *"I will look to learn, I've got this"* is declaring that running is over and it's time to get down to business. Really owning those words and executing it, is the definition of taking charge of your life! Can you imagine the outcomes in life for this person after adopting and living into a new sentence like this one? They have made room for absolutely amazing things to happen!

SENTENCE #4 *"I must be comfortable, I did my part."* → **"I'll do something new, I will do what it takes."**

This is a very common sentence among people who are very successful but seem to lose power in one or two key areas of life. These people are usually very comfortable with their lifestyles until they see a picture of themselves on vacation, or are told by the doctor to lose some weight because of health complications. These people think they decently work out and eat right. In reality, they eat a limited and unhealthy diet full of rich and tasty comfort foods. In life, they only value taking the safe route. They value security over most everything else. They steadily gain five to ten pounds every year for some time and are at peace with how they look and feel until that wakeup call. They are the kings or queens of their lives and have a pretty good control over everything. Their weight is the one thing they are quietly uncomfortable with. They have times of working out regularly and eating healthy and they do get results. Then they get comfortable and regain the weight and do it all over from the beginning again. People living this sentence never reach out of their comfort zone and never receive any of the great blessings that lie outside of their comfort zone. They play it safe gaining and losing the same ten to twenty pounds for decades. They have the same friends and go to all of the same places too. Inside they are dying slowly running on a hamster wheel. The new sentence encourages growth and renews a pledge to taking continued effort in all areas of life. It promotes reinvention.

Sentences are powerful, but they are not real. They are created out of thin air in our minds. They are coping mechanisms formed in our youth. They were chosen by default and will always remain present in your life. Carrying the same sentence around through life is like being a handyman with only one tool in their tool belt. Now that you are aware of what your sentence is you have the power to work, around, over, and with it. You have access to a new tool kit filled with tools. It is fine if you want to use your original tool for certain situations. You no longer have to show up to hang a ceiling fan and all you have is a hammer. You now have access to screwdrivers, wire cutters and wire splicers.

You should also understand that all sentences serve you well in one area and can kill possibility in others. You will never create a better reality than you historically have, until your mindset shifts and you decide to take new actions accordingly. If you tap into the power of your mind, you can begin to see it is possible to insert sentences, to operate from, that elevate you and positively affect the things that matter most to you. With regular practice you can shift mindsets like a Tetris master. There is no ceiling to what you can accomplish with your body. There are no limits to how many people you can help, or how you can impact the world. Circumstances can never be more powerful than you are when you become the conductor of your sentence. You get to intentionally create a wondrous and fulfilling life.

CHAPTER 13

NOW IS REALLY ALL THAT MATTERS

"What you do in the present will shape your future"

You may be wondering "How is it possible to change the sentence that has ran your life for so long?" Do you just say it aloud? Then all of a sudden, all of your actions change? No. It is not that simple. One of the first things needed is a profound connection with the present. Being present harnesses a high level of concentration. Get rooted in the present. A sentence created to cope with problems in the past, running your present actions, will compromise your future. The only important time is now. What you are thinking and doing in this very moment is creating your future. Writing this book is creating a version of my future for me to live into. If you have fat thoughts about yourself now, you will be fat tomorrow. If you think yourself to be poor now, it is likely you will be poor later. Using the power of now is one of the quickest ways to get on track with your best you. What can you feel, do and be now to create a future you love? As far as you are concerned, there is no other time but now. Excuses, other people's opinions, and reasons keep a lot of people away from doing the things they know deep down in their heart they should do. Excuses, perspectives, and reasons are all created out of thin air. If you live a life that is full of excuses, you live in an unreal world. You aren't living in the present.

> **ACTION: STOP** whatever you are doing, right this second, do fifteen to twenty pushups, fifteen to twenty sit-ups, fifteen to twenty squats. Then pick up the book and resume reading.

I want you to pay attention to the reasons and excuses that automatically popped into your mind whilst considering doing this quick workout. Notice what stopped you from taking action right now. Notice how you easily rationalized not taking immediate action. Start thinking of ways you can in this moment mentally override these thoughts. Did the risk of being embarrassed stop you? Did laziness stop you? Or, did you do it without question? Are these thoughts that you constantly do battle with? Have you already established a new sentence or mantra that has empowered you? Can you take new action right away? Right now is all that matters, it is the only time you are currently living. Do this light workout within the next twenty four hours. Do you commit? _____ (yes or no) Salute to those who have already done it.

TACKLING "BUSY"

"Busy is a disease that only happens in our minds."
Andre A.Van Lun

Being present in the moment means giving all of your focused attention to one action, person, place, or thing. Paying attention to too many things at the same time will leave you scattered and ineffective. Releasing the need to focus on a variety of things at once turns you into a specialist at whatever you are doing. Shouldn't you be a specialist in living your better life? A wise mentor of mine advised me to stab deep instead of cutting shallow. Focused efforts are deep stabs. Shallow cutting is trying to do it all. You gain a new found clarity and dissipation of confusion when you decide to focus on one thing in the now. You will find that you also make more lasting connections with others because you actually listen to people without being in your own head when they are speaking. People love to be heard. Human beings can only give their best effort to one thing at a time. If you multitask, something will eventually fall through the cracks. I am not saying that you should not accomplish as many things as you see fit to do, but that you should allocate an exclusive and concentrated time for each thing. Nothing else should happen at that time. Anything that gets your undivided attention has a better chance of flourishing. Focused attention aligns you with your "better".

After a meditation session, once you are in a quiet place and your thoughts are calm, it is a great time to prioritize things and set up times to give them your undivided attention. Once you do this, "busy" will dissipate. You will start to experience being "occupied" with one activity as opposed to being busy with your entire life all at once. You will feel that things slow down a lot when you do this. You may even find that you are more guarded with your time. You will have to say no to more commitments. This will be fine and you will not be missing out because the overall quality of every daily experience, business deal, fun activity and interaction with other people will vastly improve. Eventually, everything will have its time and the better version of you will be present to enjoy this new found balance.

THE SEGMENT INTENDING PROCESS

A very effective technique that anchors you to the "Now" and pre-paves the future is "Segment Intending" (I got this one from Abraham Hicks, Law of Attraction). This is the process of stopping for a moment to check in with your inner self. You define what you want to occur, in the very near future as you move through your day, segment by segment. Throughout a day we can move through many communities and worlds.

You can break them down into various segments: getting the kids ready for school, dropping them off, driving to work, going to the gym, walking into a meeting, answering a phone call, picking up the kids, preparing the dinner, sex etc. If every segment can go perfectly how would it look? See it before you enter the segment. Segment intending is taking a couple of moments to deliberately intend what you ideally want to happen. It is tragic to think of how many people never do this. You look at your inner state of being, you deliberately plan what will happen through each segment of the day. You, in essence, declare exactly what you want to take place during an upcoming event. You choose who you want to be, and what you want to feel in each segment. You have to become present to your current thoughts and feelings and project what you want to experience in the next segment of the day. The person you are in each moment can create favorable situations or horrible ones.

Let's say you were about to leave work and meet a friend for dinner.

Before you get in the car, you say to yourself that you intend to arrive safely and on time. Intend a low stress drive. You can make driving a time to reflect on how good it will be to see your friend. You can even expect to get a good parking spot. You can hope they are in a great mood. Just before you open the door, to the restaurant another segment is beginning. You also simply state the intention that you will have a fun and productive meeting. You shift feeling in that moment when you open the door with that energy. You also anticipate the sense of enjoyment you will feel after your dinner. You increase the odds of having a great dinner. What will you bring to the party? The energy that you bring to any situation matters.

By segment intending, you become present to what you want to create now. You have intentionally pre-paved what will happen. You go into every situation armed with an intention. Wow! The person you are in that instant immediately shifts and so does the balance of power in your life. Most people do not do this. By doing this you automatically go from a victim of circumstances to the powerful creator of your life experience. Whether you know what you expect or not, we often get what we believe and expect out of life. It is a universal law. Many times while segment intending, you will literally feel your entire disposition changing as you set forth the intentions of each segment of your day. Rolling through life on the default setting created by our environments is comfortable but not "better". Why should we not create a tailored life? Imagine harnessing the power to create favorable conditions through your life and not living in a washing machine of circumstance. There is a great amount of focus, stability, and peace in this process. It is something that can be practiced all throughout the day so it is easy to become good at rather quickly. Sometime you win and sometime you lose but take time to notice after one week the way life changes for you. Take a look at how much more fun you have exercising and preparing nourishing meals for your body. Segment intending doesn't magically change all people and circumstances around you, but it sets the tone for who you are, and who you will be in the upcoming experiences. That changes everything!

Being "occupied" is a totally different feeling than being "busy". There is hopelessness engrained in the act of being busy. It's easy to stop being occupied. Have you ever attempted to stop being busy? It's nearly impossible. This is because being "busy" is a state of angst being created in our minds. It is brain bound. It has no form and it is vague and cannot be measured. Many times it is the bi-product of not being present and focused on the doing of a single task at a time. Thinking ahead to what you will be doing or incessantly reflecting on the performance of something that you have already done will usually lead to a busy and overwhelmed mind-state. If you struggle with being busy consider doing less but doing it way better. Schedule specific times to do and focus on only one thing to the best use of your ability. It will drastically change the outcomes in your life.

The biggest obstacle my clients run into with incorporating powerful new habits into life is busy and overwhelm. I asked them to define "busy", and a lot of times they've answered "I have a lot of things to do but I have no time." I like to ask questions! So, I ask people "Can you show me a "busy"? Even a busy intersection is simply an intersection occupied, rapidly and often, by one to four cars. Any more cars occupying that space will result in an accident. A busy mind is very similar. Some busy people tell me that their to-do-list for the day has up to twenty items. I still reply "this is not busy". I see a list of goals that have to get done before the day is finished. Each thing on the list has its own time. Each singular objective requires its own course of action. There may be overlap but at the end of the day, you can only efficiently do one thing at a time. There is a great difference between being "busy" and accomplishing something worthwhile.

You can choose to be busy, muddled, and confused. Or you can take one thing at a time and focus all of your brain power on that thing and complete it with excellence, in a designated timeframe that you have chosen. This forges willpower. The more things you do in this fashion, the more it will diminish the amount of things cluttering your head up. It will also drastically increase the amount of things that will get done! Nothing feels as good as a thing done to the best of your ability. (This book is such a thing for me.) When you feel too "busy", stop and make time to reset and reconnect with the present. What are you doing right now? You are reading this book that is all that is happening! Take time to enjoy a state of calm and clear your mind. Pay attention to your breathing. Busy is the lack of assigning priority. Occupying your time adds that structure. For the most part in life, priorities get done. If you find yourself feeling busy and overwhelmed, understand you have made a decision to be in this state. If everything is a priority, nothing is. You will find yourself "busy" and less effective. Make peace, fitness and exercise a top three priority. Make it a matter of self-care. You can do this because you are the only person who dictates what will become a priority for you. Values are set by you. Schedule a designated and appropriate block of time for the completion of everything you do. Avoid getting to it mentally before you do so physically. Anxiety used improperly is detrimental to living.

It is very possible that eating right and exercising is something you can fit into your life if you choose to have a shorter list of things to accomplish. Doing fewer things to the best of your ability may prove to be far more rewarding. There is something to be said for embracing quality over quantity. One of the most important things you can do for your fitness is to write it down as a hard item in your schedule. It must occupy a forty-five to sixty minute slot every day until it becomes second nature. Set alarms in your phone to do it. Your health and your purpose go hand in hand. In my opinion, stress is one of the leading causes of people not living optimized lives and suffering from illness and disease. Stressed is what we become when life doesn't match our dreams and ideals. On top of it, we often have no mental coping tools to deal with reality. Choosing to become organized and assigning time blocks for tasks will diminish stress levels. It is a coping tool when life is coming at you fast and furious. Living in the "now" gives you power to gain control over your life as it comes and raises your effectiveness in the face of it. You then have the peace of mind to conquer "busy" forever. Structure can grant you freedom.

If you are one of those people who say "I have it in my head, I don't have to write it down", remember this is your old way of doing things and it has gotten you to what you have now. If you are looking to create a new reality that surpasses your current reality be rigorous with your language. You are who you say you are. If you continue saying "I don't write things down, I just get them done", you will never get a chance to see what writing your goals out, collecting feedback and accomplishing those goals can do for you. My worlds began expanding both professionally and personally when I changed this practice. In the beginning I found it hard to write down or update outcomes. I used to be that person with the busy mind who stashed all of the details in my mind and never wrote anything down. My life worked fine like that for many years but what is important to me to grow. I now unload my mind when I write out my tasks, goals, and objectives. This creates room for the solutions and insights to flood in. There is no limit to what you can accomplish when you put down an old mindset that served you in the past but no longer does so.

The most successful people in the world know that we are who we say we are. They recognize the power of their words. Especially the words that they utter to themselves. In the moment their words are released into the air and land in the ears of others, they consider what they have declared to be accomplished. It is seen as already done. They enjoy a certainty not afforded by most of us. They know that the new actions they will take in their present will create their new future. They own a confidence and a trust in themselves that translates to power in everything they do. There is no quicker way to create that kind of power and trust within yourself, than to live life firmly planted in the present. Create the belief that when you say a thing, write it down and commit to it, it is already done. This way of living translates to being able to live a powerful existence. Live your word with integrity. Give all your attention and energy to what is taking place in your life at this very moment. Always ask yourself: "Are the actions I am taking now aligned with the declarations that I have made?" Constant adjustments in your actions may be needed daily to make them line up. What you want to create comes into focus. This is where you move from living in a world of survival to creating a world based on what you desire the most in life.

This is intentional living. It takes this kind of knowing and clarity to be able to single out priorities and take constant action. Believing that there is no other option besides the realization of the goals you have defined, is paramount to success. Insert a little cockiness. Life will be life but you are inserting an intention into your life. You will no longer find yourself weak and powerless against excuses and reasons that pop up from your default sentence or a limiting mindset. It becomes easier to drown out objections that a default mindset (created when you were a child) will make. You will manage to choose to make life-changing decisions in the moment, and move forward with new initiatives created from your soul. Remember it is difficult to optimally function from a cluttered mind. Stop and clear it often. Achievements that come from a clear and deliberate space are unbelievable. They boost your swagger.

DOES THIS SERVE ME?

"Leave the past in the past to make room now for creating a new future"

It is hard create a new reality if you are wasting time cyclically living out various versions of the past. You need a clean slate. We humans often carry the past into our present. This always yields a new iteration of the past that seeps into our future. Many people do not live in the moment because they relive their past over and over again. Why allow ugliness from the past to trail us into the beautiful new life that we are creating? You do have the right to be selective in what you choose to take from the past. You can choose to learn from the negative experiences and cherish the good ones. It is a very human thing to choose to live the worst things over and over again. When you confront something from the past and release it, it no longer has any power over you. We must decide and believe that the life we live now is more important than the life we have already lived. Let go of the emotional discord that we carry in our heart and heads due to navigating a negative. Trust yourself to be able to do so. I did it and I'm no more special than anyone else is. I was just able to admit to myself that to move forward I had to purge negativity from the past. I had my identity wrapped up into what I had gone through. Some people rather repeat the same regrettable actions, and carry the same negative mindsets, instead of risking and believing in doing something different. Oddly enough we can become comfortable in reliving and repeating what has failed us in the past.

I have watched countless people who had been out of exercise for long periods of time try to pick up exactly where they left off. They never address the underlying mindsets and hidden beliefs that stopped them in the past. The ones that made them quit exercising and instead gain twenty pounds. People don't bother to confront the mindsets that would make someone stop marketing their services just as their business is picking up steam? Many of us feel like we are ready to take on transformation again. We leave behind the humility. It takes humility to own up to being hindered by thoughts that we are accustomed to having. We want a whole new lifestyle without dealing with the underlying thinking that made failure or stagnation our outcome. Until that mindset is altered or changed, the outcome will be the same as before. The cycle of failure will continue. It is just too difficult to pick a new initiative and stick with it indefinitely if you are constantly tripping over your past.

We all know how packed gyms are in January with eager exercisers ready to take on the year. We also notice how that ninety percent quit before March. They usually quit for the same reason they quit the last five to ten years. The mindset that has limited them has never changed. Adding "better" actions on top of an old mindset equals short term change or little to no change at all. Imagine spilling grape juice on a canvas you were working on in order to paint a landscape. Then imagine just painting on top of the stain. That stain will continue to bleed through the work that you are creating. So many people go through life adding good paint on top of filthy stained canvases. This section is all about cleaning the canvas of your mind. The past is the grape juice. Clean as much of it away as possible. When you do clean your canvas you can create a masterpiece. In life, the past is to be referenced, not lamented on, or ignored. Those who ignore the past are doomed to repeat it. New and focused actions are the key, not "better" or "different" actions. If an action is "better", what is it better than? It is better than some past action that occurred. That makes it based on the past. If an action is "different", what is it different from? It is different from an action that has already occurred. Is there any wonder why people continue to get repeated undesirable results? Multiple failed attempts at exercise, finding the right partner, making money etc. call for a new injection of imagination. Something new needs to be done. Courage and audacity are necessary for creating new outcomes.

Everyone knows people struggling with something that happened to them a long time ago. Many people are at a standstill. Something that has happened is still running their lives. The past can make us lose out on present opportunities. Carrying the burdens of your past into your present time on earth will block the view of your ideal future. Have you heard people say: "I do not have good luck, so it doesn't make sense for me to take a chance at it"? In the very moment they said those words failure became their new reality. This happens all the time. They choose to believe in things that are not empowering that limit their greatness. Most times, these conclusions are based on happenings in the past. It is likely that they have been unlucky in the past. They identify with it now. Every single time that you choose to definitively cut something out of your life based on something that happened in the past, you lose a staggering amount of possibilities. Cut things out of life wisely. Not ever working out because the last time you were sore for four days negates all the benefits you could get by choosing a less strenuous weight training routine. A definitive statement like "I will never be rich" is true for those who consciously or subconsciously believe that because they were raised poor that they will always be poor. That statement cements that reality. Luckily for us, past results do not control future outcomes. A better statement would be "to this point, I have not made myself rich but it is on its way." Exploring new types of exercise may result in having breakthroughs in consistency. So many single people definitively say "There are no good men/women out here." In reality, there are millions of dating options for them to explore. We should know and expect the best or at the very least the "better" in life. We kill possibility with the negative definitive blanket statements that we lend the power of belief to. It's possible that you may just need a brand new canvas.

I know many people are probably rolling their eyes and thinking to themselves "Well then, how will I ever discover what works for me?" Shouldn't I be eliminating options as I go forward? I am not saying you should never learn what not to do. I am also saying do not be so quick to write your options off based on past failures. Instead, ask if there is a lesson to be picked up from a past failure. There are always lessons. When you decide to cast away an activity, person, or a thing permanently, you also lose the good parts and blessings it may yield as well. You forfeit possibilities that you may or may not be aware exist. Too many of us spend a lifetime hacking away at our possibilities and making our worlds smaller. We wake up older than fifty, in lives that are equivalent to jail cells. The past keeps too many of us lonely and lacking connection. Too many of us are moving through life in bodies we do not love.

Be creative. Step back and seek to use critical thinking. Don't jump to abandoning all efforts. Don't give up dating when you encounter and asshole or two or three. Look for a new imaginative solution. I believe it is beneficial to look at things from the following perspective: "Does this action serve me or not?" Don't resort to swift judgements about if a thing is "right" or "wrong". So many times I am asked "is this food a good food or a bad food. People ask wealthy people "is this the right move to become rich?" People ask those of us in successful relationships "Am I dating the right person?" "Is this the right thing to do?" The best answers to all of these questions are internal. The better answers take a combination of mind logic and inner self to arrive at. "How does eating this food make my body feel?" "Will I really execute this particular type of wealth building program, Does it resonate with me?" "Does this relationship serve me or drain me?" The answers are always on the inside of us. Stop and listen often. Train yourself to hear you. The real you.

Relying on the moral filter of "right" or "wrong" alone is not the best way to make complicated decisions. Morality often gets in the way of critical thinking. It causes many people to cling to old ways of being and to forego taking new actions. Morality can eliminate possibilities when a person becomes attached to a certain way of doing what is "right". As long as it doesn't harm others it can be "right" for you right now. Healthy may include a cheat day of eating for you. Do it. If meeting new people is the best way for you to find a good life partner don't swear off being social because you are religious. Don't force yourself into online dating just because it is the "right" way to go for the majority. Do swear off dealing with people who offend your energies. We love to be right! When it comes to exercise and proper eating, "right" can mean so many different things for so many people. Everyone's psychology and body chemistry is different. Don't depend on conventional "right" and "wrong" to uncover your perfect blend. Keep as many options open as possible.

Remain open while figuring out what works for you. It leaves you the ability to make changes and be fluid. Don't quit dating, exercising, or investing. Make course corrections in the moment instead. Quit dating people who don't serve to elevate you. Invest in financial vehicles that fit who you are and are set for growth. Anchor the actions you take to align to the great whys in your life. If you do these things, when life happens, it will not knock you off of your path. You will have faith in your efforts. You will be taking guidance from your spirit in real time before choosing a path of action. Using the question "Does this serve me now?" brings the spotlight of awareness to the present. It helps to maintain a sense of purpose and focus. Decisions become easier to make. You can surf through life better if the only things that you consider partaking in are those that serve your greatest callings.

People are insistent on carrying the past into their present and then asking themselves why a future of familiar struggle is what they experience. This is equivalent to asking "I am doing almost exactly what I have always done, with the same energy, why am I not enjoying success?" Let's ask better questions: "What is a new way I can attempt to achieve my goal?" or "Who can I contact to share a new perspective with me, or a whole new approach?" "What new way of thinking do I have to adopt in order to shift my energy around this area of life?" There is always a way of thinking that serves you to get you to your goals. Hunt for it. Ask you "What energy will it take to be a match for the outcomes that I desire?" The hard part is putting your own customized approach together. In some things in life you just have not found your way yet. Be patient and compassionate with you. Give yourself grace. If you are committed and have a "no matter what" mentality you most definitely will make it. Learn to ask you better questions or hire someone to ask you wise questions. Life coaches and mentors change the game for people living intentional lives. They illuminate blind-spots. Blind-spots are the areas in life that you don't even know exist yet for you to work on. Once they are illuminated then you can put in the work to change them. They cut years off of the process towards success. Put together a group of people who think differently than you do and can serve as your own personal board of directors. Call on them when you are stuck. The sum of many minds focused on a single issue are greater than their efforts separately. Putting down the past makes room for future progress. Do not allow raw feelings and emotions to keep you on the sidelines too long when it comes to taking new actions. This is one of the true hindrances to doing the hard and super beneficial things that matter most.

By default, I naturally have a Type "A" personality. I am also a pessimist by default. My entire life I have had to work on creating a "positive" outlook on life. I had to navigate a lot of traumatic situations. I found out early on, that a negative outlook on life attracted more negatively for me to be annoyed by. I didn't have that luxury. I soon realized that better thinking was magnetic as well. What people call positive thinking is simply better thinking. In the midst of a dark childhood I always felt that better was in the cards for me. Even when there was no evidence that that was true. I had to steer my thoughts from an early age. I wanted a better life like I wanted air. Learning how to drive as a teenager and young adult pointed out how magnetic my dominant thoughts are.

If you have driven in the New York Tri-State area you will know that you can drive anywhere on the planet. It is that nerve wrecking. By the time I was driving age I was pretty sure that everyone in New York and New Jersey were terrible drivers. For my entire first year of driving I knew in my cells that I would be in a few car accidents. I expected to be in a wreck every time I turned the key in the ignition. Before long, I was hit by two other drivers, hit two deer, and involved in five accidents. It happened just as I expected it would. Two times deer ran in front of my car while I was driving on the highway. A driver decided he didn't like the jug handles in New Jersey and tried to make a direct left turn from a major highway right in front of me! He caused a five car pile-up that day. I remember the judge suspending his license. He totaled all five cars including mine. I am very lucky to be here to share these stories with you. One accident happened within the first two months that I bought my dream car. I now know that I had some latent feelings and beliefs of anxiety about receiving the things that I really wanted. I had a really hard time enjoying good things and I always felt as though they would be taken away. In my childhood they often were. I felt that I didn't deserve nice or good things. To tell you the truth I still sense a bit of a blockage there. If I am honest, as soon as I drove the car off of that lot I subconsciously expected to be in an accident.

EVERYTHING IS CONNECTED

I now believe that there is a governing and unseen force that is greater than us humans. Many people call it God. Others call it the Universe. I have even heard the scientific and learned among us call it a quantum field. In my eyes, this force responds to what we expect to get in life. You will get nothing more or nothing less than what you can imagine, believe, and expect. The prolonged thoughts and signals sent out from our minds attracts and repels matter. The overall vibration of your being attracts things, people, and circumstances. Expect being fit and amazingly healthy for a lifetime and it will come to pass. Your actions will bring it to pass. Expect to be broke and struggling with money you will get that too. Expect to be lonely and unhappy… You will find a way to be.

There is a snowball effect at play. Life has a funny way of giving you exactly what you strongly think and feel about most. Positive or negative it doesn't matter. Nature doesn't care about morality. Spend time training up your concentration on the things that you desire and you will find that they show up in reality. Inspiration becomes commonplace. Science now proves that our thoughts have actual measurable frequencies. You can never attract being thin while having fat thoughts. Set your private and personal expectations. Intentionally condition your own thinking. Society conditions us to think and believe against our own interests. Take an inventory of the most common and dominant thoughts in your head. Write them out. Recalibrate them as you see necessary. Set them to reach where you want to go. Allow them to fuel your goal setting efforts. Set your expectations and energy the same way that you would set GPS coordinates for a desired destination. Your inner self, deep down inside, will guide you to which actions you must take to reach your destination. Ignore any current mindset and mental chatter forged in the fires of survival and compliance with the status quo. The negative chatter is populating the google bar with the wrong search terms. Use your thoughts intentionally to create a life that you love.

Rebel against any negative default mental conditioning that was imposed upon you by your experience of life. Sometimes beliefs and ways of being that have served you in the past need to be discarded to make room for you to arrive where you have decided that you want to go next. Unlearning is hard. You need a clear and concise connection to the quantum field. When I stopped expecting car accidents to be a part of my reality I stopped being involved in car accidents. We all powerfully call various situations into our lives with our thoughts and the energy of who we are at a certain moment. The reason this true is because our actions, large and small, are fueled by our inner paradigms and beliefs. We have control over who we be and the thoughts that we entertain. Awareness of who you are now and what you are attracting is key. Can you think back to times in your life that you created the context of how things were and they continued happening exactly as you expected them to over and over again? Whether you perceive the outcomes as positive or negative this is not a coincidence. The place you are with your level of health and fitness is exactly as it should be. Where you are with your relationships mirror what you believe about yourself and others. Our bank accounts also show our true beliefs pertaining to money. With steady, focused, and repetitive work you can determine whether or not any situation will remain the way it has historically been. We each get to determine if it will change as well. From time to time, I think that we all get stuck in loops where outcomes that we don't like repeat. We can intentionally break the loop. Our dominant thoughts have a momentum. Always ask "What context or heart felt perceptions am I bringing to this area of life?" Be honest. Shine the spotlight of your awareness on your own thinking.

RELEASING THE PAST

Many people are crippled by the past. This eats at who you currently are. It blocks what you ultimately want to achieve in life. It blocks the view of your purpose for being. What is keeping you back from taking care of yourself, loving yourself, and doing what it takes create a life worthy of you? Make the choice now to take that power back. You are the director of the movie that is your life. A lot of people get out of shape or become overweight or obese when something tragic happens in their life. This tragic thing only happens once. Many people carry the hurt for years. I have been guilty of this myself. I have relived trauma over and over in my mind. I did it to the point that past trauma colored all of the things happening in my life. It became my new reality. Our minds cannot discern if something is happening or has already happened. Negative visualization has negative results in the body. Thoughts can make us release hormones that occur during fight or flight while we are sitting still in a chair. Our bodies are governed by hormones. This makes our thoughts even more important. When we play very real reruns of pain and tragedy. We feel the feelings that we felt when the bad occurrence took place. Nothing good ever comes from putting those type of energies out into the world. Strangely enough, some people get a payoff by playing the role of perpetual victim. Many people love the attention being a victim brings through life. They love the fact that responsibility is usually taken away from victims. They found it easier to get through life in this role.

Those people also end up carrying great burdens mentally that manifest physically. A death in the family only happens once. After a certain amount of time grieving, some people insist on perpetuating the death over and over in their mind. Putting yourself through the pain and torture of experiencing that loss isn't constructive. It is not my place to tell people how to heal from loss, but if you never do, then you may as well have died when the person that you love did. Living in a state of perpetual pain robs us of time and the quality of life. I am not saying you should be cold and callous, but do not lose your life because someone else did. That it is not the answer. You can choose to live powerfully in the face of life or death. Honor the person who left us by living well yourself. Spend the potential time that they did not get to enjoy. Making the choice to take ownership of the situations and mental processes we put ourselves through, can help us make better choices around who we become.

Feel all the feelings of the loss, failure, or adversity. Set a time to allow yourself to feel better. Whether it be twenty minutes or a year write the date and time out and adhere to healing by that time. When the time comes allow the feelings of loss and pain to go as the time you have designated has gone, never to return again. Setting a date to feel better doesn't mean that what you mourn was unimportant. It means that your life is too important to squander forever. At the "better" time you can then create a plan to move forward in a productive and powerful way.

What happens when we have ongoing happenings that resurrect traumatic feelings? This is one of the hardest situations to navigate. An example that comes to mind is racism. Although hundreds of black men aren't hanging from trees throughout the nation anymore as they were at the turn of the century, black and brown men are imprisoned at over three times the rate that their white criminal counterparts are. They are also shown killed in the streets by citizens and police alike, on an almost daily basis. This picks at the scab of the festering wound of racism in America. By constitutional law prisoners are modern day slaves. According to the prison policy Initiative by the Bureau of Justice Statistics per every hundred thousand white people, three hundred and eighty whites are incarcerated. For every hundred thousand black people two thousand two hundred and seven are incarcerated.

Trauma is activated over and over again by the existence of systemic racism. For generations in America black and brown men have been physically and psychologically affected by overt oppression. Now systemic oppression both psychologically and physically imprisons black men. It was James Baldwin who said, "To be black in America, and to be relatively conscious, is to be in a rage almost all the time." To this day in America the outcomes of generations of oppression still permeate society from education, housing, to the criminal justice system. Laws had to be passed in order to attempt to legally give black people footing. Laws rarely eradicate discriminatory practices on a day to day basis. Black men, who look like me, face a legacy of pain and discrimination that lingers from generational trauma. We must conform or be abused and imprisoned. "Comply or die" is the law of the land when it comes to policing black men.

Now with modern technology, footage pops up daily that confirms what blacks have always known in our communities. Black men and women are often treated with fear and disdain. Darker skinned Americans are not treated fairly. Police brutality is old news to us, but new to the eyes of the public. Healing is difficult with the environment as it is. Despite how hard it is I find that the answer in the face of ongoing assailants is to flex excellence. Being impeccable on as many fronts as possible has to be the answer. Being impeccable young black boys. Being impeccable family men, heads of household, and husbands is the burden that black boys and men must carry. No mediocrity or mistakes are allowed. That is until America becomes an anti-racism society. Anything else will not combat the discrimination that blacks face. Just existing is not an option for us. Whenever an unarmed black man is killed you will see that his past is brought up and any mistakes he's made put on display. Black men are the only Americans killed here and then asked to produce a resume to justify their right to live. The folly of youth is not afforded to young black men. They are tried as adults more than any other demographic. In the face of ongoing trauma causing circumstances, being the best version of yourself gives you a fighting chance. You get a shot at happiness and intentional living. When that tact fails then move. A change in environment can work miracles. Deciding to build yourself up to overcome obstacles on all levels is the only suitable answer. I willfully and vehemently avoided any situations where I could possibly have gotten into any type of trouble. I was lucky to be adopted by a woman who informed me at a very early age of how I'd be treated if I got in trouble with the law. That is one of the only reasons that I do not have a police record as a black man in America.

CHAPTER 14

DECISIONS DECISIONS DECISIONS

There is a great difference between choices and decisions. Many people make decisions instead of choices. They also make decisions when choices should be made. What's the difference? When making a choice, you have retained the option of pivoting. You can choose one thing and then choose a different course midstream. Choosing is fluid. Making a choice also implicates you as the chooser. When you make a decision, all other options are no longer able to be considered. The decision is given a life of its own. There is no coincidence that it usually takes a lot to overturn a decision once it is made. You will find that it is way easier to change your mind when you own up to making a choice. Decisions are overthrown in court. We are all allowed to make choices without reasons being attached to them. I defiantly chose and then decided to live a life of my own creation.

The suffix "cide" is in the word "decide". The same suffix as in suicide, homicide or pesticide. "Cide" means to kill. Using that word kills off possibilities and removes responsibility by the person who decided. Decisions are propped up by reasons and logic. Taking responsibility for who you are in all areas of life, is key to creating an expression of life that you want, and maintaining it. Decisions are usually made based on reasons and rob power and ownership from the decision maker. "I decided not go to the gym today, it was raining". "I chose not to go to the gym today." Many of us use choices where only decisions will do, and vice versa. Deciding to become a millionaire is a good thing. There is no wriggle room in it for not doing the necessary money management techniques. Assuming ownership over your choices will affect how and what you choose. Avoid giving the ownership of a path chosen, to a circumstance or reason, take total responsibility for it all. You should be the leader of your own life. Great leaders take responsibility whether they win or lose. Either way they earn respect. Decide to be fit. Respect the many choices you make in your mind in order to follow through on your decision consistently. The language you use is extremely important. Life happens in language. I will talk about this further in a later chapter.

The definition of insanity is doing the same thing over and over, hoping for different results. This is exactly what people do each year, during resolution season. A lot of people mentally live in the future when it comes to getting fit. Many times, they get tired of the process because physical results do not come fast enough. The question is: "Who am I being now that has my results hindered?"; "Will my current daily thinking get me closer to realizing my goals?" People say: "I will exercise when I get enough time", "Someday, I will have the time to cook and prepare food like I should", "Someday, I will hire a trainer or a personal chef". Someday is not a day of the week, it will never come. Putting off doing something now to do it in the future makes absolutely no sense. You cannot act in the future, you cannot act in the past. The only time you can take action is now. Change happens in an instant. It takes no time to mentally change a context or mindset. Even if you are slogging through a workout you feel tired, and are hating every second, it can be shifted. Imagine if in the middle of your routine, a camera crew walks in from a television network and promise to write you a check of ten thousand dollars upon completion of your routine. From that second on, will you be tired? Your entire being and demeanor will shift in seconds! That workout will magically become a pleasure and you will speed through it smiling. The mind has that type of driving force and power. Our health and longevity is worth far more than ten thousand dollars.

Getting to the point of knowing and believing is what takes the most time. In the moment you have decided to make the goal nonnegotiable, it is done! Letting go of comfort and embracing the feel of temporarily failing at a task is what takes the most time. It also takes time to accept that we deserve the great outcomes attached to the changes that we will make. It truly takes time for many people to get their actions to match their words. That is why reestablishing trust and integrity in oneself is such an important step to take. Take immediate action when excuses and limiting mindsets start to spring up. Even a small action can create motivation and momentum. Choose a word that empowers you, maybe even a workout statement slash persona, or chant that you will say in your head to make you take that first step. Choose a personal motto or mantra!

Change and transformation happen rapidly when you believe. It's time to be real enough with yourself to stop engaging in self sabotaging tactics that have been hardwired in the subconscious mind. In the instant you make a declaration to create something in your life, unseen forces start to move to make it happen. Your life will change to adapt to the new spiritual momentum. You are more than capable of achieving your goal. The desire wouldn't have even appeared to you if you weren't. Vocally declaring your word and using your pen to make it tangible, are the ignition button to taking new and sustained actions. In the very moment that you wrap your head around these concepts, you have created a spiritual shift and your body must follow. Preparing your mind, and spirit, is the main dish. Action is the seasoning that makes the dish of an epic life pop.

CONQUERING REASONS AND EXCUSES

"Whether you believe you can or cannot, you are right" ~ Confuscious

I went to the "Bodies Exhibition" in Atlantic City, New Jersey. Looking at the human body from just the point of view of its functions, as science does, you will be shocked and amazed at how complex and precise we are made. (I suggest that you see this exhibit wherever you can across the country.) In it, human cadavers were sliced, diced, dismantled, dissected and preserved down to the very thinnest visible microfiber of flesh, bone or other tissue. An entire human body was dissected in such a way that the neurons were extracted from the body, stained and preserved. You could see how intricately placed every single nerve ending was from fingertips to toe nails. From a physical standpoint, we are amazing creatures. Even though this is true, we are so much more than just our bodies. We humans have an awareness that sets us apart from other animals. Science tells us the functions of each and every organ in our body. We mostly know what each cell does and how each system and organ works together. We can outline how sensations and data are extracted from our surroundings processed, and how actions are taken based on how that information is processed. The frontier that remains uncharted is the study of the "I" we refer to every single day.

Our consciousness springing up as a result of the sum of all of our parts is largely unexplained. How does who you are as a conscious being experiencing life on a physical level, fit into the function of all of these moving parts that make up our bodies? This is what we have been looking at in this book. We are looking to become aware, conscious in order to powerfully seize control of your own mind, body and soul. Awakening our total beings to take action consciously and deliberately in order to create life is important. How does the part of you that experiences life and cannot be scientifically described affect the look and feel of your body? Experiencing great health and abundance is a life-long process of inward and outward learning. Are we consistently applying the findings and things we believe will enrich life for ourselves and the world? One of the things that enriches life is the physical use of the body. The answers to these questions are the answers that alter lives. Give time to own the ability to slow down, quiet yourself enough to identify and take notice of who we you really are in the face of life. Discernment of what actions serve us in this physical realm becomes easier when you look within to tap into inner wisdom. That wisdom will allow us to expertly navigate the external circumstances of life. We must make the effort to stay connected with the inner wisdom that we all possess. That inner wisdom will fuel efforts we need to habitually take. Doing the things that tend to our dreams regardless of circumstances becomes easier. Refreshing our sentences, reciting great affirmations and mindsets that serve you, get you plugged back into conscious thought. It's important to stay connected to the energy that connects us to our dreams. As children we were pure consciousness. The how is an after afterthought. That connection to consciousness has largely been compromised for so many of us over the years. Get back to it!

We create thoughts in milliseconds and can perform complex activities in the supercomputer called the brain. Human beings are amazing creations. Here are some powerful actions that you can sprinkle on your life. These seasonings will mentally and physically create an environment where the possibility of a strong fit healthy body, financial freedom, and beautiful professional and personal relationships occur.

THE SEASONING

- Live your word.
- When you wake up, choose to live from a place of intentional creation - Recognize your internal greatness. - Don't default to a place of survival. - Trust in your own inner strength and the God within over external circumstance.
- Make it a priority to tell yourself that you are becoming the "better" version of yourself with every passing minute and live into that reality.
- Take actions consciously from a place of peace instead of turmoil, fear and chaos. You will begin to make amazing choices.
- Define the benefits of living your dreams with a vision that you can refer to often. Don't compare your life to other people's life.
- Embrace learning.
- Always remember that you are not your mind! Your mind is your tool to use to create a life worthy of you.

The focus should be placed on creating a life worthy of the awareness within you. A space where abundance, contribution, and meaningful relationships thrive. Know that your external environment and circumstance are dictated by your internal state of being. Gaining control and awareness around any area of life just takes the will to do so and practice of new ways of thinking. Be a person who is grateful for all the things that have occurred and will occur. Pay special attentions to the things that show up to serve you. Be aware that anything holding you back from achieving the body, finances, or relationships can be figured out.

CELEBRATE YOUR WINS

A powerful step that you can take that subliminally grants you trust and power within yourself is celebrating your successes. Become allergic to your own bull shit and excuses. On the other hand, make sure that you celebrate and acknowledge your wins. When you hear your brain conjuring up reasons to not take action on celebration, stop those thoughts in their tracks before it develops momentum. The more times you keep your word, and do what you say you will, the more times that you will create progress and momentum in all areas of your life. Celebrate the discipline in your life. We avoid doing this to the peril of our dreams. Some people are scared to actually win.

They are afraid to be rich, healthy, and happy. They don't know themselves in that light. They are afraid to be stretched past the struggle. Get to know you in a different light. Tell a new story. Every tiny step that you grow forward must be acknowledged. You will believe in yourself and follow through with worthy initiatives in life. The difficulty that you will experience in being present and hearing the internal wisdom within you will become less and less. Living intentionally becomes easier and easier when progress is acknowledged. Failure will become less and less part of your reality as well as you focus on progress.

When you say to yourself "I am going for a run at 5pm today", you will know it is done before you leave your home for work in the morning. It becomes easier to pass on the chips and choose an apple at lunch instead. Celebration makes you responsible. It becomes easier to save and invest that five hundred dollars monthly. Think about it. When you realize that you are making progress you should already feel yourself becoming healthier and richer. In reality you are! When you do get a workout in or live your promise to yourself you should feel proud that you triumphed over laziness and procrastination. Whenever you take a new action that you would normally not have, celebrate that too. You've achieved what many want to achieve and few actually do. You are shifting! Do something that you love doing for you in celebration. When you confidently choose to ask for that promotion you deserve, and you get it... Celebrate! When you mustered up the courage to take action on an intimidating project, don't dismiss or overlook this either. The subtle recognition of internal growth is so necessary. It invites more new action. No one will see it to be able to pat you on the back but you will. Do it! Most type "A" personalities never take the time to celebrate and savor a win. We mostly say "Okay that was great. This is done. What's next?"

Acknowledgement and celebration of who we are, becoming holds us to higher level of achievement in the future. Don't be scared to be a winner later. When you fail you will notice it. Do the same with your wins. Shine the spotlight of awareness on both sides of the equation. Learn from the losses and propel yourself forward by internalizing wins and progress big or small. Get to know you as a winner. Strengthen the neural connections associated with taking new actions and reaping favorable results. Practice winning.

We are for some reason hard wired to acknowledge the failures we encounter in life and ignore accomplishments. Progress should be acknowledged always. Fulfillment is elusive without realizing the gravity of accomplishment. Your child can have all A's on his/her report card but the C+ in social studies will stand out. We ask them "What happened here?" Face it, we are a detrimentally critical bunch of creatures. Acknowledge every small step taken in the right direction. Doing this builds up self-image and belief. Over time you develop a self-image that is allergic to being stagnant and addicted to the dopamine release experienced when you grow into a match for a version of life that you've intentionally created. Doing things that are difficult (for you) but beneficial adds fuel to your forward progress and reestablishes trust and belief in you. This is one of the powerful antidotes to creating excuses and reasons to quit or fail. Goals acquired should be celebrated and seen as a symbol of progress around who you are becoming. There is absolutely no reason, doubt, or circumstance that can stop people who truly believe in themselves. Self-efficacy is so important. It is the faith in oneself in their ability to accomplish a thing. If you believed that you could not fail what would you attempt to create? What kind of life would you set your sites on? Who would you help?

REASONS AND EXCUSES ACTIVITY

ACTION: Get a piece of paper and write down something that you want to achieve. Write "I want to get a six pack" for instance. Divide the paper in two halves. Label one side "Reasons why I want it." and the other side "Reason's why I cannot have it". Take two minutes and write the reasons why you want the six pack: "I will look and feel younger", "I like the way they look", "Others like the way they look", "I need a smaller waist", "I love being able to see my toes." The list goes on. Take another two minutes to write down the reasons why you feel you cannot achieve this goal: "It is too hard to diet", "no one in my family has one", "I do not have great genes", "I love sugar too much", "I hate doing abs" or "I'm too old". Take four minutes to write out pro and cons. Tally up how many reason's and excuses you've created not to have a six pack. Could you list more excuses or reasons if you had ten more minutes?

The point of that action exercise is to point out that whether noble or terrible, that reasons and excuses are easily pulled out of thin air. They come from absolutely nowhere and do not take long to create. Many people create entire lives by only consulting reasons or excuses. In my opinion it is lazy, weak and unintentional. We set a goal and then either qualify it or disqualify ourselves from achieving it, by consulting reasons or excuses that we pulled from thin air. Most don't consult deep within themselves to come up with an answer to the question: "How much do I want this?" and then definitively declare "I will have it" or "I won't have it". We then consult reasons, excuses, and circumstances as to why we can't have what we want, instead of relying on a "whatever it takes" mindset to fuel our progress. We have been programmed to readily allow the mind to talk us out of achieving exceptional things. Most of us do not take time to decide whether or not certain actions align with who we seek to become. The real truth of the matter is, that you can randomly take any one or two self-manufactured reasons or excuses and operate from them. In the end, regardless of what you choose, the situation will turn out. Since any random reason you create can work out, why not consciously choose to take action on things that empower and inspire your soul? Majority of the time, why not select choices that thrill you and spark you?

SOULSET

Living an exciting life, and maintaining that energy is great fuel for self-discipline. Nothing moves without discipline. The actions and goals that are aligned with who you are, and who you want to become, is where self-discipline is naturally in large supply. When is the last time you had to struggle with self-discipline doing something that you love? Better yet, when was the last time that you were doing work that was greater than you? Work so aligned with your soul, that you felt as though you were being used by a power greater than yourself? Did you need extra motivation to do it? I have never struggled with staying disciplined when it comes to helping people realize their own potentials. I love teaching, learning, experimenting, and sharing in order to leave others better off than I met them. I didn't know it at the time, but the major driving force behind me becoming one of the best, world-renown personal trainers and life strategists had a lot to do with me living into my soulset of "better".

After a long time of navigating life as a child who was abandoned and abused, I temporarily gave up on caring for other people. I was in survival mode most of my life. I was angry most of my life. I didn't really care for or trust other people. I hated collaboration. It took me experiencing many years of consistent love and trust given by a woman who didn't give birth to me, to help me begin to believe in humanity again. After a lot of introspection, self-development, study, and willpower I arrived at the conclusion that since I had undergone such a dark and ugly childhood that I would search out and become a part of the "better" in the world. "Better", specifically pertaining to humanity. I wanted everything around me to be better. I needed myself to be better. I desired that others become their version of better. Growing up I hated my environment. I hated the lost state of the people in the ghettos that I lived in. I hated the despair, the drugs, the anger, and the feeling of lack that saturated every orifice of my existence. I also hated that at fourteen when my mother moved us just forty minutes away, into a middle classed white town that none of that existed. All of those environmental constrictions to happiness were absent in the lily white town just across the bridge. A history of being precluded from resources and being heavily policed didn't exist there.

There was breathing room to live, grow, and flourish as a human being if you wanted to. That right existed freely! For the first time, I could afford to think about healing. This lead to me helping not only myself but others as well. I vowed to be a part of helping others find their "better" while actively hunting for and creating my own. My soul became set on doing it. See, focusing on "better" can be seen as frivolously being optimistic. For me, having hope and becoming internally fueled to change wasn't optional. I would have went clinically insane due to harboring the wrong thoughts. Everything surrounding me in my old reality was horrific. If I continued to allow my environment to run my show I could have easily become a monster.

Is there a better way of serving people than aiding them in their personal quests to overcome the age old struggle against obesity and unhealthiness? I don't know, but that is where I started. Start where you are and move towards your goals. I discovered that passion in the military at age seventeen. Helping others with difficult and personal work, that on the surface, did not immediately yield tangible results, was helping me with my own personal growth. It actually forced me to put my health and mental wellbeing first. That was an immense struggle. I was used to being put last, by society, foster parents, and the community around me. I was very comfortable putting myself last in my own life. I had to work hard to overcome that tendency. I still work on this now. Having this tendency helped me to connect with my clients. They were usually those shepherds among us who were doing the same. They neglected caring for their own bodies and their health. It never made the list. Although the exact stimulus isn't the same, the human emotions experienced as a result of personally adverse circumstances are universal. Abandonment and neglect can be felt by a child who has both parents. It can be felt by a wife. It can be felt collectively by a people, as it is felt in many black communities in America. It was felt by me. I started living according to my soulset by helping others attain positive change within their own bodies. A soulset is acknowledging that the forces that created all things actually wants to work through you and your existence. It is a prime directive. Our soulset usually puts us in a position of service to others. Surrendering to that call is what grants liberation and undying internal motivation. Lean into that call no matter what it looks like. You will find fulfillment. Our life's journey (however ugly or easy) often prepares us to work in accordance with our soulset and our calling. It requires being ego less and open to being used (by God or higher powers) to move life forward for others on this planet in either a large or small way.

All of the hardships of my life prepared me to live into alignment with my soulset of helping people locate and realize their version of better. Growing up and moving from foster home to foster home I got an awesome glimpse into the good, bad, and ugly of humanity. I was a pro at observing and deconstructing human behavior by age six. I had to be. I was protecting and looking out not only for myself but an asthmatic younger brother as well. My brother and I's very survival depended on that skill as we navigated our journey. At a very young age I saw and experienced a plethora of human emotions. Most of them negative. I experienced all emotions in HD clarity from compassion, fear, frustration, loss, complacency, promiscuity, anger, and hate. I got to see first-hand what neglect and a lack of resources can do to American communities. I also dealt with both of these in my life as an individual. I was neglected by my both biological parents and society at-large. I grew up feeling like I was "other". I felt I didn't belong anywhere, and that there was something very wrong with me and extremely right with me as well.

My entire ghetto community was filled with abandoned buildings, crack heads, and crack houses. The country abandoned us and showed us what they felt our worth was every day in both subtle and not so subtle ways. As a kid I knew that being black, poor, and parentless wasn't a winning lottery ticket. It was a reflection of how the nation felt about our community. The filth and graffiti in the hood further cemented what we were supposed to think of ourselves as residents of the hood. The fact that it remained for decades, even centuries, shows how the government felt about us as well. I witnessed and remembered how even the cops avoided our cries for help. I powerfully identified with helping people who were good at neglecting themselves as well. My soulset of helping people realize their version of "better" was realized in me learning personal training, life coaching and strategizing the achievement of life goals. It just felt right. Following the work that makes your soul feel awesome, is our most important work. This is the work that has potential to transform the planet. Helping others realize potential and their versions of "better" while seeking my own "better", every single day, is my work. When I am doing this work with people whether speaking, leading trainings, or working as a life-strategist, leadership coach, and consultant nothing else matters to me. I am in bliss! When I am lifting weights I feel that same adrenaline rush. The feeling of belonging that I felt in this kind of work was like nothing else I have ever felt.

I created the word "soulset" to explain the directive from my soul. The directive that kept me faithful moving towards doing whatever it took to assist myself and others in acquiring our version of "better". When I am traveling to enjoy some relaxation and see the many beautiful cultures across that globe I do not need a shot of motivation to get my bags packed and get my ass on a plane. I do not need extra help to get up out of bed and do the work that earns me money to be able to survive this system that we live in. When you are tapped into a soulset no one needs to push you or motivate you. Motivation is manufactured internally. You find it easy to stay the course. No matter how challenging the road becomes, if you are living according to your soulset, you remain inspired and divinely connected to God, universe, or whatever you call the thing that created all things. Our talents become the physical tools that we can rely on to help the God in us be expressed in our actions.

Passion, as well as the divinity in you, must always be consulted when setting goals. Logic, excuses, and reasons must also play a part in your decision making process. Use both so that you will be focused on achieving worthy goals. Selecting worthy big picture goals that excite you and scare you a little bit is key. So many mess up and waste huge amounts of energy, money, time and other resources due to selecting goals that society says are important. They haven't consulted with themselves on the deepest most powerful levels of their being and consciousness. They work really hard and achieve the goal, just to find that the reality of having hit said goal did nothing for them on the inside. Worse yet, if they had to hurt others in order to achieve them.

Misaligned goal setting is the cause for so much unnecessary stress and struggle. Society subliminally programs so many of our wants and desires. We must guard our minds and the thoughts that we entertain. It's a necessity to deep dive within and defiantly do what you find on the inside. Discern what was implanted by the external world and what is directed from the wise observer within. It takes tapping into a deeper part of who we are as humans. Not only will you find purpose and passion when you look there, you will find self-discipline to do whatever needs doing in your life. Those who can't do this work end up working from a paradigm populated with reasons and excuses that others have implanted there. Reasons and excuses that other people have indoctrinated into their subconscious is what they work from. Defy the motives that society has implanted in us.

The power that reasons and excuses have is that they conjure up new crops of thoughts and ideologies that strengthen their position. These new thoughts and ideas complement the original reason or excuse. It mentally becomes easy to justify inactivity or inconsistency. It can also become easy to justify taking new and powerful action. Over time, subconsciously a reason or excuse can mature into a belief that is regarded as a truth. This is a risky thing. Have you ever had a single thought and then found that similar thoughts are manufactured about it, in rapid succession in your mind? Have you ever had one bad thought and then noticed that multiple bad thoughts start building up on top of it? Have you noticed your energy shift for the better as the result of a single good thought? Worrying starts with one simple thought that escalates on to another one and then escalates to another one far worse, causing stress and anxiety. Thoughts have a snowball effect

Worries serve no purpose whatsoever. They are psychological, physiological, mentally negative responses to actions that have not even occurred in reality. Worry, is a negative stress-filled joyride through the magical "Land of Make Believe"! There are far more rewarding investments of your time, energy, and effort. It is easier to be at peace with the idea that "things will turn out how they turn out". Believe that you get to have a say in how things turn out with the actions you take. Believe and trust in your own strength. Know that you will survive. Surviving is the worst it will get. Know that a reason, an excuse, or even a worry can be manufactured out of thin air. If you function from those three alone, you will have outcomes that don't necessarily serve you.

Self-discipline is best fueled by purpose and passion. They are internal and personal qualities. They are super important when considering whether to create any outcome in your life. They also require that you be connected with what internally lights you up and brings you happiness and fulfillment. Self-awareness is so important. Think about and take ordered actions for the sole purpose of discovering what makes you feel fulfilled. Consider both your mindset and your soulset. Straight lines and curves govern our universe. These two pair together nicely. A pairing of the structured, stiff and logical with wavy creativity and emotion is needed for balance. Keep eyes on what intellectually stimulates and satisfies you as well as what supplies purpose and fulfillment to you on the inside. Feeling extraordinary at the very essence of your being should also be a paramount goal when evaluating thoughts and actions worth taking.

Can you become more un "reason" able person when it comes to intentional living? Are you willing to become a person who does not only function from reasons or excuses drummed up in the mind? Will you allow true power and wisdom from inner guidance system to move you? Your inner being (the part of you observing this show called life) must have a say in the creation of a life worth living. State what you want to accomplish and choose to acknowledge only actions and choices that serve in the completion of that goal. Scary and thrilling goals work best. They cause you to feel. They tickle your soulset. Practice operating from less reasons and excuses. Teach and condition yourself to become fine with choosing something because you choose it.

Choose to do something because it lights you up inside. Then decide to be unreasonable in your pursuit of getting that something done. Too many of us are living without the spark in us that we were born with. Somewhere along the line in our journey from child to adult we have had imagination and true excitement beaten out of us by society. Not all of us have, but many of us have. That childlike wonder is lost in so many lives. Choose working out and healthy living in your life, not only because of the benefits that you can list. It may be easy to lose sight of those benefits if the results are not coming as fast as you think they should. Choose to live that way simply because you can imagine and feel how blissful it would be to embrace health and well-being as you age. Do it because you are on a constant quest of life where you focus on "better". Never settle for less than better health, better laughs, better self-expression, better relationships or better finances. All of that comes as a result of focusing on better thoughts. Dare to enjoy an entirely better expression of living.

No reasons or excuses needed. "Better" can be a soulset that you embrace. It has moved me a very long way through life, with an unrelenting power. It can fuel your entire existence as well. That way, while working, if results come right away or not, you will still adhere to the process of living healthy and being fit. Choosing to live a life unreasonably and intentionally makes it near impossible for you to fail due to outside circumstances. It takes a clear and powerful connection to your soul. What has been your soulset up until this point? What powerful undying directive moves the observer in you? Have you run from it for years? Do you live towards it every day? Mindset usually gets all of the love but #soulsets matter too. What unwavering theme has your soul set for you to be living? Chances are that you haven't consulted the core of who you are yet. This is necessary to be able to mentally process what your soulset is. A soulset is your core directive for living. It is what you are here on the planet to do. It is your function. It is your soul's agenda. Your authentic purpose for being here on the planet resides here. Are you aware of yours? The vision that you hold and the emotions that you get to experience as a result of aligning with your soulset is powerful. Just thinking about it will pull you forward through all odds. My soulset is to spark "better" in others. It is the agenda that I am here to move forward in humanity. I am here to be a catalyst for "better" thinking, feeling, and doing for myself and others. I am here to uphold "better" treatment of those who are disenfranchised through no fault of their own. This includes those who are and have been abandoned. Children and youth signify potential and possibility for the entire human species in my opinion. They represent the possibility of "better" for me. I work hard to move the needle forward for those among us who society has cannibalized and abandoned. You do not need reasons to fuel your continued efforts when working in alignment with your soulset. You trample on excuses when your soulset is tapped into. Your imagination opens up to help you find solutions. Remain emotionally tethered to your soulset. Anyone who's accomplished anything great in human history has been unreasonable and purpose filled. They concentrated and embraced discipline. They lived in accordance with their soulset.

I discovered mine by taking a true inventory of all of the things that lit me up and excited me in life. I had very few of those things as a child. As an adult I accumulated more. Somewhere along the line I mentally decided that I hated my circumstances enough to seek out better. Even though as an abandoned foster kid raising my brother, as we hopped from home to home, I didn't feel worthy of "better." My soul consistently and quietly called me towards seeking "better" not only for myself but eventually for others. That looked like me assisting some of the planet's most successful people to accomplish things they thought impossible in an area of their lives that they neglected... Themselves and their bodies! Lightning struck me on a cellular level the first time I got a chance to lead one of these driven professionals to better health. It struck as I lead a group of soldiers through a training exercise or a workout. It struck when I was asked to do a leadership presentation for my first executive group. It strikes again powerfully today as I lead leadership workshops for disadvantaged youth in foster care. This very minute it fills me as I write the words to this book. I have learned to follow my soulset and my bliss. Starting in dismal circumstances helped me to embrace being a light to others and an access to their "better". Better was the only direction that I could go where I started from. Perfection wasn't the directive. Striving for the "better" in everything and experiencing self-expression was the common thread. Fit bodies better expressed who the humans that I helped were.

CHAPTER 15

DEVELOPING SELF DISCIPLINE

Yesterday's "Crazy" becomes today's "Brilliant" when people diligently choose to be un "reason" able in the pursuit of a worthy goal. If reason is relied upon alone it will always inform you of how to stop the pursuit of a dream. You will be shown reasonable limitations. Be unreasonable when it comes to following dreams and living into experiences that excite and thrill you. Discipline is the tequila in the margarita named success. You can't experience the greatness of the drink without tequila. There were many reasons why people believed that humans would never fly. That did not stop the Wright brothers from attempting to construct a plane until they succeeded. The prospect of flying through the air thrilled and consumed them. Harriet Tubman was so unreasonable in leading slaves from Maryland to Philadelphia by foot in the eighteen hundreds. Freedom for her people lit her up and thrilled her to the core. Her soulset was "freedom"! Tap into the same human drives and internal power that the greats before us used to achieve great personal success and transformation of other human lives. All human beings have this ability. We all can access self-discipline. As a matter of fact we all have used it to create outcomes in the past. Decide what major driver or soulset will move you. Listen for it in the still of your mind and act from it now! Self-discipline is one of our most powerful tools. Excitement makes it accessible. When is the last time you have truly been excited to accomplish something? Here is how you can build up your discipline and willpower. Practice it every day. Do everything with your full attention attached to it and see it through to completion. Start with small simple daily activities. Something like having breakfast can become one of those discipline muscle builders. *EXAMPLE 1. Cook a healthy breakfast. 2. Eat your food without doing anything else. No going on your phone, no watching TV. Just be present with your food. Chew it thoroughly. 3. Wash dry and put away your dishes. 4. Acknowledge that breakfast is complete.* Do this with as many things as possible, all day long. Complete tasks thoroughly, better than good, and to the best of your ability. Remain present and complete things in great detail. People who can consistently complete small things in disciplined fashion build a reputation of capability, focus, and strength, with themselves. They soon complete projects. They go on to use their pumped up muscle of discipline that they forged day by day, month by month, and year over year to accomplish things that others deem impossible. My mother forged discipline in me by giving me chores and seeing that I completed them to the best of my ability every time.

Know that it will cost you some mental energy to clear the obstacles that will arise along your journey to developing willpower. Structure supports willpower and willpower will set you free. It is important to set your top five priorities for the day and live into them daily. Set them from the night before. Know that you are greater than any distraction or adversity that you will encounter along the way. As of today you have 100 percent track record in making it through hardships. Action keeps that momentum going. It is especially easy to work from desire and purpose when the mind is clear and free of distraction. Now that you are aware that excuses and reasons are manufactured out of thin air, it should be less likely that you allow one of them to derail the goals you'd like to realize. No outside circumstance should trump your inner resolve. Leave no room for what other people say to run your life. Struggles associated with money, or any outside things cannot stop your progress. Turn up the volume on your inner voice and mute the outside world when it comes to affecting change in your own life. Remember to make a practice of meditation. Meditation is not about stopping all thought. It is about stopping to tap into and gain perspective on your thoughts. Meditation is about slowing them down to be able to see them, evaluate, and release them. Gaining perspective over the flow and quality of your thinking gives you power. I can't stress the importance of trying meditation apps and Youtube videos that help us (the type A intellectual, introverted, thinkers) to meditate. They have been very instrumental for me and my clients. There are some of us for whom it is extremely hard to adopt a meditation practice. Meditation was impossible to me in the beginning. I lasted a sad three minutes before deciding that it sucked and "wasn't for me". I stuck with it though. In the last 10 years my life the fulfillment levels have been immensely transformed for the better as a result of diligent work.

The surface things that stop us when adopting life changing habits are a lack of time, money, motivation, discipline, lack of faith, fear, laziness, etc. Whatever your go-to drug is for making it "OK" to quit on a dream, make a brave and conscious choice to override it now. Reconnect with your prime directive for living. Every creative dream and desire within you is a plea from the soul, universe, force around us, or God for you to make it into a reality. We should all give those inclinations more power in our lives and give less power to outside circumstances. A sound body aids and empowers all dreams a person can set.

THE LIFEBLOOD OF TRANSFORMATION

"You are in the driver seat of your life, now!"

Hopefully, at this point of the book, you are more aware of what has been going on within you on a subconscious level. You have hopefully identified one or more of the default mindsets in place that have historically prevented you from continuously taking action around what matters most to you. We uncovered that there are some things that you "don't know" that you "don't know" that have been in place that may cause you to self-sabotage your growth as well. You know that in order to become aware of those things, you have to interact with others and learn from their perspectives. You have been made aware of the value of practicing meditation and approaching tasks and priorities from a peaceful mindset. You may have also discovered that you can switch mindsets (at will) that cater to you succeeding from moment to moment in whatever endeavor that you want to pursue. You may have also differentiated your higher-self from the crazy unpredictable and reckless yet creative super tool that is your conscious mind. You even have a powerful new word "soulset" to describe a prime directive that tethers you to meaning and fulfillment in life.

You know that you are not your mind. You also have been exposed to the importance of the concept that you are who you declare yourself to be. You have been made aware that no matter how real a reason or excuse may seem, it was pulled out of thin air and it does not have to be your reality or truth until you accept it as such. This logic even holds true for findings from experts. You also know that taking action leads to motivation. You are the sole controller of your life. None of this information will make a difference in your body or life without the following tools in place. The following things are the things that separate people who simply *know* what to do to and those who actually *get it done*. Nothing feels as good as "done" does. Knowledge indefinitely remains potential and becomes power only when action is poured over it. Think of a Sundae. A sundae ain't a sundae until you pour that chocolate syrup on top. You will never push past pain and preconceived set limitations. It does not matter if you have the means to achieve a thing if you lose sight of your why. Your why (soulset, prime directive) will help you in tough times to hold onto integrity.

THE POWER OF INTEGRITY

Integrity is everything! The definition that I like best for "integrity" is: A person, place, circumstance, or thing that is whole, complete and undiminished. If something does not have all of its parts it cannot be said to have integrity. Integrity is either present or not. If a four legged chair has only three legs it has no integrity. It is not whole and complete and undiminished. It may still stand, but it lacks integrity. If you work out on a weight bench and it missing two screws, it has no integrity. It still may function but it is not whole and complete. It is weaker than it could be. How many of us live lives just like this? We do not lack integrity due to any physical handicap. We lack integrity due to harboring limiting mindsets, beliefs, and perceptions that have been consciously or subconsciously turned into truths. The lack of integrity is caused by the lack of importance we place on our inner worlds. Broken promises we've made to ourselves cause the most damage. Our inner worlds create our outside realities. Unfortunately, many times the world we live in does not make it easy for integrity to thrive. It should always be that what a person says and what that person does matches to the letter. Integrity is absolute. Many of us live, work, and play in communities where it is okay for people to be reckless with their word. It is tolerable in our society for circumstances to have more power than our words or the promises that we make. This is not true for those of us who stand out and regularly win. We reside in a physical world where all that we are is our word. Yet, we play with it like it is unimportant. Standing by our word should also include standing when unfavorable circumstances occur. There is immense power in your word if it is laced with integrity. The lack of integrity in our society has truly altered many things in our culture today. Society says life is a blessing but a struggle. It says, in many ways, that you are not good enough. It encourages us to be content with merely surviving and getting by. It doesn't promote being used for a greater purpose that benefits the whole. It is important to rebel against popular thinking in order to maintain your integrity.

You made it to this book and have read this far because deep down you desire not to be affected by the world, you'd rather happen in the world. Without integrity that can't happen. Nowadays people give their word to take actions they have no intentions of seeing through. We have to fill out legal forms and contracts to conduct both personal and business deals nowadays to ensure parties keep their word. Employers hook up cameras all over the workplace to check and make sure that employees work honestly. Divorce is at an all-time high in America. Obesity is the number one preventable cause of death. Many times obesity is the physical manifestation of broken promises that someone makes to themselves. The days when "Yes" and a firm handshake meant something are long behind us. Integrity is power, the power to make things move just because you said so. Why would you throw that away with reckless abandon? If you say you will be somewhere at eight AM, you should be there at eight AM. If you declare you will make four visits to the gym in a week, the front desk person should see you four times that week. If you borrow money and promise to pay it back in a certain time frame, you should pay that debt on time, possibly with interest. Do you know any people who have great integrity? They are people who can say they will make something happen out loud with no idea of how it is going to happen, and they get it done every time. That is you.

People call them lucky. When these people speak, others listen, and the world wonders why their lives appear enchanted. When these people speak, others respect them and believe in their word. They have an unsaid leverage with people, they have an edge. Most importantly, these people respect and believe in themselves to accomplish anything. If you do what you say you will do all of the time, you will stand out and people will truly take notice. Regardless of what area of life it is people will respect you. You will also notice the amount of times you have to apologize for shortcomings will be greatly diminished. Getting into the best shape of your life simply because you said so, is a thing that takes a great amount of integrity and power.

Hundreds of years ago, a person's word was held in very high regard. You can see it in the language they used. Your words could get you challenged to a duel. There was a great chance then that you'd die in a duel that day. People spoke in absolute terms. They made pledges, oaths, declarations, and stood by their words. They lived and died by the words they spoke. The power of the being was expanded exponentially. People took a stand and action from their purpose. Things were created in that time period that we consider modern marvels. Wholeness and completeness around the things that you say are important. Integrity always equals power. People with integrity are able to create by simply uttering the words. Words have absolutely no strength without integrity. There is no trust when integrity is lost. Death of self-belief is a tragedy. People lie to themselves more than anyone else can lie to them in their lifetime. A breach in integrity will always result in a breach in power and success. Any area of life lacking integrity will experience cyclical breakdown. It is important never to hold anyone to a higher standard of integrity than you can demonstrate. Work towards being impeccable.

Most people make promises with the greatest intentions. Intentions alone never bring results. Have you ever heard people say after getting a present they don't particularly like "It was the thought that counts? The reason that is true is that the giver enforced the intention with the action of giving. Even if the present wasn't a good fit. Good intentions can be found a dime a dozen but the follow-through is the most potent part of a declaration. Intentions actually make the people who created them feel good. Too many people give out their word and make promises with sincerity but without aligned actions. We need to make these promises to ourselves and others with a sense of integrity and commitment behind it. The action taken makes the intention real. The difference between sincerity and integrity is huge. One hints to the intentions that a person has and the other hints to the commitment and follow-through to completion that a person is willing to implement. People who make a commitment are people who will not fail to reach their goal, no matter what comes their way. They have consciously chosen to enter an obligation and become dedicated to making their word come true at all costs. This is a trait I found in every single successful person I've met in my life. I have met and worked intimately with thousands. In the majority of their lives, they exude extremely high integrity.

ACTION: Take time to briefly reflect on one area of life that works exactly as you like it.

1. Write out three major accomplishments that you saw through to the end.
2. Write down one area in life that needs improvement now. Write three major steps that you know that you should take but have not taken in that area yet
3. Set completion dates for doing what you know that you should in the weaker areas.
4. Finally, tell two people what you are working towards accomplishing. Use the attentions of others to hold you to integrity.

INTEGRITY RENEWAL

In the areas that work in your life, you have an abnormally high amount of integrity. In those that don't work, integrity is low or your starting line in that area of life is further from success than you could imagine. When you fail do not despair. You still do have an access to power. Integrity can be renewed. Most of us don't inherently know this but it is true. That is why so many quit when the road gets bumpy and their integrity suffers. They mess up and then believe that "the game is lost so why even continue to try?" It may be hard to do but most of us can earn a clean slate to begin again with renewed energy.

The first step is to renew integrity in a lagging area of your life is to admit to yourself where your integrity has been broken. When trust is completely severed with another person or even yourself a huge action displaying trustworthiness must take place to mend it. You can never fool yourself. There are some simple ways you can take action around reestablishing your integrity to yourself. One of the first things you can do is start to reestablish your integrity with people around you. If there is anything you promised to do for someone, or anything that you promised to give to anyone and have not done so, go back and make good on your promises.

No matter what it is, no matter how big or how small it is, make it happen. Even if it has been a long time restore your integrity. Remember to acknowledge each completion. Notice the feeling of completion you feel when you go back and do what you said you would in life. Notice how the people react when you show up with a promise fulfilled. Many times people will look at you as if you are crazy. Many will tell you not to worry about it. It is a very good way to have people in your life regard you in a new manner. Eventually, you will too. If you are now in the process of taking responsibility for your physical health and your life, it is great to have people seeing you this way as well. It holds us to a higher standard, and helps us to become our word. Become your word and set the bar high with the words you use.

Impeccable integrity drastically changes things and relationships that you are involved in. As far as health and fitness are concerned, promises you make to yourself and keep will alter your body significantly. Integrity can help you shift the historical state of your body. Can you imagine your body miraculously starting to change simply because you said it would and all of your actions automatically mirrored this new reality? The power of your word can be that strong. Integrity is the access to true power and will lead to the physical manifestation of greatness within you. Since you actually intend on fulfilling your promises, you will find that you give your word to far less situations. Learn to make less promises. This is one of those cases where less is more. People will respect it.

Integrity is not something you can gain and keep intact without remaining vigilant with it. We each can feel when we are out of integrity. Babies can tell. We just get really good at lying to ourselves as we age. It's important to remind yourself that you are human and that there will be times where you will fail. Remember that both failure and feedback serve as the breakfast of successful people. So eat it and get right back up. If you tell yourself you will go to the gym at six o' clock, six o'clock rolls around and you do not make it, recognize you have failed. Do not ignore it, own up to it. You will undoubtedly start to justify your lack of integrity. Briefly explore the excuses or reasons you gave in to and notice if it is something that you fall victim to often. If you consciously choose to skip this workout session, take a second to notice that as well and your reasons for doing so. Process what you feel. The worst thing you can do is have your integrity blindly compromised by you. Acknowledge the break in your integrity. Set a time for you to get over the feelings of failure. Not acknowledging the failure, or feeling bad about it for too long is how one missed workout becomes a week of missed workouts. The key is to not let breaks in integrity, especially when it comes to investing in your wellbeing, mindlessly pile up. Check yourself before you wreck yourself. Feel the inadequacy. Feel the pain of distrust in you and then release them. Wipe your slate clean so that you can make a new contract with yourself. A contract that is not built on the failure and dirty energy of your past break in integrity.

Deal with them swiftly and powerfully. In this case, you can reestablish your integrity by choosing a new time that day or the next to get that particular work out completed. Do so once the cloud of negative emotion has passed. The trick is to be specific and be committed in your new contract. Declare a new time, place and duration as well. Get specific. It is a good thing to add a few more minutes of exercise for missing your last session. Over deliver on your new promise. Your relationship with any person will deteriorate if you break a few great promises without restoring your commitment to deliver. The same deterioration in trust takes place with yourself subconsciously if you continuously break your word to yourself.

You cannot escape yourself, you have to live with yourself all of the time. Think about the power people have lost with you when they tell you what they are going to do something and then flake on you. If you were in great need would you call on them? People with a pattern of untrustworthiness will have a hard time convincing most of us to believe them when it counts. Why are we able to accept the broken promises that we make to ourselves better than we tolerate broken promises others make to us? Hold you to a higher standard. The more broken promises to yourself occurring in a certain area of life, the more that area will not work the way you want it to. You will always find a struggle and hardship in that area of life. When it comes to exercise and fitness, long term results only appear when people have an ongoing relationship with integrity. That also goes for our finances, our relationships both personal and professional.

With practice, meditation, and the other mind centering practices I have outlined in this book, you should be able to once again hear when your integrity is in jeopardy. There should almost be a flashing red light and a siren going off in your head that tells you when you have to keep your word or renew it once it is compromised. No longer ignore or justify when your word is compromised. Like anything else you practice, it will become a second nature. The key is to regain your integrity in each situation as soon as possible. The most common reason people do not like to fess up to a failure is because they are overly concerned with "looking" bad. Many times, we attach a negative connotation to failing at delivering on something and spend more time dwelling on the fact that we failed than we do fixing the problem. The contexts of "Good" and "Bad" also can really restrict what we see and get out of life at times. There are instances where putting down morality is beneficial. I would be lying if I told you that this was always easy to do. Sometimes, no alarm goes off to even alert you that you lost your integrity. This is where other people come into play. A really honest good friend or a spouse can let you know when you slip. Remain open to the perspectives of your board of directors. It is sometimes the only way you can see something through another set of eyes. All of this really takes practice for some people. Going back and fulfilling the promises that you made to others will also mean admitting that you did not live up to your word. It does not even have to be big things. I once had a client whose body took longer to respond to physical activity than normal. No matter what he did, we did not get the results we should have. Aside from him ditching the cake and diet cola, I promised him I would purchase him a reflective vest so that he could bike and run after work when it got dark early. Weeks passed and I never got the vest. My integrity was broken. He graciously told me not to worry about it each week. I admitted to failing him. Then I made it a priority to get that vest. I purchased the best reflective vest on the market. I over delivered. He was now able to walk or ride his bike after work. That added one and a half hours of physical activity to his day. His cardiovascular endurance skyrocketed and those stubborn pounds of body fat began to melt away.

ACTION: REESTABLISHING INTEGRITY

- Admit to yourself you have not lived up to your word.
- Acknowledge and feel the emotional fallout from broken integrity and set a time period to release it.
- Declare a new commitment with the person or yourself. This time, make this declaration with renewed intention to deliver *no matter what.*
- Do your word and over-deliver this time. Do a little more than you originally set out to do. ACTION!

For many of us, it has been many years ignoring the fact that they never kept their word with certain things. We flake on the management of finances. We continuously fail to water our great relationships. Take a couple of minutes to reflect on how much breaking your word has cost you. The great thing about life is that as long as you live it, you have the power and the ability to make a change. Change happens in an instant when you have trust in your own abilities. Go back and reestablish the trust you have in yourself. Acknowledge that you have fulfilled your declaration and acknowledge yourself for each and every small accomplishment. Look for any sign of progress in your thinking and doing daily. Celebrate it! Every time you fulfill a promise that you have made to yourself, you should see it as a victory. Celebrate it! The more victories you have, the more trust you will develop in you. The declarations we make once we have an expanded level of integrity in all that we do, carry a different sort of weight to them. This is the garden bed for establishing a new mindset. Hopefully you can now feel the weight and power of doing what you say. You are creating passion and obligation to do the things you say you would that was not there before. You will develop a momentum. Wants and desires are instantaneously transformed from "someday" dreams and whims to goals and results when you add commitment, will and action.

Below, expose, kill, and transplant the mindset that has cost you further progress in the past. Then write in a new mindset that you will adopt in the area of life where your integrity has most historically suffered.

I am establishing a the following mindset for _____

I Lay To Rest:

_____

it is the old mindset that has kept me from attaining and maintaining _____ *until this point.*

Here I Commit to Living From:

_____

that will replace the old default mindset

FILL IN

Each day is an opportunity to live out our word and notice situations that occur when we do not do so. In practice, we become people who realize the highest levels of trust in our abilities. Remember self-efficacy is everything. We become people who mentally eliminate limits in what we can create. A fit and healthy body is simply another thing that we can create here in this lifetime to further achieve our soulset and purpose. The most important type of integrity is the integrity that you have with yourself. Even after reading this entire book and implementing all of the tactics, if you do not trust yourself you will still struggle. Subconsciously, you have to establish a new self-image. Capable and effective is how you should see you. Step outside of the comfort zone.

It takes effort and vigilance to do this work but it is so worth it. Integrity needs to be strengthened and renewed on a daily basis in all areas of life. You must be willing to call yourself out on the pretexts you create to avoid making real change. Acknowledge the promises you make, keep them. Make fewer promises to yourself and others. Remember to be grateful and celebrate the outcomes you will produce. Set goals and reward yourself for achieving them. Trust and believe in yourself once again. You are more than capable of transforming your physical being once you transform your mind and allow inner wisdom to guide the way. Always do internal checks to see who you are being in certain circumstances and if that way of being aligns with your goals. Do not allow yourself to subconsciously become resigned or okay with things not working out the way you want. If you do become aware that you got stuck *1. Take a look at your level of integrity. 2. Inventory the amount of gratitude that you have expressed for where you already are in life.* When gratitude and integrity are at high levels in any area of life, you will notice that things begin to work in your favor.

SUPER GRATEFUL

Gratitude is a vibration that creates a context in life where things that serve you happen more frequently. Use it! Gratitude is profound and it invites increase your way. It always feels really good! A priority in life should be feeling really good! This lesson perhaps took me the longest to master. I just had to include it in this work. Have you ever noticed that when you have feelings of gratitude, you automatically lighten up and sit up a little straighter? Being grateful for your ability to see, walk, or even think clearly, puts you in the right frequency to experience the best that life has to offer. It is hard to be angry and upset with yourself or others when you express feelings of gratitude for the things in your life that you already have. Gratitude serves your existence and can extinguish self-inflicted mental misery. I now look at gratitude as a full on spiritual state of being. Gratitude is an immediate antidote for the intense self-centered negative spiral of emotion that we all have found ourselves sliding down at one time or another. Although I had to navigate some ugly and intense external circumstances they paled in comparison to the numerous times I cruelly rehashed them in my mind. It perpetuated decades of depression in me. Intense focus on our hardships, failures, shortcomings, and missed opportunities all have one thing in common. They are selfish and self-centered thoughts. They are ego focused. I explained the compounding nature of our thoughts in a previous section of this book. Nothing creates more momentum for misery than our internal negative thoughts gone unchecked.

Expressing gratitude for what you have, where you are in life, and even what you will achieve in the future is very important for setting the stage for realizing more of the things you want. Being grateful for something is the easiest way to tell the universe what type of things you want and expect. I noticed we tend to constantly sulk, talk, and focus on all of the things that do not serve us. Negative news is the loudest. Taking a complete inventory of life is powerful. Every one of us has one area that just takes a little longer to get where we want it to be. Our starting points in regards to said thing may just happen to be very far from its achievement. Being in foster care set me at a disadvantage for having and enjoying trusting and loving relationships. Some people genetically have sensitivities to carbohydrates. They gain weight at the very thought of them. They have a harder road to achieving a six pack. We will never traverse the distance between our starting points and success as long as we focus on the symptoms alone and ignore underlying causes. When we work out, we look at ourselves in the mirror saying "if only I could tone up my_____!", "This stomach will not go, no matter what!" We may have lost significant amounts of fat elsewhere and can't see it. We may have even trained to the extent we are able to get off of medications that have harmful side effects. Exercise may have made anxiety a thing of the past. Yet, we remain fixated on the stomach. I have witnessed this multiple times that until we learn to be grateful for the other ninety-five percent of progress, we will be stuck at a standstill in our progress. Where attention and energy goes, everything grows. Be grateful.

I remember this one client named Chelsea who rapidly lost thirty pounds. She went to the gym, she ran three miles every other day, and she lifted weights with me two days a week. She went from relatively inactive to very active. She got stronger. Her endurance improved tremendously. She was able to see definition in her arms, legs and even her back, a hard area of focus for her. She was so overly concerned about her midsection. It took longer to show definition than the rest of her body. (It does for most people) She barely talked about how happy she was to have definition in her arms and legs and that her pants sizes have gone down considerably. At the end of assessments Chelsea would always stop and say "if only this fat in my midsection would go away". She told me "no matter what I do this stomach will always stay the same." (Even though I noticed it too had shrunk along with the rest of her she didn't) I immediately told her that she was right if she believed that was her fate. If you keep telling yourself something long enough, you will subconsciously believe it and unknowingly take action from it. It becomes your truth. She had a lot to be grateful for but couldn't see it.

Have you ever heard of the expression "what you resist will persist?" The same adage is made real when it comes to the human body and focusing on one area that may not be where you want it to be. One of the reasons I believe charities and many other initiatives and movements that start out with good intentions but never succeed is because more thought, time, awareness, focus and energy is spent focused on the problem. I believe that charities focusing on cures or the promotion of taking new actions are on the right course to make a change. Why have anti-war demonstrations when you can have peace rallies? The overall tone of our thoughts should mirror the realities that we want to experience.

If you have a personal trainer, your body is not created during the time you spend with him or her. This is true of a wealth advisor, life coach or any other professional that you hire. If you have a gym membership, your body is not created in the limited time you spend in the gym. Your body is created the other seventy-five to eighty percent of the time outside of the gym. Your habits run the show. Who do you become in those moments? Who are you when you are left to your own devises? If you subconsciously believe that you will never have results, you will conduct yourself as a person who never will have results. The passion will not be there, the drive will not be there, the resilience to stick it out will not be there either. You will not eat, exercise, or execute living a life that creates an environment conducive to being in shape. According to what you believe deep down inside, it simply makes no sense to do so consistently.

Through some life-strategy coaching I got Chelsea to acknowledge her triumphs. I got her to understand that most humans gain first and lose last in the midsection. I also reminded her that genes dictate which fat deposits diminish in size first, second, third and so on. She started to see things from a place of possibility and was able to manage expectations. One of the main laws in life and nature is that what you expect with great passion will become reality. Mike Dooley is a great motivator and inspirational mentor of mine. You should really take a look at his website, Tut.com. He has trademarked a phrase that I believe is pertinent as it comes to getting into shape, reviving your financial landscape, or enjoying powerful relationships. He says "Thoughts become things". When I first heard this my first response to this was *"Why not choose better thoughts then?"*

Be super grateful! This is expressing gratitude for outcomes that haven't even shown up yet. You can do this authentically because you know that you are willing to do whatever the work may be to make it so. Celebrate walking into the dream home. Celebrate landing your dream job. Celebrate that sexy body of your dreams because you know that you will find out and execute whatever it personally takes you to get there. This is self-efficacy and gratitude combining to have a success baby. This is the reason why the rich stay rich and the poor stay poor. The rich do not believe in poverty for themselves and the poor do not believe in abundance for themselves. Their realities reflect that, and so do their actions. These observances go far deeper than money.

Poor people win the lottery all the time and most times it does not make them rich for long. It just makes them have more money. If they are broke on the inside, they will once again be broke on the outside, many times worse. Nature is governed in a way that physical outcomes often match spiritual energies. There is a balance and order to things. Make it your job to be meticulous with your focus and balance. There will be things happening in life that are not optimal for you but always make it a point steer your thinking back to gratitude. Like attracts like. You'll notice the things you think about most ultimately correspond with the things in your life. Then you can exercise a level of control over them and a newfound faith. Find faith in yourself and that unseen power that has created all things. Always picture yourself looking and feeling the way you want your reality to be. Just before bed is the best time to reflect on what you are grateful for. The subconscious mind is very suggestable then. Practice writing five things regarding your ideal reality in a notebook every night.

LANGUAGE, ART, & POWERFUL WORD PLAY

"What you say to you controls your actions. Your actions control the tangible outcomes in your life."

According to various sources of research the average person speaks anywhere from seven thousand to as much as sixteen thousand words a day. That is not even counting the most important words of all, the words we use when quietly speaking to ourselves. The power of your word is unbelievable! People that have mastered the skill of speaking things into existence are people who understand the strength and power associated with their word. These people live intentional lives that inspire others and add greatness to our world. People call them lucky and blessed. Self-talk and language are super important.

One of the absolute most insane and ancient commitments we have left is the covenant of marriage. It is insane by definition. "Till death do us part?" Loving someone forever for the rest of your life and sticking by someone's side no matter what, is a crazy thing! Making this covenant in front of people and actually signing a lawful contract makes it even more serious. The utter gravity of these vows should be a deterrent in and of itself if you are not ready to exercise the power and integrity of your word. This is an absolutely ridiculous commitment to make and in my opinion. As ridiculous as it is, it is absolutely beautiful. The integrity needed to keep a marriage together and allow it to grow is sealed with two powerful words: "I do". If people really looked at the words they used when getting married and made them "real", many would run! The statistics say that forty to fifty percent of first marriages fail in the United States. Second and third marriages trend even higher. Why do many couples not decide to maintain being ridiculous and unreasonable when it comes to keeping their union alive? I think many people have not taken inventory of the gravity of the words involved. Granted that a marriage is whatever you make it these days, it is traditionally something much deeper than simply stating intentions you may keep. Some wedding vows should have clauses to lend to the integrity of the union. Some would read: "I do, until we have really tough financial times", "I do, until we no longer see eye to eye" or "I do, until I get tired of you leaving the toilet seat up". "I do, until you get sick and this shit isn't fun anymore." Way too many people place no thought into the words they use. Words take ideas, feelings, intentions, and emotions, from the unseen spirit realm and our minds then makes them real. Sometimes in seconds! These things are made audible, tangible, and transferable. This book is a stream of words and consciousness. As I am writing it I have 101,458 words written. I used a lot of words to convey emotions and thought!

There is an absolute disconnect in most people's minds between the power of their words and their state of fitness for example. In the first five minutes of meeting someone who wants to get into great shape I can pick up maybe five clues as to why they are not in the shape they want to be yet. The words they use show their leaks in power. Phrases that they use lack the power it takes to continuously get up and do something that is hard. Exercising in these modern times is a very intentional practice for the majority of us. You can make it through life without addressing your physical health. We have to intentionally invite convenience and abundance into life with the way that we speak. Language should always be chosen wisely. Many people like to use vague words that absolve them of any responsibility. Words are very powerful whether you choose to acknowledge them or not. Life is created in language.

The way you speak and the words you choose shape your life. Words ultimately shape your body. Your body is shaped through self-talk first, then the gym, and then the kitchen. We have conversations about money in our mind and then we spend and use our money accordingly. We speak in stories to ourselves about people that we know and don't know then we treat them accordingly. I would like to propose that all that you are is your word. The words you speak to yourself as well as your words you speak to the outside world make up the complete picture around all things in our lives. The power of language and wording becomes even more evident as we start to write things down. Now that a thought was floating around in your brain is on a piece of paper it is granted a tangible power.

ACTION: Divide a sheet of paper into two parts. Write down the most common phrases that you use when it comes to any area of struggle in life. In the same column, write down what actions and outcomes you believe those words have produced in reality.

On another paper write down what you envision as your ideal outcome in that area of life to be. Working backwards, write down the type of language you believe that you will need to get you the ideal outcome and ultimately the results you want.

The purpose of this exercise is to being your awareness to the language that you use and give you an access to altering it in your favor.

"It has been said that sticks and stones may break my bones but words will never hurt me". Let me be the first to tell you that this statement is fuckery. Words have the power to linger, cripple, and maim a person deep down to the core. Dependent on who they are said by they can also ignite drive and action. They can serve as a source of progression or stagnation for a person for many years. This is especially true if people do not have the mental tools to stop words from repetitively looping in their minds. Remember repetition can usher any thought true or false into the subconscious mind. There are too many instances where the words repetitively said to a child at a very early age proved to be words that shaped their lives. How many strong sentences or phrases can you recollect that came from a family member in your childhood? I bet that without digging too deeply, you can remember some words and phrases that had great impact on you. Words that come from others, especially those that you respect or admire, have the power to thwart or propel progress in an instant. Verbal abuse as a foster kid growing up in the hood kept me paralyzed for years in many areas of living. As an adult, I made it a priority to spend any resource I needed to in order to overcome these words.

How many careers were launched due to a respected mentor's words of encouragement? How many great corporations were created by an elementary school bully who teased a random child in the school yard? That kid grew up to prove himself a person of great value. How many suicides were caused by words? So many people run through life using reckless and powerless language and attracting uninspired existences. If you cannot say it, then does it exist? If it exists, how could you relay its existence or any of the possibilities around it to another person? Until the word "Gravity" was defined by Isaac Newton, could there be a way of defying it? Because gravity was defined we now have planes, satellites, and rockets. Think of cultures that do not have language throughout history. What were their customs and how was their culture? Conquerors throughout time burned libraries, books, and outlawed languages for a reason. If you do not know how to say it, can it exist? A word defined comes with a string of possibilities attached to it. It was for this reason that slaves in America were forbidden to learn to read. Cultures with no language are limited in what they create. Cultures with language are shaped by words and the way they are communicated. Individual people with limited vocabularies are limited in what they can express and create in the world as well. Language is participation. What are you participating in when you speak? Changes in our language can result in changes in actions and ultimately in their lives.

When we use a word, its context allows us to paint a picture. When asked about their exercise and fitness, many people would say "I try to eat better, exercise, or drink more water". Does this sound powerful? There is absolutely no power in any of those statements. The person who speaks this way is doomed to fail in the reaching of this goal. How would you feel if your doctor said that he was going to "try" to do a high-level brain surgery on you? Trying insinuates that people do not believe in their ability to get the job done and that failure is a likely outcome. "Trying" will always lead to more "Trying." Do whatever it takes to stop "trying" in life. Make all-out attempts at the doing of a thing.

A place of learning and not mastery is where anyone starts, even if some first-time attempts are better than others. Here is something absolutely scary but effective. Start to use the words "I will do it". Use this even in situations that you are not confident of your ability yet. It adds power to any action you take. It holds you to a higher standard to live your word. You may want to add the caveat that you will make your very best attempt at DOING it. This is much more powerful than saying to yourself that you will "try" to do something. Usually, perfect practice and gaining more knowledge about something instills a stronger belief in your ability to do it. That is why it is important to always be learning. Add the word "temporary" when reviewing failures that you encounter. These practices will inevitably lead to less "trying" and more "doing". You only get paid for "Done" and you can only get fit through "Doing". Malcolm Gladwell states that one should spend at least ten thousand hours in practice to become a master. I say perfect practice because practicing it wrong still does not help performance. Perfect practice implies learning and being guided to do a thing properly. "I am doing" or "I want to" moves the responsibility of action into your court. It gives you ownership of what you must do. The definite tone of these words makes you accountable for taking action. Self-talk (Language in our head) creates motion and makes it deliberate. Start to listen to the way the most dynamic people in your life speak. Listen to the way that the unhappy people you know speak as well. You will notice patterns. Make mental notes. Look at all of the things in life you are "trying" to do and honestly gauge the progress and achievement in those areas. You will find out that the only things you say you are "doing" get done. Doing leads to done, you will be surprised at the outcomes you get while using that word. Purposely leave yourself less wiggle room to get out of your commitments to yourself. *"I will go to the gym tonight. I will save one hundred dollars a paycheck."* VS *"I will try to make it to the gym. I may save one hundred dollars a paycheck"*.

FROM "BUT" TO AND"

A simple word that kills a lot of possibilities is "but". Most times, when an action that we know is beneficial should be taken, the first thing to kill all possibilities in that arena is the word "but". "I want to work out today *but* I am so busy." "I want to retile the kitchen *but* I do not have enough money." "I want to get into great shape *but* I hate to work out." "I wanted to ask you out *but* I was afraid." The word "but" is a possibility killer. It would make a lot of sense to use that word a lot less. One simple fix is to replace the word "but" with the word "and". *"I want to work out today and I am too busy." "I want to retile the kitchen and I do not have enough money." "I want to get into great shape and I hate to work out." "I wanted to ask you out and I was afraid."*

ACTION: Write out three to four sentences that fit your life in the manner above and switch the "but" in each sentence for an "and". Then have fun brainstorming how to create from the "and". You will be able to see possibilities and roadways that lead to you getting what you want. Be unreasonable and unstoppable in the pursuit of your answers.

Many times, one simple word in the right place causes your brain to think of ways to solve a problem as opposed to losing momentum and never taking any beneficial action. Replace the sentence "I want to get into great shape but I hate to work out." with "I want to get into great shape and I hate to work out." Looking at this sentence, you can start to ask questions that may help solve the dilemma. Start to think about the fact that there may be another way to get into good shape besides working out in the traditional sense. You can play a sport, participate in adventure races, or do yoga or Pilates. You can look at why you hate exercise, confront it head-on and then choose to have an all new mindset to live from, when it comes to exercising. You will find that you have many more possibilities opened up to you by just changing out one simple word. Words send out a signal to the universe that help us to decipher and frame what you see in reality. Always choose words that serve you. Keep in mind that when you choose to become the best version of yourself, you add to the entire world we live in. Your speech should lend itself to healing and inspiring you. The way you speak to yourself and the words you choose will determine your relationship with exercise and proper eating. Literally speak yourself fit. Work every day to establish language that makes a strong connection between where you want to be and where you are in life. Speak to what you want to happen in your existence.

Some only talk about things they do not want to experience in life and then step back and wonder why they happen. I couldn't afford to do this as a depressed foster kid growing up. Bad environment and bad thinking would have killed me one way or another. For me there have only ever been two ways of thinking. There is bad thinking and better thinking. I realized early on that I make everything better or worse with my mind. Everything I was experiencing was something I didn't want. Something deep within me knew that if I was to beat my surroundings my vocabulary and the way that I spoke aloud would have to elevate my existence. If you are a black person in America from the ghetto and you wish to move your station up in life, eloquence will take you far. Learn how to communicate either in writing or verbally. I learned this at a young age while attending private schools that my adopted mother made me go to. I hated them then, but thank God for them now. You had to speak well in class or you got hit with a yard stick. Shame was used in a beneficial way. It kept us in line and made being exceptional the only option. It was a Caribbean run school in the heart of Brooklyn. It was super strict!

It took me much longer to understand that speaking to myself in a positive manner counted as a bridge from survival to thriving. So many talk about how incompetent they are, how sick they are, and how incapable they are to themselves. You should not be surprised when reality morphs to confirm these things over and over again. By speaking in a way that elevates you and then having the integrity to live from your words, you can alter any circumstances in your life. This is why affirmations do work. The possibilities are endless. Speak in terms of "I can" instead of "I cannot". Speak in terms of "fit and healthy" instead of "fat and sick". By purposely changing your words, you alter the context of what you think. The way you speak and see things will start to mesh together. You don't even have to believe it at first. Just work on the quality of your language. Choose words that help you do the things that benefit you most. Speak in definite terms that people will hold you accountable for. Most importantly, hold yourself accountable to make the words you speak come true. Be patient. It does not matter if, in the past, you found it very difficult to follow through and finish on initiatives. You can choose to relate to yourself differently. Decide to see you as a reliable person who delivers on their word from this moment forward. Go back and review the section on building self-discipline like a muscle.

If you truly embrace the importance of living with integrity and choosing wisely the mindsets and things you commit to, you will find that you already have what it takes to transform your life. You will notice when you are off track and have what it takes to renew your integrity and get back to doing the things that get you closer to your goals. Elevating the quality and direction of your language is something you can practice right now. Start to speak with trust in yourself to make things happen. Live from the will to take actions that match the direction of your dreams. Other people will begin to believe in you, you will start to believe in yourself as well. Ask yourself constantly: "What am I saying to myself?" or "What is the overall tone of the language I use with others?" Gauge if the answer to that question is uplifting or limiting. Ask yourself from time to time: "What am I thinking about most and do my actions match?"

EBBS & FLOWS

> *"Change is constant, nothing that we perceive to be either good or bad will last forever."*

The universe we live in is governed by ebbs and flows. There inevitably will be ups and downs in life. Change is the only constant and it doesn't care what you perceive as an "up" or a "down". Change happens. From time to time in your efforts to find what better and awesome looks like, you will fail. Expansion and contraction are part of life. No one experiences one without the other. Life has seasons. That is why social media is so inauthentic. Most people only show expansion and growth. They display the highlight reel. The people that we see in the best physical shape in magazines, on television, and on billboards have times when they are not in as good shape as you see them in. Those pictures usually don't see the light of day. The photos of the past due bills never quite accompany the vacation pictures with the Rolex's and the women.

Comparison to those fake and unattainable goals are a source of pain and feelings of inadequacy for so many of us. I have done some fitness modeling and bodybuilding and trust me, absolutely no one always looks their sharpest at all times. This goes for all fitness influencers and IG fitness models. Even the wealthiest of us experience pullbacks in their portfolios. Even people surrounded by family experience love falter and have family issues. This is the plight of humanity. There are times in life when you are very fortunate and everything seems to be going your way and there are times when nothing is working the way you believe it should. Your commitment to your version of excellence should stay constant. Hold onto it with all that you have. Expect that in every pursuit there will be ebbs and flows. Expect adversity. Expect favorable outcomes to cost you more than you'd expect. They will take longer, cost more, and ask you to become more. It is par for the course for those who are advancing individuals.

In nature, there are hot seasons and cold seasons but the most important thing to consider is who you are in the face of these changes. The real you is the observer. Who you be on the inside is the only constant. Some call this the God within us. Some call this the soul. Call it the real you. That authentic part of you must rebel against the societal programming around us. That is the part of us that must buck the status-quo and remain focused (against all odds) on better. The better mindset, the better thought, the better action, the better perception, are all yours for the taking. You have a coat for the winter and shorts for the summer. The same adaptability is needed in your mind when choosing what mindset to adopt and live from in a given area of life. If you stay aware and own who you become in the face of change and adversity, you hold true power. All processes and distinctions shared in this book are geared toward giving you that awareness. Hopefully you find the strength and power in your life, the power to be able to manufacture motivation to do the hard and beneficial things regardless of what is going on around you. No matter what circumstances may come your way, you will be able to find strength and motivation to continue to take action towards a goal. External and superficial motivations are not enough. You must have a deeper purpose to have the energy needed to live an intentional and purpose filled life. If you have children, you can attach exercise and eating right to the possibility of witnessing your children grow up and become contributing members of society. You may have set up the goal that you want to run a business that makes an impact in the world. Waking up your own personal health and possibility is a definite asset to the formation of anything that is important to you.

Defining a purpose in life, big or small, will be one of the keys to you being able to consistently do hard things that transform life. Get your soulset tattooed onto your body (not required). It's that important though for real. Identifying with an agenda bigger than you can be your tattoo. What will you live for and support? I have a special place in my heart for children in foster care paying for the mistakes that others have made before them. Part of my purpose is serving them. Taking actions that align with me doing this is of the utmost importance to me. I know what it is like to feel as though you have no one in your corner. I stand for displaying what "better" can look like and facilitating better for them in the real world. I see every abandoned child as possibility. I am them and they are me. No one who'd lived a life like mine ever came back to tell me anything that would have helped me access my own version of better. I am now blessed to do that for others.

Go back to your childhood and find what you enjoyed doing back then. Look at who you wished you could have met. Why not be that person for someone. Most times, your purpose is attached to some activity you have let go long ago. Life got in the way, and that is why it is so hard to see now. Do take time to meditate and reflect on it. If you have already defined this, you are far ahead of the game. Always ask yourself what inspires you? Always research what you say is really important to you..

Once your purpose is chosen and known to your conscious mind, you will have accessed one of the greatest forces known to man. Once you discover your purpose or soulset, it will act as the anchor for your actions. It moves you from successful to becoming significant. Success is you winning. Being significant is you helping others access their success. Alignment of thought and action is all that you have to maintain. Living from purpose is living in the zone. Think of Neo in the movie "The Matrix": Everything slows down in his world and he is able to fight agents previously stronger than him with one hand. Life just moves out of your way and things tend to happen for you with far less resistance when you have clarity of vision. You will be able to tap into that power even when things around you are not at their best.

You will be able to find ways to save and invest, do the workouts, and stop procrastination in its tracks. A clear vision pulls us through the hard parts. That is why my company is named "A Vision Lived" Clear vision is the antidote. Mindsets that hindered you before will be uprooted and replaced, not only when it comes to exercise and fitness but when it comes to making your passion and purpose clear to the world. I grew up poor, abandoned, and moving from house to house. I felt like a burden to others. This gave me a very limited view of money. I was raised in survival mode thinking it was difficult just to stay alive. I also believed that there was never enough. I researched and read so many books about wealth because it was an unreal vision and dream for me. I read thirty to fifty books a year for a decade. I still do. I have significantly changed how I view money. I live an abundant life and support a few charities and initiatives that help underprivileged children. The research and the mentors that I have hired over the years have transformed my money thermostat. I live my purpose. Doing what I "ought to" for years (investing and saving) has allowed for me to now do what I want to with my money. This goes against society norms. We are taught to earn to spend. The status quo be damned... I learned to make my goals priority!

RONNIE

A former client of mine dreamt to help people tap into their greatness and help them see that they can live empowered lives. She was a life coach who helped people prioritize their lives and provided them with structure and effectiveness. She came to me stating she needed my help to get her body to match the person she was on the inside. She allowed herself to get out of shape to the point where she was taking many medications. She had lost sight of her integrity in this area of life. She was aware enough to find me.

For six months we worked hard to get her body in alignment with her soulset which was service. She dropped thirty pounds of fat in that time period and put on eight pounds of muscle. She remodeled herself. More importantly, she was able to get off of most of her medications and her business took off. The subtext that had dominated her life up until this point was: *"How can I help you? I will be better tomorrow."* This mindset cannot be applied to health and fitness. She kept saying that she would exercise the next day. That was until we made a small tweak. I asked her to look at her exercising and working out as yet another way for her to inspire her clients. Her life was a testimony of grit, resilience, and the ability to overcome obstacles. She had ascended from being sexually abused and beaten to being a beacon of light for abused women.

She was extremely gifted at helping people see their strength and power and put it to use. At the same time she lost her own. We got her to realize that she had stopped using the tools that got her to such success in life. She realized that she as using an old injury and being on many medications to justify being inactive and obese. We had to tap into her purpose of service to others. I had to show her the impact that her clients were not getting because of her lack of energy. I showed her the fallout from her not being as healthy as she could be. We strengthened the connection to her clients by making her health a priority. She was able to tap into a newfound dedication to fitness. She seized control of her own physical health once she saw how it impacted and influenced others. Some people are shepherds. Her soulset was to serve and empower others. We re-connected with that. It was made clear that her physical transformation would impact transformation in her client's lives. Her sentence did not even have to change much. The way she related to it did. The "It will be better tomorrow" part changed into "I will give my best today". That is an absolute win-win situation. With a sentence like "How can I help me?, I'll give my best today." How could she ever fail in the gym?

THE FOCUSED ON BETTER METHOD

Process for Manufacturing Internal Motivation

1. Admit to yourself that you have a challenge or an issue going on around taking a certain productive and beneficial action. Do not make yourself wrong. Hang the morality hat up.

2. Tell yourself that you will make a change in the actions you take. Make room and create the expectation that you will make something different happen mentally.
3. Identify your default sentence. Connect the dots and see how it conspired to put you into your current situation.
4. Swap the default mindset for one that serves you in the situation. Create a new powerful sentence to operate from. Choose who you will be in the face of the challenge at hand. Write it down.
5. Create a new realistic physical plan of action. With integrity, commitment and purpose. Declare the execution of your plan with your new mindset and mantra in place.
6. Expect the start of a new action to be difficult. Outside circumstances may not always line up to make your goal achievement easy. Expect that you may slip but your commitment and resilience will make it happen no matter what.
7. Take the time to learn from setbacks. Renew Integrity and pair your objective with your purpose for living or whatever is most important to you in life.
8. Make choices and actions that are aligned with the new sentence created in step four repeatedly.
9. Share your goals and action steps with others who you trust. Speak in terms of it already being done and realized: language.
10. Intentionally execute plan of action: implement. Repeat steps 1 to 10 as many times as needed until it is done.

These ten steps are combined to give you the power to accomplish anything and maintain it for a lifetime. From situation to situation you will find that, like anything else, it will become easier and easier to use with repetition. You will also see that some steps are easier for you than others. Use it dynamically, skipping from number to number as your abilities allow. Always refer back to areas in this book that renew strength. Take a look at some distinctions to make it through the tougher parts of your journey. Work on creating an environment conducive to success around things that were historically hard for you to accomplish.

We can create bodies and mental environments that give us the ability to achieve things formerly thought impossible. No more settling for not having anything that we desire. We no longer are victims of our subconscious minds. We no longer have to throw away an entire gamut of possibilities because of a limited mindset created by us when we were youngsters. Motivation to do hard things on a consistent basis has to come from within. Manufacturing it from inside is what counts and keeps you. You can use any manner of inspiration to construct sentences and stories that drive and move you to taking continued action in life. The ability to have a great connection with what is mentally going on inside you is key to making lasting transformations. Never lose that connection by living on autopilot.

The goal is to be a dynamic, morphing, and transformational individual in the face of life. The goal is to be becoming someone who is doing and creating things that are most important to you. Why not seek to be able to handle situations as they come because we are in touch with who we want to be in the face of life? The vision is clear. It is near impossible to be exceptionally effective while operating from a hidden sentence that was manufactured by a toddler years ago. It was a very powerful toddler, but I prefer to take the reigns as an adult and see what wonders can be created. It is also debilitating to lead a life where your personal likes and dislikes box you in and seclude you from great experiences that expand living. Learning about yourself and your surroundings has to be something that trumps any limiting context you can create. The ability to first learn about yourself and share your gifts from a unique perspective is something you do have the ability to do. It is something that we all do when we experience being in "the zone". Create a calm internal environment within you. Practice taking control of your feelings and emotions it is a priceless skill. Developing the ability to actively choose who you are in the face of life is the best gift you can give to the world.

When things start to feel like they get out of hand or become overwhelming, you should first aim to get back to the calm and unbothered version of yourself. Meditate and take it back to your natural state of peace and calm. This is the best way to access the quiet yet powerful directives of your soul. They show up like sparks and splashes of clarity. They show you the next step to take on your journey. In times of stillness you will get more and more clear directives. By paying attention to those directives, you will be able to carve out an existence in this world that not only inspires others but benefits you as well. De-clutter your mind and ask yourself often. "How can I personally flourish and be devinely used in service of others?" and "Is who I am being a match for making it happen?" Once you have done that and possibly even plotted out a plan of action, it is important that you take action right away. Do not wait until the time is right. Do not wait until every little thing is in place. When you are inspired from within take action now. When given a sliver of inspiration, go for it! Start a new beneficial habit. Something as simple as taking a walk daily can alter life drastically. Walking may not be the only thing needed to get you into shape but it definitely begins to form a habit that will change what is currently going on. Consistently doing something small and pointed is much better than inconsistently doing something great, once in a while. Remember that you create an environment in your brain and in your body by repetitively taking action. What we practice with intention is conducive to us all accessing the better version of ourselves.

Integrity will actually set you apart from the rest of the world. Having a high level of integrity makes the things you want deep down inside of you manifest into the world. It also attracts others that will help champion your cause. No one ever created anything great without the help of others. Use language that eliminates failure from setting like concrete anywhere in life. Look for the learning in it. Quitting is impossible. Share your goals with a trusted few. Especially share them with people that will hold you accountable for what you say. The little voice inside our minds that gets annoyed when people hold you accountable, would love for you not to. Do it anyway! That voice is not your boss any longer and has to actively be overridden. There can be no Plan B in your mind. The premise of a Plan B takes away the effectiveness of plan A. Your only options are to win by incorporating necessary actions.

Everyone is capable of making the commitment to themselves to be their "better". One of my favorite questions I ask in order to motivate myself while exercising is "If I do one more, will I die?" The answer is always no. There are many times I felt like the answer would be yes but if I am being 100% real it is always no. Even when I trained a 210 pound body to run a marathon and lost thirty one pounds in only nine weeks, the answer to that question was still no. I didn't die taking the next step. I lost seven toenails in the process, and cramped up, but I made it. The human body is super resilient to the rigors that we put it through. If you have done a lot of the activities in this book and taken to heart the distinctions set forth, you may be in a place where you have a lot more clarity, awareness and strength over your mind. This will translate into your ability to sustain healthy and wealthy habits that really work for you. The next time you approach the creation of a hard-for-you-to-do habit you know that you can give it your all. You will be able to establish a mindset that defies your default if it must. You are essentially a new person in this very moment. You can forget about the old you doing the same things that limited you in the past.

TAKE AWAYS

Creating this mind flow is like tending a garden. Focusing on better takes small consistent efforts. It takes always being aware of your old mindset and evaluating why you do things. It takes the will to get to know yourself and to stop functioning from reasons and excuses created by your old default mindset. It is important to establish new actions in alignment with what you want to achieve in reality. Do not allow the comfort of the actions that you usually take, to make you move on autopilot. It is important that you acknowledge them and actively change course to your new mantra.

Old habits die hard, especially when you are unaware that they are running things behind the scenes. It's easy to slip right back into them. Always evaluate your integrity. Be aware of your mental hang-ups. Remember, don't make yourself wrong for failures along the way. Willfully flourishing is not an issue of being right or wrong. Enjoying increments of better in life is the main goal. It is really a matter of doing what you say you will do. Scrutinize your default settings when it comes to areas of life that don't work how you believe they should. Defy those old habits and develop new ones. Practice self-discipline, focus and concentration daily. Read that chapter often. Through repetition and spending time being present every day your goals must manifest. This process will really change who you are in all of life. This whole process will make you a dynamic and thinking person in the areas of life that matter the most to you. You have to be willing to clean shop mentally and establish a whole new paradigm in your life.

We are all excellent procrastinators. Some of us are so good that we do not even know we do it. Be real! Whenever you feel you are about to do your procrastination activity, an alarm should go off in your head! Are you a social media addict? Do you eat when you are bored? Do you have a favorite series that you binge watch? Do you make other people's problems yours to avoid handling your own inauthenticity? Make that alarm going off mean that you take immediate action towards reaching a single goal. The hardest part of anything is just getting started. You have to overcome inertia to get moving. If you are able to point out all the pitfalls you have fallen into in the past, you can choose to avoid them going forward. Write them out. Make it plain. The past should be used only as a point of reference. It shouldn't be a pool that you disrobe and swim in. Confront yourself at every sign of wrong doing, release it, and then choose a new action instead. Exercise will lead to more exercising. Investing will lead to more investing. Put those dollars to work. Do not allow mental pitfalls to stop that momentum. Accepting a mental pitfall and allowing it to go unchecked is the only thing that will stop your progress. When you are able to control your mind or at least have a heightened level of calm and awareness, you will gain a better lock on your body. Keep clearing out the weeds in your mind. Your meditation is gardening.

Utilize the tools in this book that make mind flow possible: meditation, integrity, nutrition, language, segment intending, hearing your inner-self, dropping the past, making choices as opposed to only decisions, and gratitude. End the obsession with being "right" and reconnect with your soulset and the real you. Last but not least, take new actions in the direction of your wildest dreams. Big or small, they all matter. Make it your business to hunt for new information about what you care about most. Research and do whatever it takes to create solid new personal and professional relationships that resonate with you. Play games within your mind that push you to become comfortable with uncomfortably moving towards progress.

Andre A. Van Lun

Know you better. Be aware of the wisdom in your body and your mental processes as you participate in new and challenging things. You now have many tools to manufacture your own motivation and function from the inside out. Consult with your higher self and uncover your soulset. Be patient with you. Your mind is not all that you are. It is a tool filled with creativity and power. Your body can be a resilient vehicle that helps you to impact the world around you. Use your heightened awareness and consciousness to see how a better you impacts the ones you love. De-clutter your mind and fill it with action steps towards being the enhanced version of you alive in your mind's eye. Choose consciously who you are in the face of failure, negative circumstances and mental distractions. When you reach your physical goals and master the process of better thinking and better living, make sure to share the powerful distinctions that helped you the most. By sharing you further solidify thinking, doing, and being habits that make your new and better reality sustainable for as long as you like.

Go against being "normal" or "average" with your mental and spiritual energies. Remember there is only bad thinking and better thinking. Commit to self-development and progress. While the world focuses on *"what do I have to do to get"* focus on *"Who must I become in order to experience_____?"*

It is time to put this book down and get moving!
Claim your better. Both you and this planet deserves
to know exactly what that looks like... POW!
Better is always within your grasp.

ACKNOWLEDGEMENTS

There have been an extraordinary amount of people, circumstances, and luck that came together to knock my life off of a track of either being a career criminal, being incarcerated, or dying prematurely. I would like to first thank my mother Travis Farnell for being the strong, beautiful, and loving anchor in my life. You informed the man that I am. You modeled and informed the woman that I have selected to build a life and family with. Thank you for taking a chance and pouring love and wisdom into me. Words can't do justice how much I love and admire who you are and how you allow God to work through you.

Big shout out to Nicole Van Lun my wife and soulmate. You loving me, pushing me, and believing in me the way you have, grew me. My soul called for you and your soul answered. You are truly my better half and I am the luckiest man on the planet to be able to have witnessed you grow as a young lady, my main squeeze, my wife, and ultimately the mother of my children. No one is you and you elevate everyone who meets you. I see you baby! Loving you has been my "better" for thirteen years. Thank you Nico Anthony Van Lun and Drece Delainey Van Lun my Gemini twins! Your impending births made me move differently and better since I was seven. I have your back for life!

I want to say thank you to every single one of my clients past, present, and future. You all at some point believed and trusted in me enough to invest in me becoming a part of you moving forward and accessing greater potentials in your lives. Thank you for seeing me. Thank you for openly sharing who you are. Thank you for your wisdom. Being a part of your journey has fulfilled me and has immeasurably added wisdom and better to my life. Our work together has transformed me.

BIG BIG BIG shout out and love to my powerful group of editors and early readers. *Bridget David*, I don't know anyone who has lived more lives and crushed more seasons of living than you have. I also don't know anyone more committed to growth and following dreams and callings than you. Thank you for your insights. *Justin Legg*, you are literally superman. You are a conqueror like myself. I see you. I admire and love your ability to communicate and mentally reframe the fuckery that life inevitably throws our way as humans. Thank you for your candid and analytical feedback. You made this book better. Your character and your desire to impact and spark thinking in others is EPIC! *Lisa Riedmiller* thank you for your feedback and input. How many books have you read? You are the English major of the group as well as an extremely successful entrepreneur. You are always "Focused on Better" not only for you but for others. Thank you for sharing your firm grasp of the English language and who you are.

Lastly, gratitude goes out to you for having picked this book up to read. It is already in you to be powerful and great. This book appeals to leaders. Consider yourself one. I hope this work helps you in a way that you need. It is my love for you that has helped me to pull this work together. Every person who reads this book has pulled me into being a better man. I live for being of service and it is my intent that this book serves you. Thanks for being interested in learning and improving yourself to better impact others. Continue building your legacy.

Printed in the United States
By Bookmasters